New Social Foundations
for Education

This book is part of the Peter Lang Education list.
Every volume is peer reviewed and meets
the highest quality standards for content and production.

PETER LANG
New York • Bern • Frankfurt • Berlin
Brussels • Vienna • Oxford • Warsaw

New Social Foundations for Education

Education in 'Post-Secular' Society

Edited by Philip Wexler & Yotam Hotam

PETER LANG
New York • Bern • Frankfurt • Berlin
Brussels • Vienna • Oxford • Warsaw

Library of Congress Cataloging-in-Publication Data

New social foundations for education: education in 'post-secular' society /
edited by Philip Wexler, Yotam Hotam.
pages cm
Includes bibliographical references.
1. Education—Religious aspects. 2. Religion and sociology. 3. Postsecularism.
4. Educational sociology. 5. Education—Curricula.
6. Education—Philosophy. I. Wexler, Philip.
LB1027.2.N48   370.1—dc23   2015003309
ISBN 978-1-4331-2278-1 (hardcover)
ISBN 978-1-4331-2277-4 (paperback)
ISBN 978-1-4539-1565-3 (e-book)

Bibliographic information published by **Die Deutsche Nationalbibliothek**.
Die Deutsche Nationalbibliothek lists this publication in the "Deutsche
Nationalbibliografie"; detailed bibliographic data are available
on the Internet at http://dnb.d-nb.de/.

The paper in this book meets the guidelines for permanence and durability
of the Committee on Production Guidelines for Book Longevity
of the Council of Library Resources.

Table of Contents

Acknowledgments

This book is a first result of an ongoing academic collaboration which enriched our lives in recent years intellectually and personally and was accompanied by vibrant discussions, and meaningful collegiality. Philip Wexler would like to thank Heinz Sünker for the invitation to work in Germany, and Lambert Koch, the Rector of the Bergische Universitat, in Wuppertal, for his support. Yotam Hotam would like to thank Adi Efal, Itzhak Benyamini, and Cedric Cohen Skalli for exciting discussions on themes of modernity, secularism, faith and politics.

We gratefully acknowledge the following permissions to reprint:

Taylor & Francis
"On the Teachings of George Grant" by William F. Pinar, published in *Critical Studies in Education*, 55:1, pp. 8–17 (2014).

"Religion, Education and the Post-secular Child" by Robert A. Davis, published in *Critical Studies in Education*, 55:1, pp. 18–31 (2014).

"The Case of Palestinian Civil Society in Israel: Islam, Civil Society, and Educational Activism" by Ayman K. Agbaria & Muhanad Mustafa, published in *Critical Studies in Education*, 55:1, pp. 44–57 (2014).

John Wiley & Sons, Inc.
"Notes on Post-Secular Society" by Jürgen Habermas, published in *New Perspectives Quarterly*, 25:4, pp. 17–29 (2008). (The text originally appeared in German in *Blätter für deutsche und internationale Politik*, 4, 2008).

Introduction

New Social Foundations: Education in Post Secular Society

PHILIP WEXLER & YOTAM HOTAM

Education and Society

The venerable tradition of thinking about Education socially seems to be coming to an end. At least for Schools of Education, there are repeated reports (Tozer and Butts, 2011) that teaching and research in what was, since the 1930s, called "social foundations" of education have been "marginalized." They have been replaced, on the one hand, by a huge shift in focus—away from the social science disciplinary approaches that defined the social, contextual analysis of education—toward the applied, toward "practice," both through teacher education and policy studies.

There is an aura of "triumphalism" about the new-found liberation among teacher education and policy researchers. This is not only understandable but also justifiable given the long history of condescension by discipline-trained researchers toward their more professional practice-oriented colleagues in education and the consequences for them personally and for their style of work that suffered from a disciplinary regime which inferiorized research and knowledge in professional practice.

This liberation from the disciplinary bases of the social foundations of education may be deceptive and short-lived—if it only helps pave the way for the incorporation of educational knowledge into nationalistic and corporate agendas of a new capitalism; one which fuses public and private, and where knowledge production and use—in which education is central—is an instrumentalized commodity in a problem centered academic world, as part of a fully commercialized wider apparatus of markets and networks: not "society."

Tozer and Butts, in their recent history of the social foundations of education (2011: 10), without tracking the transformation of the wider world but in observing only about education, wrote:

> Social foundations of education are caught between two powerful and competing movements, neither of them very compatible with the historically critical traditions of social foundations research and teaching. One of these movements is the standards-based movement in pre k–12 teaching, with its emphasis on standardized achievement tests, curricular alignment with the state and national standards and professional teaching standards. The opposing position is a market-driven orientation that emphasizes the deregulation of teacher preparation and the elimination of the 'monopoly' of colleges and universities on teacher certification programs.

Regimes of Social Knowledge

If the disappearance of the social in the marginalizing near-death of the social foundations in teacher preparation and policy analysis (plus a supercharge of legitimacy to the residual traditional elite status of psychology in education and in cognitive and neuro-sciences) turns out to be part of a new regime of overall social knowledge production in what Holmwood (2011) and others (see, for example, Slaughter and Rhoades, 2004) analyze as part of a shift in the mode of economic production from an industrial corporatism to a digitalized post-Fordism, then this liberating re-direction may be an example of how incorporative, reproductive hegemony works. Critics of the disciplinary domination of the social foundations of education may have won a "pyrrhic victory."

For sociology of knowledge and for critical theory (Horkheimer, 1972), changes in emphases and distribution of academic research and teaching are neither simple, deserved triumphs of truth and justice nor the accumulative knowledge of research. In this view, paradigms change not only for "internal" reasons having to do with research in academic organization itself but also for "external" reasons in the wider context in which knowledge is produced, transmitted, consumed, and used.

Holmwood's critical sociology of academic sociology offers a valuable illustration with implications across the range of knowledge taught in colleges and universities and, indeed, perhaps especially in their professional branches. Like "practice" triumphalism, critical sociologists have seen an advance and liberation from the post-World War II institutionalization of positivist empiricist sociology in the new wider economic production apparatus and its academic reverberations. Holmwood (2011), however, argues instead that (2011: 537):

...although disciplinary hierarchies have been destabilized, what is emerging is a new form of instrumentalized knowledge, that of applied interdisciplinary studies. Part of the disciplinary displacement is an "applied," problem-centered knowledge, which is based in economic categories and which represents closer and more direct linkages between research and application and between the state sector and private corporations, in the newer networks and coalitions of "a new spirit of capitalism."

The inter-disciplinarity of applied social studies is not, he argues, the critical inter-disciplinarity of the modern corporate-industrial and academic disciplinary past but one that has no place for the critical interests of such boundary crossings. The "reorganization of knowledge" leads to an

...increasing integration of university research and economic goals (which) has given rise to a new emphasis upon the 'co-production' of knowledge ...; knowledge production is increasingly trans disciplinary and is part of a 'larger process in which discovery, application and use are closely integrated. (Holmwood 2011: 545, quoting Gibbons, 1994 and Slaughter and Rhodes, 2004)

In such a regime, not only do private interests gain in a corporatist melding of state and economy but so do "researchers in professional disciplines such as management (and here, we want to add, also Education), struggling to wriggle out from under the condescension of more established and more 'academic' disciplines" (Holmwood, 2011; 548, citing Novotny, 2003). The price is a loss of critical distance and capacity traded at the door of practical integration and, with that, the Archimedes point, the pivot for critical vision and transformation which they provided through contextual, perspectival, and social analytical theoretical frameworks.

Social Movements

Along with positivist empiricist orientations to knowledge, the modern corporate and attendant disciplinary regime brought with it—though no longer with a view of the social totality of "society"—the specific resistance and oppositional movements of the disfavored and dis-privileged minorities which found their voices in the expanding opportunity structure of the modern university. Holmwood notes the importance of these voices for the development of a critical sociology in the 1970s (2011: 541). Wexler argued similarly, early on, and specifically with regard to education (1976), that a "new sociology of education" was emerging with a critical interest displacing the taken for granted assumption of a scientized social paradigm deeply rooted in American Progressive thought. A paradigm shift occurred in that subfield, fueled not by the accumulation of positivist research from within the universities but from without, an external force in changing paradigms from sources in social movements rather than simply form disciplinary traditions (Wexler, 1976, 2009). Holmwood observers (541):

> Steinmetz (2005) associates the rise of critical sociology in the 1970s with the rise of new social movements that were challenging the Fordist settlement (and its ideological quietude), for example, feminism, gay rights, postcolonialism and other components of a new left.

Wexler's contextualization of sociological research in education pointed earlier to the anti-War movement (Vietnam), the movement of a cross section of the American Afro-American population, and the movement of students against the universities themselves. The way that social research in education was conceptualized began to change then toward a more socially critical rather than apparently "neutral" scientific positivist approach, reflecting the world views and interpretive schemata of the contemporary movements to affect ideas about equality, knowledge, and organization in education.

The new regime of knowledge production not only eclipses critique in favor of more efficient sectoral integration and a faster integrated track between research and application fostered by coalitions and consortia of nation state and economic actors, but it instrumentalizes knowledge as a "double eclipse of reason" (551) and makes the category of the social—a contextualizing Archimedes pivot for acritical perspective—redundant. Even that critique which "remains" is eclipsed and instrumentalized.

This is the second side of what remains after the death of social foundations in Education and its supersession by teacher education and policy analysis. The elision of the social is denied by an "appearance" of the continuing critical capacity which a social analysis provides to education. Tozer and Freeman (2011) refer broadly to "critical social foundations." These critical foundations are now the routinized institutional versions of the social critiques of the historical new social movements of the 1960s and '70s. "Critical pedagogy," "qualitative research," and "diversity" (social justice) are their newer and more popular incarnations. Yet, if the new knowledge regime in education under the naïve victory banner of "integrated," "applied," or "practical" ("professional") has surrendered the critical capacity of socializing education, the so-called "critical" foundations have given up the power of analytical explanatory critique in favor of the use of concepts for the otherwise laudable goals of political mobilization and inclusion.

There has already long been discussion of the dead ends of "critical pedagogy" and even the hand-wringing of the critical pedagogues themselves, forfeiting "practice" for the newer status neighborhoods that gentrified the disciplinary slums as now "cultural studies" and even "critical theory" and "Marxist theory" (Gur Ze'ev, 2005). The loss of the analytical power that is at the heart of social critique in favor of the political gains of mobilizing, inclusionary symbolic stances, which has been at least one practical consequence of the academic incorporation of the critical pedagogy voice, is only worsened by the success of "qualitative research" in education. The contemporary view that "qualitative" is by its mere declaration or perfunctory performance a research achievement is no advance at all. When qualitative research relies on the assertion of description, albeit the now clichéd "thick description," as an adequate replacement for insensitive positivism then it forfeits the potential power of research to understand and explain, and not merely to describe and display (even when it also serves as a biographical reflexive occasion for the researcher), then critical qualitative research is neither critical nor research.

Likewise with "diversity." Both at the level of educational life and educational theory and research, the critical impulse toward diversity was to break open the façade of social reality that hid every form of disempowering difference from a narrowly sampled elite representing itself as the population, as society itself. In research, this was the function of the so-called "neutrality" of science. But this "diversity" has become a formulaic harness on practical, research, and theoretical innovation despite its understandable resilient rage in the face of social and social scientific repression. Should we say it has become a "repressive desublimation" (Marcuse, 1955: 196), paying for inclusion with the price of sacrificing deeper criticism of the historical social structures and cultures that generate the demand for sameness, for category, for stereotypes and cliché—and which impede the critical imagination for the beneath and beyond surface appearances? "The critical" in education has won a victory no less pyrrhic than has the practical. Between them, they unintentionally celebrate the loss of the analytic power of "society" and "the social" in education.

This routinization of critique, born in the new social movements, as it now appears in "critical social foundations," is partner to the instrumentalization of knowledge that has displaced elitist exclusionary social disciplines in education. Between instrumentalization and routinization how do we now find the critical social, and what might be its implications for Education, in the future, in a new social foundations of education?

From Movements to Knowledge

Between the social movements which commodify and commercialize knowledge—unsettling the disciplinary university in favor of a problem-centered, trans disciplinary, applied educational apparatus, along the path to full instrumentalization—and those charismatic claims for a more democratic inclusion of the full range of social identities which end up as routine formulas for identity politics—together, closing the door on "society"—historical social change brings "new-new" movements to the fore. These social movements go deeper into the social core than the democratization of legitimate identities, transforming the structure and culture of society and, with that, the character of education and the possibilities for new regimes of social knowledge.

Three transformative social movements stand out in the present. The revolution in the forces of production, which is digitalization, and its network infrastructures is no "upgrade" in the economy but rather a total societal transformation that reaches the far corners of inner as well as outer worlds, no less an upheaval than was the industrial revolution when it supplanted feudalism. Simultaneously, the alienation and disembodiment which modernity seemed to require and encourage—the loss and destruction of the body and of nature, the organic integrity of the self and ecological totality at the planetary level, is what now aims to be reversed by a wide range of new age and environmental movements. And, along with this, there is a revitalization of the pre-modern, though in almost unrecognizable new ways. The "spiritual revolution" and the "post-secular society" (Habermas 2001), like the digital and ecological revolutions, carries with it the possibility of different regimes of knowledge and education and in so doing brings back "society"—although in ways unfamiliar and anathema to the modern, industrial, de-socializing world of secular instrumentalism.

Each of these transformations requires rethinking the meaning of society and the social historically, both generally but also for knowledge and education. In this book, we begin with this last movement, the post-secular, and try to show lines of new developments that bring back an altered "social" in education and so lead toward a "new social foundations of education."

Post-secular Society

A return of the religious, or else a "religious turn," is one of the central transformations that seem to draw the attention of contemporary scholarly research in the humanities and social sciences. This social change, as Gorski, Kim, and Torpey (2012: 1) argued, "has surged onto the academic agenda, marked by the increasing scholarly use of the notion of the 'post-secular'." A "post-secular" emergent society is about the return of religion. While the debates concerning post-secular emergent society have been prominent in critical thought in the humanities and social studies of the last decades, this topic is only now beginning to enter the field of education (Fischer, Hotam, & Wexler, 2012; Jacobsen & Jacobsen, 2008).

The term "post-secular" refers to two interconnected topics. The first is about changes in contemporary society: a return to religious and/or spiritual quests characterizing contemporary society. The question is whether empirical evidence now demands a revision, if not abandonment, of the secularization thesis that has dominated the social studies in recent decades. There is already a great deal of empirical and theoretical work analyzing such a return of religion to the social arena. For example, in the *New Blackwell Companion to the Sociology of Religion*, the editor, Brian Turner (2010: 654), observed about what he calls "the religious turn" that "… there are various transformations of social and political life that have placed religion as an institution at the center of modern society […] We might argue that public space has been re-sacralized insofar as public religions play a major role in political life." (652).

The second topic is discursive. It is about the ways that social scientists, historians, philosophers, and culture critiques turn their attention and analyses to religion and theology. This scholarly turn of attention reflects the apparent return of the religious to everyday social life. The (re-)turn indicates an ongoing process of radical change in which social return and scholarly turn are in interaction.

In dating the rise of public awareness to religion back to the early 1980s, Jose Casanova (1994), for example, outlined the "post-secular" as a new era in which we are witnessing the "deprivatization" of religion in the modern world (5). More recently, Charles Taylor (2007) conceptualized such a (re-) turn of the religious somewhat differently as "a time in which the hegemony of the mainstream master narrative of secularization will be more and more challenged" as much as "a new age of religious seeking, whose outcome no one can foresee" (534–535). From a European perspective, Jürgen Habermas (2001) pointed mainly to change in public consciousness that still had to "adjust itself to the continued existence of religious communities in an increasingly secularized environment" (13). For him, however, such newly required adjustments that characterize a "post-secular" era are confined to the future role of religion in the otherwise modern and secular society (Habermas & Ratzinger, 2006; Habermas, 2008). Conversely, Hent de Vries (2008) saw in the "post-secular" an unequivocal process of "reenchantment, if not outright remythologization" (xiii) of the modern and secular world which is accompanied by a parallel "materialist turn" in current religious studies (6). In a somewhat similar radical tone, Žižek (Žižek & Milbank, 2009), perhaps one of the most vocal thinkers today spoke of the return of theology "with a vengeance" (4) and of the social return to "a quest for the truth of Being in the World" (13). From a social science perspective, Thomas Csordas (2009, 1) writes: "The sleeping giant of religion, whose perpetual dream is our collective dream as a species has never died, and it is now in the process of at least rolling over and at most leaping to its feet." In the same vein, we focused (Fischer et al., 2012) on the "meltdown" of the old binaries between religious/secular and philosophy/theology as a main characteristic of the "post-secular"—a view that is, to some extent, shared also by others (Blond 1998; Jacobsen & Jacobsen, 2008).

These no doubt divergent views have, nonetheless, common grounds in what we term a (re-)turn of the religious, that is, the twofold argument regarding the return of religion in society and the turn of the scholarly attention to and in the wake of such a return. These different takes on the "post-secular" share common ground in being repeatedly contested by defenders of the mainstream narrative of modernity. Though there ought to be sufficient empirical evidence to lend some support to the arguments for this change, still the "post-secular" remains a contested term for those who do not wish to acknowledge a delimitation, or even an "end," of the "secular age" (Taylor, 2007).

Interestingly, the views regarding the "post-secular," some of which are cited briefly above, articulate the relations between the modern/secular world and the realm of religion/theology historically because they commonly accentuate the religious heritage as the origins from which the modern/secular world matured. The historical emphasis on the religious heritage as the origin of the modern/secular world is certainly not new. Such historical framing may inform an understanding of the process of secularization as a developing separation of the secular world from its religious past. The success (Habermas, 2006) or failure of this process may be, in this framework, debated. Yet, it should be also noted that almost an entire generation of leading twentieth-century continental scholars, such as Hannah Arendt, Max Horkheimer, Karl Löwith, Eric Voegelin, Leo Strauss, Hans Blumenberg, and Hans Jonas, to name a few, have challenged this disconnection, seeing modernity on the whole as secularized Christianity, or Judeo-Christian (Aschheim, 2007; Hotam, 2009; Lazier, 2008; Schmidt, 2009). This scholarly legacy requires an engagement with the lingering presence of the theological realm of meanings within the modern and secular and as part of its character. Sometimes termed the "dialectics of secularization" (Schmidt, 2009; de Vries, 2006; Žižek & Milbank, 2009), this complex entanglement between the lingering presence of the Christian (or Judeo-Christian) worldview and a turning against it is still viewed today as the mark of modernity. It is not a binary but a dynamic dialectical complexity which defines relations between the sacred and profane in the modern/secular world (Fischer et al., 2012).

One of the implications of the thinking of a "dialectics of secularization" lies in that it enables us to traverse the borders of a secularized Christian context. Both Jewish modern nationalism (Hotam, 2013) and Muslim-Arab modernity are dialectical, displaying the complex entanglement of the secular and the profane. As Talal Asad has argued (2003), the concept of the secular, though historically born within the Christian-European context, can and should be employed in non-Christian societies that experienced or are experiencing modernization. The point to note is that other social frameworks may share the same dialectic structure of the relations between the profound and profane, though not necessarily the same "history" that refers to the Christian West. We may, for example, shift our attention geographically and culturally to readings of contemporary social and political turmoil in the Middle East. In such a geographic and thematic shift, from "the affluent societies of Europe" (Habermas, 2006) to the Middle East and from secularized Christianity to Jewish, Muslim and other modernities, "post-secular" societies may appear in different places and social contexts in a range of different guises. A current "post-secular" emergent society may imply, for example, a transformation of orthodox religiosity in one context, theocratic revolutions in another, and the proliferation of new age spirituality in still a third (Fischer et al., 2012). The "post-secular" and the (re-)turn of religion are then richer and more divergent phenomena, relevant to a wider map than what has until now been commonly assumed.

Education in post-secular society

One of the challenges of education is to offer a new theoretical horizon for critical analyses of education in a society that no longer limits discussion to a "secular West" or dichotomizes society and religion, making religion the excluded term. It is the challenge of addressing what has been mostly left out by critical thought: the relation between religion and society, the secular and the sacred, faith and political action, and to engage and influence accordingly new lines of work, theoretically, empirically, and practically.

In being dedicated to a critical analysis of education in a post-secular society, and by means of combining selected papers of scholars from around the world and across different fields of studies, this book offers a resource for the challenging of the old distinctions and for the possible drawing of innovative theoretical and practical horizons for "new social foundations" for education. The first group of chapters consists of two theoretical frameworks for thinking about post-secular society. Since its original publication in 2008, Habermas' "notes on post-secular society" acquired the status of an intellectual "ground zero" for later discussions of post-secularism. "Global changes and the visible conflicts that flare up in connection with religious issues" argues Habermas, "give us reason to doubt whether the relevance of religion has waned" (this volume: 3). Thus, in arguing that modernity no longer implies the continual advance of enduring secularism, Habermas invites a "change in conscious-ness," and a more "reflective" secularism that would be politically opened to the views and convictions of the "subculture" of believing citizens. Holding in this way to a stark and, as we have suggested above, by now heavily debated division between the secular and the religious, Habermas offers a way to nego-tiate between the worldviews that aims at defending, perhaps even saving, the modern democratic social order in which "all subcultures, whether religious or not, are expected to free their individual members from their embrace so that these citizens can *mutually recognize* one another in civil society as members of *one and the same* political community" (this volume: 9). Indeed, it is this very view presented by Habermas that Alexander's chapter is designed to challenge. For Alexander, Habermas fails to ask *why* secularism may be in decline. In posing this particular question by means of rethinking the two conceptual tra-ditions that inform secularism—liberal rationalism and critical social theory—as much as discussing their educational implications, the chapter argues that "the fundamental problem that brings post-secularism to the fore is disen-chantment with the very disenchanted worldview that lies at the heart of both traditions." The task, and especially that of education, then, lies not in balancing liberalism with critical social theory, or secularism with religion, as Habermas would have it. Rather it lies in formulating re-enchanted visions of the good "so that people will find them meaningful moral resources both for living their own private goods and contributing to a common public good across difference, without falling prey to the excesses that have often prevent-ed such a common life."

The second group of chapters invites a comparative examination of differ-ent modern, social, and educational traditions and their relations to religion and spirituality by presenting a variety of theoretical and practical perspectives that contextualize education historically and socially. Bill Pinar returns to the writings of the celebrated Canadian philosopher George Grant (1918–1988) from the 1960s–1980s. It demonstrates Grant's early critique of the instru-mentalization and the disappearance of questions of meaning and significance in modern thought and education, alongside his wish to transgress this "fate" of modernity while reintroducing the relationship between freedom and tran-scendence, philosophy and theology, piety and education. The paper exempli-fies then an early historical example for the questioning of the secular/sacred divide within the modern western educational thought and practice, showing perhaps what the post-secular might mean for curriculum as exemplified in such earlier example.

From a similar historical interest in challenging the great divide between the secular and the religious in modern western society, Bob Davis's chapter seeks to illuminate in particular the place of religion and religious experience in the education of the young. It draws attention to the importance of religious identity and affiliation in the prevailing accounts of childhood, which he attributes to an intrinsically religious character of the controversies in which the understanding of childhood has been inextricably implicated from the early modern period onwards. In so doing, the paper challenges the widespread belief that liberal education is rooted in a simple division between the secular/religious, calling for the need for education that engages with a more complex understanding of the relations between the two.

Hotam's chapter examines the unique case of Waldorf Schools and the "secular theology" of Rudolf Steiner against the background of the historical context of its creation and actualization. It demonstrates the relations between early twentieth-century Life-Philosophy and Steiner's hopes to overcome what were for him the faith/reason, spirituality/science dualisms in stage models of educational development and in curricular syntheses of rationality and spirituality. It is therefore a type of a "religious Enlightenment," the chapter argues, that is being played out in Steiner's pedagogy. Such a rereading of the Waldorf education highlights the methodological value of "contextualization" in domains of education—pedagogy and curriculum—too long thought of as categories and types, extruded from their generative contexts. Here, historically contextualized curricular and pedagogical case study becomes a model of how not to fall prey to contemporary assertions of the spiritual displacement of the secular but of their integral and harmonious "entwinement" in a fuller way of being and educating.

The contextualization of dualism also underlines Ergas's analysis of contemplative practices in today's public education. The heart of Ergas's interest, however, lies in the curricular adaptations of Eastern, notably Buddhist, contemplative practice as actual curriculum. Starting out not from Christian symbolism and theology as does Hotam, but following the Eastern, particularly Buddhist, path, Ergas's emphasis is on the direct application of spiritual practice to curriculum and pedagogy and, like Hotam, gives lie to the de-contextualized, anti-spiritual, and, then, dualistic understandings of spirit and reason. He also demonstrates how science and empirical knowledge are not posed as constituting an antinomy to spirituality and the soul or to educational movements which try to access and activate the neglected dimension now coming to the fore but, instead, how they can fit together harmoniously.

His inquiry is to show how such an educational practice and its articulation can either serve the claims of a new, alternative, "out of the box" education, a "paradigm shift" in education or, instead, work within the "box" of education—sometimes paying the price of overly integrated secularized adaptations that serve the instrumentalized interests of the what he calls the "economic narrative" which is to say state/market post-modern capitalism. Or, instead, offers an effective, but also spiritually enhancing integration of science and spirit, bringing contemplative practice into the "box" of contemporary hegemonic educational theory and practice, but also, in changing it. There is a "spectrum" of possibilities that emerge beyond dualism, and Ergas calls up Weber to help understand how to go beyond the most simplistic instances within the current dominance of the economic narrative.

The last group of chapters is composed of three historical, social, and anthropological illuminating analyses into one case study—that of the Arab and Jewish communities in Palestine/Israel which, albeit entangled with the secularized "Western" tradition, transgresses its borders. The chapters point then to the importance of showing the value of studying non-Christian, non-European forms of the secular and post-secular and presenting the subtleties of difference between secular and religious educational movements even within the same "religious" arena. In focusing on the curriculum used in the Arab public schools maintained by the Government of Mandatory Palestine in the 1920s and 1930s, Suzanne Schneider's chapter demonstrates how the British local administration promoted secular education as a means to avoid the development of a secularized Arab population while, at the same time, promoted religious education as part of a universal moral system rather than a particular political-theological tradition. The chapter presents then a historical exploration of the same complexity that ties, rather than separates, religious and secular notions in modern education. Schneider's meticulous analysis of Muslim education in Mandate Palestine is particularly useful methodologically in that it not only juxtaposes an alternative to Christianity in the non-secular but also shows how Christianity, especially Anglo-Protestantism, constructs both the religious and the secular differently from the Islamic, especially, but also the Jewish. Here, the nuanced historical treatment of how education is politically understood and deployed conveys its dependence not only on religious traditions, though importantly so, but also on distinguishing between a universalizing understanding of "moral education" and "socialization" and a particular one, leading perhaps to a different concept of "Bildung." Modern, Christian, Protestant education serves the de-politicizing purposes of colonialism as "secular" (i.e., Protestant) education against the internally disparate approaches to the particularistic reconstruction of Moslem traditions in different ideas about how it works in relation to religious history/Bildung and contemporary (then, in Mandate Palestine) nationalistic political mobilization interests.

Indeed the different uses of religion in the constructing of modern education that is designed to serve the Muslim community in today's Israel stands at the center of Agbaria and Mustafa's contextualizing of two contemporary social movements—a secular and a religious Islamic—in the field of education. The chapter presents a comparative micro-level analysis of the involvement of the two Palestinian civil society organizations and in so doing addresses the complex interplay between religion, civil society, and the State. Highlighting the role of Islamic perceptions of civil society "in carving an alternative, sub-State at the local community level and transnational at the global level, spaces and routes for political mobilization and educational activism" the authors recognize the impact of a new struggle for political hegemony between a religious-communitarian and a civic-State approach that shapes the national and civic identity of the Palestinian pupil in Israel. From the micro, or "meso," sociological perspective, the paper then places organizational analysis not in a static framework but in a dynamic historical one of social movements. In that sense, the paper's demonstration of such social movements is not only valuable for illuminating central "case studies" today, but for engaging with dynamic social phenomena, showing how these are meaningful not only in relation to wider general theoretical debates, but in relation to historic social movements, giving a more dynamic and contextualized meaning to such case studies.

If the first two chapters of this section present historical and social analysis of Muslim education, a parallel engagement with contemporary Jewish education in Israel is highlighted by Stern's ethnographic study of Neo-Hasidic religious Zionists. Stern brings the lens of specificity to the post secular educational discussion first by offering a particular new Jewish view of spirituality and then situating that in the context both of historical Jewish thought and especially in light of the successful institutionalization of the religious Zionist ideal of a national Jewish renaissance. This successful institutionalization, from the Zionist point of view, is now being challenged by the socio-historical changes which make Israel less socialist and more capitalist or neo-liberal. They do not, however, make Israel necessarily more secular, which means that the struggle for the Israeli future is being fought out not as is commonly assumed and broadcast in the conflict with the Palestinians but in the intra-Jewish community conflict and contradiction between the view of Jewish spirituality as necessarily communal, collective, and, ultimately, nationalistic and state-based on the one hand and, on the other, as reflected in a new, individualistic but not capitalistic ideal of state-oriented spirituality that recalls the orientation of the practical, social forms of Jewish mysticism that appear as what we put under the one umbrella of "Hasidism." This reappearance now of a new-agey version of Hasidism that Stern and others call "neo-Hasidism" shows how the post-secular can not only accommodate and flourish within the rationality of secularism but how it emerges, within religion, to make spirituality a vehicle of individualism—and so, ultimately modern but also post-secular. This emergent Jewish *episteme* is displayed in the methodological medium of "ethnography," here meaning observations and interviews with contemporary individualistically oriented new age spiritual young Israelis who enact this habitus contradictorily with the territorially contested terrain of nationalism and capitalism. It is still another practical and empirical effort to overcome the secular/sacred dualism in education and society.

References

Asad, T. (2003). *Formations of the secular: Christianity, Islam, Modernity.* Stanford, CA: Stanford University Press.

Aschheim, S. E. (2007). *Beyond the border: The German Jewish legacy abroad.* Princeton, NJ: Princeton University Press.

Blond, P. (Ed.). (1998). *Post-secular philosophy: Between philosophy and theology.* London: Routledge.

Casanova, J. (1994). *Public religions in the modern world.* Chicago, IL: University of Chicago Press.

Csordas, T. (2009). *Transnational transcendence.* Berkeley: University of California Press.

de Vries, H. (Ed.). (2008). *Religion beyond a concept.* New York: Fordham University Press.

Fischer, S., Hotam, Y., & Wexler, P. (2012). Democracy and education in postsecular society. *Review of Research in Education, 36,* 261–282.

Gorski, P. S., Kim, D. K., & Torpey, J. (Eds.). (2012). *The post-secular in question: Religion in contemporary society.* New York: New York University Press.

Gur Ze'ev, I. (2005). *Critical theory and critical pedagogy: A new critical language in education.* Haifa, Israel: University of Haifa Press.

Habermas, J. (2001). *Glauben und Wissen.* Frankfurt: Suhrkamp.

Habermas, J. (2008). Notes on a post-secular society. Retrieved from http://www.signandsight.com/features/1714.html

Habermas, J., & Ratzinger, J. (2006). *Dialectics of secularization: On reason and religion.* San Francisco, CA: Ignatius Press.

Holmwood, J. (2011). Sociology after Fordism: Prospects and problems, *European Journal of Social Theory,* November, *14*(4), 537–556.

Horkheimer, M. (1972). *Critical theory: Selected essays.* New York. Herder and Herder.

Hotam, Y. (2009). Overcoming the mentor: Heidegger's present and the presence of Heidegger in Karl Loewith's and Hans Jonas' postwar thought. *History of European Ideas, 35,* 253–264.

Hotam, Y. (2013). *Modern gnosis and Zionism: The crisis of culture, life philosophy and Jewish national thought.* London: Routledge.

Jacobsen, D., & Jacobsen, R. H. (Eds.). (2008). *The American university in a postsecular age.* New York: Oxford University Press.

Lazier, B. (2008). *God interrupted: Heresy and the European imagination between the world wars.* Princeton, NJ: Princeton University Press.

Marcuse, H. (1955). *Eros and civilization: A philosophical inquiry into Freud.* Boston; MA: Beacon Press.

Schmidt, C. (2009). *Die theopolitische Stunde.* Munich: Fink.

Slaughter, S., & Rhoades, G. (2004). *Academic capitalism and the new economy: Markets, state and the new economy.* Baltimore, MD: Johns Hopkins University Press.

Taylor, C. (2007). *A secular age.* Cambridge, MA: Harvard University Press.

Tozer, S. E., & Butts, R. F. (2011). The evolution of social foundations of education. in S. E. Tozer, B. P. Gallegos and A. M. Henry (eds). *The handbook of research in the social foundations of education* (pp. 4–15). New York: Routledge.

Turner, B. (2010). Religion in a post-secular society. In B. S. Turner (Ed.), *The new Blackwell companion to the sociology of religion* (pp. 650–667). Chichester: Wiley-Blackwell.

Wexler, (1976). *The sociology of education: Beyond equality.* Indianapolis, IN: Bobbs-Merrill.

Wexler, Philip. (2009). *Symbolic movement: Critique and spirituality in sociology of education.* Rotterdam: Sense Publishing.

Žižek, S., & Milbank, J. (2009). *The monstrosity of Christ: Paradox or dialectic?* Cambridge, MA: MIT Press.

Part I

Perspectives

1. Notes on Post-Secular Society

Jürgen Habermas

The controversial term "post-secular society" can only be applied to the affluent societies of Europe or countries such as Canada, Australia and New Zealand where people's religious ties have steadily or rather quite dramatically lapsed in the post-World War II period.

These regions have witnessed a spreading awareness that their citizens are living in a secularized society. In terms of sociological indicators, however, the religious behavior and convictions of the local populations have by no means changed to such an extent as to justify labeling these societies "post-secular" even though trends in these societies towards de-institutionalized and new spiritual forms of religiosity have not offset the tangible losses by the major religious communities.

Reconsidering the Sociological Debate on Secularization

Nevertheless, global changes and the visible conflicts that flare up in connection with religious issues give us reason to doubt whether the relevance of religion has waned. An ever smaller number of sociologists now support the hypothesis, and it went unopposed for a long time, that there is close linkage between the modernization of society and the secularization of the population. The hypothesis rests on three initially plausible considerations.

First, progress in science and technology promotes an *anthropocentric understanding* of the "disenchanted" world because the totality of empirical states and events can be causally explained; and a scientifically enlightened mind cannot be easily reconciled with theocentric and metaphysical worldviews. Second, with the *functional differentiation of social subsystems,* the churches and other religious organizations lose their control over law, politics, public welfare, education and science; they restrict themselves to their proper function of administering the means of salvation, turn exercising religion into a private matter and in general lose public influence and relevance. Finally, the development from agrarian through industrial to post-industrial societies leads to average-to-higher levels of welfare and greater social security; and with a reduction of risks in life, and the ensuing increase in existential security, there is a drop in the personal need for a practice that promises to cope with uncontrolled contingencies through faith in a "higher" or cosmic power.

These were the main reasons for the secularization thesis. Among the expert community of sociologists, the thesis has been a subject of controversy for more than two decades. Lately, in the wake of the not unfounded criticism of a narrow Eurocentric perspective, there is even talk of the "end of the secularization theory." The United States, with the undiminished vibrancy of its religious communities and the unchanging proportion of religiously committed and active citizens, nevertheless remains the spearhead of modernization. It was long regarded as the great exception to the secularising trend, yet informed by the *globally extended* perspective on other cultures and world religions, the US now seems to exemplify the norm.

From this revisionist view, the European development, whose Occidental rationalism was once supposed to serve as a model for the rest of the world, is actually the exception rather than the norm—treading a deviant path. We and not they are pursuing a *Sonderweg*. Above all, three overlapping phenomena converge to create the impression of a worldwide "resurgence of religion": the missionary expansion; a fundamentalist radicalization; and the political instrumentalization of the potential for violence innate in many of the world religions.

A first sign of their vibrancy is the fact that orthodox, or at least conservative, groups within the established religious organizations and churches are on the advance everywhere. This holds for Hinduism and Buddhism just as much as it does for the three monotheistic religions. Most striking of all is the regional spread of these established religions in Africa and in the countries of East and Southeast Asia. The missionary successes apparently depend, among other things, on the flexibility of the corresponding forms of organization. The transnational and multicultural Roman Catholic Church is adapting better to the globalizing trend than are the Protestant churches, which are nationally organized and the principal losers. Most dynamic of all are the decentralized networks of Islam (particularly in sub-Saharan Africa) and the Evangelicals (particularly in Latin America). They stand out for an ecstatic form of religiosity inspired by charismatic leaders.

As to fundamentalism, the fastest-growing religious movements such as the Pentecostals and the radical Muslims can be most readily described as "fundamentalist." They either combat the modern world or withdraw from it into isolation. Their forms of worship combine spiritualism and adventism with rigid moral conceptions and literal adherence to the holy scriptures. By contrast, the "new age movements" which have mushroomed since the 1970s exhibit a "Californian" syncretism; they share with the Evangelicals a de-institutionalized form of religious observance. In Japan, approximately 400 such sects have arisen which combine elements of Buddhism and popular religions with pseudoscientific and esoteric doctrines. In the People's Republic of China, the political repression of the Falun Gong sect has high lighted the large number of "new religions" whose followers are thought to number some 80 million.

Finally, the mullah regime in Iran and Islamic terrorism are merely the most spectacular examples of a political unleashing of the potential for violence innate in religion. Often smoldering conflicts that are profane in origin are first ignited once coded in religious terms. This is true of the "desecularization" of the Middle East conflict, of the politics of Hindu nationalism and the enduring conflict between India and Pakistan and of the mobilization of the religious right in the US before and during the invasion of Iraq.

The Descriptive Account of a "Post-Secular Society"—and the Normative Issue of How Citizens of Such a Society Should Understand Themselves

I cannot discuss in detail the controversy among sociologists concerning the supposed *Sonderweg* of the secularized societies of Europe in the midst of a religiously mobilized world society. My impression is that the data collected globally still provide surprisingly robust support for the defenders of the secularization thesis. In my view the weakness of the theory of secularization is due rather to rash inferences that betray an imprecise use of the concepts of "secularization" and "modernization." What is true is that in the course of the differentiation of functional social systems, churches and religious communities increasingly confined themselves to their core function of pastoral care and had to renounce their competencies in other areas of society. At the same time, the practice of faith also withdrew into more of a personal or subjective domain. There is a correlation between the functional specification of the religious system and the individualization of religious practice.

However, as Jose Casanova correctly points out, the loss of function and the trend toward individualization do not necessarily imply that religion *loses influence and relevance* either in the political arena and the culture of a society or in the personal conduct of life. Quite apart from their numerical weight, religious communities can obviously still claim a "seat" in the life of societies that are largely secularized. Today, public consciousness in Europe can be described in terms of a "post-secular society" to the extent that at present it still has to "adjust itself to the continued existence of religious communities in an increasingly secularized environment." The revised reading of the secularization hypothesis relates less to its substance and more to the predictions concerning the future role of "religion." The description of modern societies as "post-secular" refers to *a change in consciousness* that I attribute primarily to three phenomena.

First, the broad perception of those global conflicts that are often presented as hinging on religious strife changes public consciousness. The majority of European citizens do not even need the presence of intrusive fundamentalist movements and the fear of terrorism, defined in religious terms, to make them aware of their own relativity within the global horizon. This undermines the secularistic belief in the *foreseeable disappearance* of religion and robs the secular understanding of the world of any triumphal zest. The awareness of living in a secular society is no longer bound up with the *certainty* that cultural and social modernization can advance only at the cost of the public influence and personal relevance of religion.

Second, religion is gaining influence not only worldwide but also within national public spheres. I am thinking here of the fact that churches and religious organizations are increasingly assuming the role of "communities of interpretation" in the public arena of secular societies. They can attain influence on public opinion and will formation by making relevant contributions to key issues, irrespective of whether their arguments are convincing or objectionable. Our pluralist societies constitute a responsive sounding board for such interventions because they are increasingly split on value conflicts requiring political regulation. Be it the dispute over the legalization of abortion or voluntary euthanasia, on the bioethical issues of reproductive medicine, questions of animal protection or climate change—on these and similar questions the divisive premises are so opaque that it is by no means settled from the outset which party can draw on the more convincing moral intuitions.

Pushing the issue closer home, let me remind you that the visibility and vibrancy of foreign religious communities also spur the attention to the familiar churches and congregations. The Muslims next door force the Christian citizens to face up to the practice of a rival faith. And they also give the secular citizens a keener consciousness of the phenomenon of the public presence of religion.

The third stimulus for a change of consciousness among the population is the immigration of "guest-workers" and refugees, specifically from countries with traditional cultural backgrounds. Since the 16th century, Europe has had to contend with *confessional schisms* within its own culture and society. In the wake of the present immigration, the more blatant dissonances between different religions link up with the challenge of a *pluralism of ways of life* typical of immigrant societies. This extends beyond the challenge of a *pluralism of denominations.* In societies like ours which are still caught in the painful process of transformation into postcolonial immigrant societies, the issue of tolerant coexistence between different religious communities is made harder by the difficult problem of how to integrate immigrant cultures socially. While coping with the pressure of globalized labor markets, social integration must succeed even under the humiliating conditions of growing social inequality. But that is a different story.

I have thus far taken the position of a sociological observer in trying to answer the question of why we can term secularized societies "post-secular." In these societies, religion maintains a public influence and relevance while the secularistic certainty that religion will disappear worldwide in the course of modernization is losing ground. If we henceforth adopt the perspective of participants, however, we face a quite different, namely normative question: How should we see ourselves as members of a post-secular society and what must we reciprocally expect from one another in order to ensure that in firmly entrenched nation states, social relations remain civil despite the growth of a plurality of cultures and religious worldviews?

All European societies today face this question. While preparing this lecture last February, a single weekend offered me three different news items. President Sarkozy dispatched an additional 4,000 policemen to the infamous Parisian banlieus, so sorely afflicted by rioting Maghreb youths; the Archbishop of Canterbury recommended that the British legislature adopt parts of Sharia family law for its local Muslim population; and a fire broke out in a tenement block in Ludwigshafen in which nine Turks, four of them children, met their deaths—something that despite the lack of evidence of arson prompted deep suspicion among the Turkish media, not to say true dismay; this then persuaded the Turkish prime minster to make a visit to Germany during which his ambivalent campaign speech in an arena in Cologne in turn triggered a strident response in the German press.

These debates have assumed a sharper tone since the terrorist attacks of 9/11. In the Netherlands the murder of Theo van Gogh kindled a passionate public discourse, as did the affair with the Mohammad cartoons in Denmark. These debates assumed a quality of their own; their ripples have spread beyond national borders to unleash a European-wide debate. I am interested in the background assumptions that render this discussion on "Islam in Europe" so explosive. But before I can address the philosophical core of the reciprocal accusations, let me outline more clearly the shared starting point of the opposing parties—a proper interpretation of what we used to call "the separation of church and state."

From an Uneasy Modus Vivendi to a Balance Between Shared Citizenship and Cultural Difference

The secularization of the state was the appropriate response to the confessional wars of early modernity. The principle of "separating church and state" was only gradually realized and took a different form in each national body of law. To the extent that the government assumed a secular character, step by step the religious minorities (initially only tolerated) received further rights—first the freedom to practice their own religion at home, then the right of religious expression and finally equal rights to exercise their religion in public. A historical glance at this tortuous process, and it reached into the 20th century, can tell us something about the *preconditions* for this precious achievement, the inclusive religious freedom that is extended to all citizens alike.

After the Reformation, the state initially faced the elementary task of having to pacify a society divided along confessional lines, in other words, to achieve peace and order. In the context of the present debate, Dutch writer Margriet de Moor reminds her fellow citizens of these beginnings: "Tolerance is often mentioned in the same breath as respect, yet our tolerance, and its roots date back to the 16th and 17th centuries, is not based on respect—on the contrary. We hated the religion of the respective other, Catholics and Calvinists had not one iota of respect for the views of the other side, and our 80 Years' War was not just a rebellion against Spain, but also a bloody jihad by the orthodox Calvinists against Catholicism." We will soon see what kind of respect Margriet de Moor has in mind.

As regards peace and order, governments had to assume a neutral stand even where they remained bound up with the religion prevailing in the country. In countries with confessional strife the state had to disarm the quarreling parties, invent arrangements for a peaceful coexistence of the inimical confessions and monitor their precarious existence alongside each other. In confessionally split countries such as Germany or the Netherlands, the opposing subcultures then each nested in niches of their own and subsequently *remained foreign* to one another in society. Precisely this *modus vivendi* (and this is what I would like to stress) proved to be insufficient when the constitutional revolutions of the late 18th century spawned a new political order that subjected the completely secularized powers of the state to both the rule of law and the democratic will of the people.

This constitutional state is only able to guarantee its citizens equal freedom of religion under the proviso that they no longer barricade themselves within their religious communities and seal themselves off from one another. All subcultures, whether religious or not, are expected to free their individual members from their embrace so that these citizens can *mutually recognize* one another in civil society as members of *one and the same* political community. As democratic citizens they give themselves laws which grant them the right, as private citizens, to preserve their identity in the context of their own particular culture and worldview. This new relationship of democratic government, civil society and subcultural self-maintenance is the key to correctly understanding the two motives that today struggle with each other although they are meant to be mutually complementary. For the universalist project of the political Enlightenment by no means contradicts the particularist sensibilities of a correctly conceived multiculturalism.

The *liberal rule of law* already guarantees religious freedom as a basic right, meaning that the fate of religious minorities no longer depends on the benevolence of a more or less tolerant state authority. Yet it is the democratic state that first enables the impartial application of this principled religious freedom. When Turkish communities in Berlin, Cologne or Frankfurt seek to get their prayer houses out of the backyards in order to build mosques visible from afar, the issue is no longer the principle per se, but its fair application. However, evident reasons for defining what should or should not be tolerated can only be ascertained by means of the deliberative and inclusive procedures of democratic will formation. The principle of tolerance is first freed of the suspicion of expressing mere condescension when the conflicting parties *meet as equals* in the process of reaching an agreement with one another. How the lines between positive freedom of religion (i.e., the right to exercise your own faith) and the negative freedom (i.e., the right to be spared the religious practices of people of other faiths) should be drawn in an actual case is always a matter of controversy. But in a democracy those affected, however indirectly, are themselves involved in the decision-making process.

"Tolerance" is, of course, not only a question of enacting and applying laws; it must be practiced in everyday life. Tolerance means that believers of one faith, of a different faith and non-believers must mutually concede to one another the right to those convictions, practices and ways of living that they themselves reject. This concession must be supported by a shared basis of mutual recognition from which repugnant dissonances can be overcome. This recognition should not be confused with an *appreciation* of an alien culture and way of living, or of rejected convictions and practices. We need tolerance only *vis-a-vis* worldviews that we consider wrong and *vis-a-vis* habits that we do not like. Therefore, the basis of recognition is not the esteem for this or that characteristic or achievement but the awareness of the fact that the other is a member of an inclusive community of citizens with equal rights, in which each individual is accountable to the others for his political contributions.

Now that is easier said than done. The equal inclusion of *all citizens* in civil society requires not only a political culture that preserves liberal attitudes from being confused with indifference; inclusion can only be achieved if certain material conditions are met. These include full integration and compensatory education in kindergartens, schools and universities, and equal opportunities in access to the labor market. However, in the present context what is most important to me is the image of an inclusive civil society in which equal citizenship and cultural difference complement each other in the right way.

For example, as long as a considerable portion of German citizens of Turkish origin and of Muslim faith have stronger political ties to their old homeland than their new one, those corrective votes will be lacking in the public sphere and at the ballot boxes which are necessary to expand the range of values of the dominant political culture. Without the inclusion of minorities in civil society, the two complementary processes will not be able to develop hand in hand, namely, the opening of the political community to a difference-sensitive inclusion of foreign minority cultures, on the one hand and, on the other, the reciprocal opening of these subcultures to a state which encourages its individual members participate in the political life at large.

Kulturkampf *Between Radical Multiculturalism and Militant Secularism: Philosophical Background Assumptions*

In order to answer the question of how we should understand ourselves as members of a post-secular society we can take our cue from these two interlocking processes. The ideological parties that confront each other in public debates today seldom take any notice of how both processes fit each other. The party of the multiculturalists appeals to the protection of collective identities and accuses the other side of representing a "fundamentalism of the Enlightenment," whereas the secularists insist on the uncompromising inclusion of minorities in the existing political framework and accuse their opponents of a "multiculturalist betrayal" of the core values of the Enlightenment. In some European countries a third party plays a major role in these battles.

The so-called multiculturalists fight for an unprejudiced adjustment of the legal system to the cultural minorities' claim to equal treatment. They warn against a policy of enforced assimilation with uprooting consequences. The secular state, they say, should not push through the incorporation of minorities into the egalitarian community of citizens in such a manner that it tears individuals out of their identity-forming contexts. From this communitarian view, a policy of abstract integration is under suspicion of subjecting minorities to the imperatives of the majority culture. Today, the wind is blowing in the multiculturalists' faces: "Not only academics, but politicians and newspaper columnists likewise consider the Enlightenment a fortress to be defended against Islamic extremism." This reaction, in turn, brings a critique of a "fundamentalism of the Enlightenment" into play. For example, Timothy Garton Ash argues in the *New York Review of Books* (Oct. 5, 2006) that "even Muslim women contradict the way in which Hirsi Ali attributes her oppression to Islam instead of the respective national, regional or tribal culture." In fact, Muslim immigrants cannot be integrated into Western society in defiance of their religion but only with it.

On the other hand, the *secularists* fight for a colorblind inclusion of all citizens, irrespective of their cultural origin and religious belonging. This side warns against the consequences of a "politics of identity" that goes too far in adapting the legal system to the claims of preserving the intrinsic characteristics of minority cultures. From this "laicistic" viewpoint, religion must remain an exclusively private matter. Thus, Pascal Bruckner rejects cultural rights because these would give rise to parallel societies—to "small, self-isolated social groups, each of which adheres to a different norm." Bruckner condemns multiculturalism roundly as an "anti-racist racism," though his attack at best applies to those ultra-minded multiculturalists who advocate the introduction of collective cultural rights. Such protection for entire cultural groups would in fact curtail the right of their individual members to choose a way of life of their own.

Thus the conflicting parties both pretend to fight for the same purpose, a liberal society that allows autonomous citizens to coexist in a civilized manner. And yet they are at loggerheads in a *Kulturkampf* that resurfaces at every new political occasion. Although it is clear that both aspects are interlinked, they argue bitterly over whether the preservation of cultural identity has priority over the enforcement of shared citizenship or vice versa. The discussion gains its polemical acuity from contradictory philosophical premises which the opponents rightly or wrongly attribute to one other. Ian Buruma has made the interesting observation that following 9/11 an academic debate on the Enlightenment, on modernity and post-modernity, was taken out of the university and floated in the marketplace. The fiery debate was stoked by problematic background assumptions, namely a cultural relativism beefed up with a critique of reason on the one side and a rigid secularism pushing for a critique of religion on the other.

The radical reading of multiculturalism often relies on the notion of the so called "incommensurability" of worldviews, discourses or conceptual schemes. From this contextualist perspective, cultural ways of life appear as semantically closed universes, each of which keeps the lid on its own standards of rationality and truth claims. Therefore, each culture is supposed to exist for itself as a semantically sealed whole, cut off from dialogues with other cultures. With the exception of unsteady compromises, submission or conversion are the only alternatives for terminating conflicts between such cultures. Given this premise, radical multiculturalists cannot discern in any universalist validity claim, such as the claim for the universality of democracy and human rights, anything but the imperialist power claim of a dominant culture.

This relativistic reading inadvertently robs itself of the standards for a critique of the unequal treatment of cultural minorities. In our post-colonial immigrant societies, discrimination against minorities is usually rooted in prevailing cultural prejudices that lead to a selective application of established constitutional principles. If one then does not take seriously the universalist thrust of these principles in the first place, there is no vantage point from which to understand how the constitutional interpretation is bound up with the prejudices of the majority culture. I need not go into the philosophical issue of why cultural relativism, derived from a postmodern critique of reason, is an untenable position. However, the position itself is interesting for another reason; it lends itself to an opposite political conclusion and explains a peculiar political change of sides.

Ironically, the very same relativism is shared by those militant Christians who fight Islamic fundamentalism while proudly claiming the Enlightenment culture either as part and parcel of the tradition of Roman Catholicism or as the specific offshoot of Protestantism. On the other hand, these conservatives have strange bedfellows, since some of the former leftist "multiculturalists" turned into war-hungry liberal hawks. These converts even joined the ranks of neocon "Enlightenment fundamentalists." In the battle against Islamic fundamentalists they were evidently able to adopt the culture of the Enlightenment, which they had once fought in the name of their own "Western culture" because they had always rejected its universalist intent: "The Enlightenment has become attractive specifically because its values are not just universal, but because they are 'our,' i.e., European, Western values."

Needless to say, this reproach does not refer to those "laicistic" intellectuals of French origin for whom the pejorative term "Enlightenment fundamentalists" was originally coined. But it is again a philosophical background assumption which can explain a certain militancy on the part of these truly universalist guardians of the Enlightenment tradition. From their viewpoint, religion must withdraw from the political public sphere into the private domain because, cognitively speaking, it has been historically overridden as an "intellectual formation" ("Gestalt des Geistes," as Hegel puts it). In the light of a liberal constitution, well, religion must be tolerated, but it cannot lay claim to provide a cultural resource for the self-understanding of any truly modern mind.

Complementary Learning Processes: Religious and Secular Mentalities

This secularistic position does not depend on how one judges the empirical suggestion that religious citizens and communities still make relevant contributions to political opinion and will formation even in largely secularized societies. Whether or not we consider the application of the predicate "post-secular" appropriate for a description of West European societies, one can be convinced, for philosophical reasons, that religious communities owe their persisting influence to an obstinate survival of pre-Modern modes of thought—a fact that begs an empirical explanation. From the viewpoint of secularism, the substance of faith is scientifically discredited either way. As such, discussions about religious traditions and with religious figures, who still lay claim to a significant public role, escalate into polemic.

In the use of terms I distinguish between "secular" and "secularist." Unlike the indifferent stance of a secular or unbelieving person, who relates agnostically to religious validity claims, secularists tend to adopt a polemical stance toward religious doctrines that maintain a public influence despite the fact that their claims cannot be scientifically justified. Today, secularism is often based on "hard" naturalism, i.e., one based on scientistic assumptions. Unlike the case of cultural relativism, here I need not comment on the philosophical background. For what interests me in the present context is the question of whether a secularist devaluation of religion, if it were one day to be shared by the vast majority of secular citizens, is at all compatible with that postsecular balance between shared citizenship and cultural difference I have outlined. Or would the secularistic mindset of a relevant portion of the citizenry be just as unappetizing for the normative self-understanding of a post-secular society as the fundamentalist leaning of a mass of religious citizens? This question touches on deeper roots of the present unease than the "multiculturalist drama." Which kind of problem do we face?

It is to the credit of the secularists that they, too, insist on the indispensability of including all citizens as equals in civil society. Because a democratic order cannot simply be *imposed* on its authors, the constitutional state confronts its citizens with the demanding expectations of an ethics of citizenship that reaches beyond mere obedience to the law. Religious citizens and communities must not only superficially adjust to the constitutional order. They are expected to appropriate the secular legitimation of constitutional principles under the premises of their own faith. It is a well-known fact that the Catholic Church first pinned its colors to the mast of liberalism and democracy with the Second Vaticanum in 1965. And in Germany, the Protestant churches did not act differently. Many Muslim communities still have this painful learning process before them. Certainly, the insight is also growing in the Islamic world that today an historical-hermeneutic approach to the Koran's doctrine is required. But the discussion on a desired Euro-Islam makes us once more aware of the fact that it is the religious communities that will themselves decide whether they can recognize in a reformed faith their "true faith."

When we think of such a shift from the traditional to a more reflexive form of religious consciousness, what springs to mind is the model of the post-Reformation change in epistemic attitudes that took place in the Christian communities of the West. But a change in mentality cannot be prescribed, nor can it be politically manipulated or pushed through by law; it is at best the result of a learning process. And it only appears as a "learning process" from the viewpoint of a secular self-understanding of Modernity. In view of what an ethics of democratic citizenship requires in terms of mentalities, we come up against the very limits of a normative political theory that can justify only rights and duties. Learning processes can be fostered but not morally or legally stipulated.

But shouldn't we turn the question around? Is a learning process only necessary on the side of religious traditionalism and not on that of secularism, too? Do the selfsame normative expectations that rule an inclusive civil society not prohibit a secularistic devaluation of religion just as they prohibit, for example, the religious rejection of equal rights for men and women? A *complementary learning process* is certainly necessary on the secular side unless we confuse the neutrality of a secular state in view of competing religious worldviews with the purging of the political public sphere of all religious contributions.

Certainly, the domain of a state, which controls the means of legitimate coercion, should not be opened to the strife between various religious communities, otherwise the government could become the executive arm of a religious majority that imposes its will on the opposition. In a constitutional state, all norms that can be legally implemented must be formulated and *publicly justified* in a language that all the citizens understand. Yet the state's neutrality does not preclude the permissibility of religious utterances within the political public sphere as long as the institutionalized decision making process at the parliamentary, court, governmental and administrative levels remains clearly separated from the informal flows of political communication and opinion formation among the broader public of citizens. The "separation of church and state" calls for a filter between these two spheres—a filter through which only "translated," i.e., secular contributions may pass from the confused din of voices in the public sphere into the formal agendas of state institutions.

Two reasons speak in favor of such liberal practice. First, the persons who are neither willing nor able to divide their moral convictions and their vocabulary into profane and religious strands must be permitted to take part in political will formation even if they use religious language. Second, the democratic state must not preemptively reduce the polyphonic complexity of the diverse public voices, because it cannot know whether it is not otherwise cutting society off from scarce resources for the generation of meanings and the shaping of identities. Particularly with regard to vulnerable social relations, religious traditions possess the power to convincingly articulate moral sensitivities and solidaristic intuitions. What puts pressure on secularism, then, is the expectation that secular citizens in civil society and the political public sphere must be able to meet their religious fellow citizens as equals.

Were secular citizens to encounter their fellow citizens with the reservation that the latter, because of their religious mindset, are not to be taken seriously as modern contemporaries, they would revert to the level of a mere *modus vivendi*—and would thus relinquish the very basis of mutual recognition which is constitutive for shared citizenship. Secular citizens are expected not to exclude *a fortiori* that they may discover, even in religious utterances, semantic contents and covert personal intuitions that can be translated and introduced into a secular discourse.

So, if all is to go well, both sides, each from its own viewpoint, must accept an interpretation of the relation between faith and knowledge that enables them to live together in a self-reflective manner.

2. Education and the Post-Secular Condition: Resanctifying Pedagogy in an Era of Disenchantment

Hanan A. Alexander

Introduction

In his seminal essay, "Notes on a Post-Secular Society," Jürgen Habermas (2008) describes the waning of the so-called secular thesis—"that there is a close linkage between modernization of society and the secularization of the population" (17). The rise of modernity, in order words, should have signaled the decline of religion, whereas it turns out that the persistence of religion amidst modernity appears to suggest a weakening of secularism. In this view, "secularism" involves at least three trends: (a) the dominance of a "disenchanted" worldview in the public domain that controls law, politics, and welfare, based on a "hard" scientific naturalism; (b) restricting organized religion to the private domain with a pastoral role of administering salvation; and (c) appreciation for the higher standards of living, reduction in risks to life, and increased existential security resulting from advanced technologies (18, 27). One consequence of this decline is what Habermas calls a "post-secular consciousness," in which rival religious and cultural traditions and attitudes exist alongside one another in modern liberal societies, side by side with secular traditions and attitudes, between and even within both collective and individual identities (20). He also discusses some of the normative consequences of this condition for citizens in constitutional democracies, including the rule of law that guarantees freedom of religious and cultural expression and from religious and cultural coercion, the right to choose a way of life among alternatives that appear in the free public exchange of ideas, tolerance and recognition of views that are not only different or foreign but possibly even offensive, and robust dialogue among rival religious and secular perspectives (28). This dialogue should be more engaged than earlier models of *modus vivendi* such as that between Calvinists and Catholics which strove to disarm quarreling confessional parties through thin arrangements for peaceful co-existence that merely monitored precarious lives alongside but not together with one another (22).

Habermas does not ask directly, however, why the secular thesis failed or why secularism may be in decline. This failure, it seems to me, and hence the onset of post-secularism, is at least in part a consequence of difficulties in the two conceptual traditions that inform secularism—liberal rationalism and critical social theory—which have themselves been subjected to serious challenges in recent decades. Indeed, I would argue that post-secularism properly understood consists not only in a description of the social processes that appear once the disappointment sets in, including the resurgence of spiritual sensibilities, whether tethered to historic religions or not, concerned, for example, with the discovery or improvement of self; belonging to, joining, or enhancing community; preserving or transforming tradition; engaging higher goods or experiencing transcendence. It also entails a substantive critique of the very secular beliefs and practices that seem to be in disarray, especially their claim to a privileged neutral epistemological stance against which other perspectives are to be adjudicated, religious and ethical traditions in particular. In this sense, the prefix "post" signals a conceptual not only temporal circumstance, meaning "contra" or "in opposition to," in addition to something that may happen *after* something else.

Habermas refers to both the liberal and critical traditions in their extreme formulations—"Enlightenment fundamentalism" on the one hand and "radical multiculturalism" on the other. He suggests that the former, found for example among French "laicistic" intellectuals, has closer ties to what he calls "militant secularism" than the latter, which is grounded in the so-called "incommensurability" of worldviews, discourses and conceptual schemes (24–26)—criticizing the one for its resistance to diversity and the other for its rampant relativism (25). Instead, he advocates a middle course in which "Enlightenment by no means contradicts the particularistic sensibilities of a correctly conceived multiculturalism" (23). However, in so far as it entails suspicion of or limitations on religion, secularism has roots in the counter-Enlightenment critical social theories that inform much multicultural thought, not only Enlightenment liberalism; and the difficulties that I have in mind relate to a loss of faith in the standards of assessment that lie at the heart of each tradition, not on their margins, which has led to disillusion with the very disenchantment associated with the hard naturalism that they have spawned.

Habermas seeks detent between radical multiculturalism and militant secularism by means of dialogical learning processes among religious and secular mentalities, in short, through education (27–29). But most philosophers would agree that the very idea of education, however understood, presupposes some conception of criticism which in the modern context has often been grounded in one or the other of the accounts of secular neutrality that appear to be in retreat. Without a defensible theory of criticism, however, the question arises whether it is possible to speak coherently of education in connection with post-secular consciousness altogether. In other words, can the dialogical learning processes Habermas proposes between secularism and religion be effectively enacted as a form of education, as opposed to say indoctrination in the moderation he defends (Snook, 1972), given difficulties with the critical standards of both Enlightenment liberalism and counter Enlightenment multiculturalism that lie at the heart of secularism in one form or another?

In this chapter I answer that education in a post-secular condition *is* possible, though not necessarily or, more precisely, not entirely as conceived by Habermas. If the difficulties that have inspired dissatisfaction with secularism are central to both the liberalism and the multiculturalism upon which it may be based, a theory of criticism suitable to sustaining an education in keeping with post-secular consciousness cannot be grounded in a dialogue between extreme, or even moderate, formulations of these views. The fundamental problem that brings post-secularism to the fore is disenchantment with the very disenchanted worldview that lies at the heart of both traditions. The problem of post-secular education, then, is not how to balance secularism with multiculturalism or liberalism with critical social theory but rather how to re-enchant visions of the good so that people will find them meaningful moral resources both for living their own private goods and contributing to a common public good across difference, without falling prey to the excesses that have often prevented such a common life in the past. We require, in other words, a concept of criticism, and hence of education, consistent with a world that is at least partially re-enchanted—a re-sanctification of pedagogy!

The most appropriate political theory for this purpose is to be found neither in the liberal-multiculturalism of Habermas, nor the classical liberalism of John Rawls (1971; 1993), following John Locke (2003) and Immanuel Kant (1997; 2002), with which Habermas also famously takes issue (e.g., Habermas, 1993), nor even in a conversation between them. It is to be found rather in the communitarian critique of liberalism initiated by Charles Taylor (1989; 1991), Michael Sandel (1984; 1998), and Michael Walzer (1985), often tied to the neo-Aristotelianism of Alastair MacIntyre (1984, 1989), and in the value pluralism of Isaiah Berlin (1969). Indeed, Habermas's post-secular turn might well be seen as somewhat of a nod in the direction of the neo-Aristotelianism from which he once tried to distinguish himself (Habermas, 1993: 113–132). Due to its critique of rational neutrality and its expanded concept of self, John Gray (1996; 2002) referred to the early modern roots of this view as an alternative face of liberalism to that of Locke, Kant, and Rawls, more in keeping with Thomas Hobbes (2002), David Hume (1953), and Johann Gottfried Herder (Berlin, 1976). Gray (1996) also referred to some of its more recent expressions broadly as post-liberalism. I prefer the liberal to the post-liberal designation, since I understand this orientation as remaining within a reimagined liberal camp that prizes community and pluralism above a narrow and uniform individualism. Called diversity as opposed to autonomy liberalism by William Galston (1991; 2002), this view entails a non-neutral account of criticism according to which citizens learn to view their own commitments from the perspective of those with whom they might disagree through a robust dialogue among rival perspectives. Although similar in some respects to the dialogue envisaged in Habermas's discourse ethics, this view is grounded in more promising assumptions. I have called the sort of worldviews that emerge examples of "intelligent spirituality" (Alexander, 2001: 139–70), the education through which one is initiated into such views, "pedagogy of the sacred" (Alexander and Ben-Peretz, 2001), and the processes by means of which one learns to engage alternatives in dialogue, "pedagogy of difference" (Alexander, 2015: 87–138).

The chapter is divided into six parts, including this introduction. In the next part I consider the sources of secularism in both autonomy liberalism and critical social theory. The subsequent part considers difficulties with these traditions, including Rawls's autonomy liberalism and Habermas's liberal multiculturalism, from a perspective that seeks to understand the discontent with secular disenchantment. Part four explores a conception of post- or diversity liberalism consistent with post-secular consciousness and part five with how pedagogies of the sacred and pedagogies of difference, grounded in post- or diversity liberalism and leading to intelligent spiritualities, are in sync with post-secular consciousness properly conceived. I conclude with some consequences for contemporary educational thought and practice.

The Dialectic of Modernity and the Sources of Secularism

The intellectual sources of secularism are bound up with two directions in modern thought, not one. Sometimes called rationalism and romanticism or, in Isaiah Berlin's (1976) terms, Enlightenment and counter-Enlightenment, these trends have been in tension with one another at least since the beginning of the nineteenth century. Max Horkheimer and Theodor Adorno (2007) came close to capturing this conflict in their classic phrase *dialectic of enlightenment*, though by this term they had in mind the failure of Marxist critical theory to capture the socio-economic contradictions within Enlightenment capitalism. Berlin (1997), however, was referring to tensions between the rational mindset of eighteenth-century Enlightenment thought, of which Immanuel Kant is probably the greatest example, and the nineteenth-century reaction encapsulated by G. W. F. Hegel (1953; 1967; 1978) and his left and right leaning descendants. The former saw a-priori reason as independent of history and society, whereas the latter placed a premium on a posteriori history and society to either reconceive reason or abandon it altogether. The hard naturalism that grounds modern disenchantment with medieval religion is tied to both of these trends and the current critique of this disenchantment belongs to the less rational side of its counter-Enlightenment strand. This less, or even anti, rational side of counter-Enlightenment thought argues against the dialectical rationality of Karl Marx (1970) and his heirs no less than the rational liberalism of Kant and his. I prefer to call this tension the *dialectic of modernity*, therefore, not merely of Enlightenment (Alexander, 2001: 21–2).

One source of the modern disenchantment that characterizes secularism, then, began with the empiricism of Francis Bacon (2002) that emerged from the skepticism of Rene Descartes (1999). This way of thinking climaxed in Immanuel Kant's (1970) response to David Hume's (2007) application of Cartesian skepticism in critique of the very empiricism to which it gave birth. Descartes (1996) questioned his own existence, responding with the brilliant idea that this very doubt proves that someone does the doubting. On this basis, Bacon (2002) proposed a naïve empiricism according to which it is possible to predict, for example, that the sun will rise tomorrow based on the many instances in which the sun has risen in the past. Hume (2007) rejoined by pointing out that this prediction, like all such inductive conclusions, is contingent, not necessary. Although perhaps true as a matter of brute fact, at least for now, this reality is entirely accidental and could have been otherwise. Indeed, we now presume what Bacon and Hume did not, that the day will come when our sun will not rise, but degenerate into the stellar explosion of a supernova.

Awakened by this argument from what he called a "dogmatic slumber," Kant (2004) distinguished between numena, or things-in-themselves, and phenomena, or things-in-relation-to-consciousness. The former refers to the world as it exists independently of our thoughts, about which we can know nothing at all, and the latter to the meeting point of mind with the outside world, which constitutes the proper subject-matter of empirical investigation.

Kant held that the logic of induction, like that of deduction and the categories of space and time, is part of an a priori rational structure that exists in our
minds independently of a posteriori experience, not outside of conscious in
the world of things-in-themselves. Necessary knowledge becomes possible,
he concluded, when that rational structure is properly applied to data ema-
nating from beyond consciousness. Our capacity to understand the world, in
other words, stems from our ability to subjugate it to autonomous a priori
reason, not from insights revealed by its creator as interpreted by one heter-
onomous religious authority or another. Indeed, religion itself must be subjugated to the same rigorous rationality executed by the individual believer if it
is to remain intellectually respectable, or rejected by the individual unbeliever
if it is not. Kant (1960) intended his conception of religion within the limits
of reason as a way to save religious metaphysics; but it actually became a first
step toward disenchantment.

This sense of secular disenchantment was strengthened by two important consequences of Kant's rational structure of mind. First, Kant's (1970)
critique of pure reason allowed the attitude to gain influence in Western intellectual circles that only beliefs based on rational deduction or empirical
induction are to be considered epistemologically legitimate, which may allow
belief in a Kantian Idea of God as the progenitor and ultimate aim of rational
inquiry but not faith in a divine creator who acts in the world with ontological
status independent of consciousness (Kant, 1960). An example of this view
can be seen in August Comte's (1988) positivism according to which the
causal reasoning of scientific investigation is the only proper arbiter of truth,
in the human as well as the natural sciences, including of course religion.

Second, Kant (1997) published a critique of practical in addition to pure
reason which grounded ethics and politics in the same a priori structure of
mind that, in his view, governed the pursuit of scientific truth. According to
this position, the right to choose a way of life lies solely with the individual
according to his or her own autonomous reason, not with the heterono-
mous authority of organized religion, provided that he or she adheres to the
imperative to treat others as ends not means. It is a primary task of any just
society to protect the unalienable liberty of individuals to choose a particular
comprehensive concept of the good, in this view, "particular" because it is
not shared in common with all citizens and "comprehensive" because it gov-
erns all aspects of life. By prioritizing the freedom to choose a concept of the
good over any good one may choose, this fundamental principle of liberalism
positions a prior reason as the neutral ground against which religious and
other particular comprehensive goods are to be adjudicated and according
to which the public square should be governed. It is within such a public

domain that adherents to these particular goods must meet in order to create a life together based on values they hold in common. This public domain is thus completely disenchanted, as seen in John Locke's (2003) *Letters Concerning Toleration* and *Two Treatises on Government* which set the stage for separating church from state, leaving room for religion and spirituality only in one's private affairs. Perhaps the most dramatic contemporary example of this trend can be found in the political philosophy of John Rawls (1971; 1993), arguably the greatest twentieth-century heir to this sort of liberalism, who defines the commons in terms of a conception of "public reason" that requires all civic claims to be based on assumptions shared by everyone. These are then to be negotiated by means of "burdens of judgment" that enable people to balance opposing views in order to create an overlapping consensus among alternative comprehensive goods. This relegates particular religious or spiritual inheritances to the personal sphere alone, precluding them from influencing civic life across difference.

But as I have said, there is another source of secular disenchantment. It can be found in the counter-Enlightenment views that reached somewhat of a zenith in Hegel's critique of Kant, with roots that reach back to Giambattista Vico and Johann Herder (Berlin 1976). Vico argued that truth is verified through creation or invention, not observation, as per Descartes and Bacon, justified by the practical reasoning of civic life that strives to embody a teleological end grounded in common sense, not one that is imposed from above as in dogmatic religion. Herder tied this civic life to diverse national cultures, each with its own distinct language and history in addition to its own faith, but governed by the people or "Volk," not by religious hierarchies. Here we find the origins of a secularism grounded in politics, culture, and language, not a priori reason, though with epistemological aspirations toward the possibility of a neutral truth that transcends local circumstances no less than those of the Enlightenment liberals.

In this spirit, Hegel (1953) challenged Kant's contention that reason can be separated from history, culture, and language, a contention grounded in the distinction between a prior and a posteriori reason upon which the liberal conception of neutral secularism rests. Once it is supposed that knowledge involves the meeting of a structure that lies within consciousness with a reality that exists outside of it—of mind with matter, so to say, or subjectivity with objectivity—it is difficult to sustain the position that this internal structure can be hermetically sealed against the influence of life in the outside world, even if we can say nothing with certainty about that external reality. Indeed, the very idea that a priori reason, deductive or inductive, should be granted epistemological priority over other grounds of truth, various dialectical or historical accounts of rationality, for example, can only be sustained if one presupposed the a priori rational assumptions one seeks to defend, which of course violates those very assumptions.

Hegel argued, therefore, that all reason is necessarily a posteriori, grounded in the dialectical progress of historical experience and expressed in particular national languages and cultures. These national cultures correct themselves across time through a process of inter-generational criticism in which the thesis of one generation is opposed to an anti-thesis in the next generation, the synthesis of which in the third generation becomes a new thesis, to be opposed by yet another anti-thesis in the fourth, and so on until liberation from error, or absolute freedom, is achieved by one nation state, at the very least, to be then imitated by or imposed upon the rest. The grounds of secular disenchantment, which were concertized in left rather than right leaning interpretations of this view, are to be found in the "cunning of reason"—the dialectic process within history that moves society forward toward absolute freedom by serving as the neutral criterion for assessing all ideas and cultures, including their respective religious and spiritual traditions. Left-leaning Hegelians followed Marx (Marx and Engels 1998) in reconceiving dialectal reason in terms of socio-economic conflicts over power, whereas the right leaning Hegelians viewed nineteenth-century Europe as the summit of social development and idealized the state to affirm established politics and orthodox religion.

It is common to distinguish between two types of left leaning Hegelians or critical social theorists, as they are often called today: modern and postmodern. Due to the economic materialism of their common Marxist lineage, both share a suspicion of religion and spirituality that is a source of secular disenchantment. Marx (1970) and neo-Marxists such as Horkheimer and Adorno (2007) are generally considered modernists. They believe that it is possible to overcome unequal distribution of power and achieve liberation even though they may disagree over the relative importance of economic relations versus the ideologies used to rationalize them. The ultimate end of absolute equality in the distribution of all resources, whether economic, cultural, or ideological, serves as the rational criterion against which all views are to be judged. On the other hand, postmodernists such as Michel Foucault (1982; 2001), Jacques Derrida (1998), and Jean-Francois Lyotard (1979), and postcolonialists such as Edward Said (1979) and Frantz Fanon (2005) follow Friedrich Nietzsche (2001) in rejecting the possibility of liberation or any other meta-narrative altogether. The former argue that awareness of the power relations inherent in all human activity may ease, but cannot overcome, the extent to which we oppress one another, whereas the latter contend that resistance to colonial practices can be a cathartic experience that restores self-respect to subjugated indigenous peoples even if their eventual extrication from the bounds of hegemony may not equalize the distribution of resources.

Habermas seeks to remedy the disappointment associated with secular disenchantment grounded in both of these Enlightenment and counter-Enlightenment origins by way of dialogue between extreme versions of each trend: French laicism on the one hand, rooted in a strident reading of Locke's separation of religion and government affairs; and radical multiculturalism, on the other, grounded in a version of neo-Marxist critical theory that seeks to equalize power relations by diminishing differences among peoples of distinct origins. A student of the Frankfurt School, Habermas's own intellectual proclivities lie in a more moderate branch of neo-Marxism. His multiculturalism seeks equality between subjective life worlds by reconceiving rationality as communication oriented to achieving, sustaining and reviewing intersubjective consensus based on claims that can be criticized (Habermas 1985; 1991). This revives the possibility of Kantian-style liberalism grounded in a conception of reason with roots in social solidarity rather than individual consciousness with a shared life far more robust than the thin public domain allowed by Rawls. But the commons of this liberal multiculturalism are no less disenchanted than those of the more radical variety or of French laicism, or Rawlsian liberalism. This raises the question: can dialogue between these perspectives, whether in extreme or moderate versions, address the malaise that secular disenchantment appears to engender? To answer we need to look more closely at the origins of the disappointment with this disenchantment within both Enlightenment and counter-Enlightenment thought.

Liberalism, Social Criticism, and Disenchantment

I have written about the consequences of secular disenchantment from a liberal perspective, referring to it as the political successes and moral failings of modernity (Alexander, 2001: 25–53); but this appears to be no less true for critical social theory, at least in its modernist varieties—Marxism and neo-Marxism. Both perspectives seek ways for people of deep difference to live together in a common civil society, the one through prioritizing the individual's right to choose a way of life over any life she may choose, the other via liberation from dominance of one group over another. But both also make it difficult to embrace any particular account of the comprehensive good. Liberal toleration has a tendency to soften comprehensive ethical commitments by entertaining the possibility that opposing views are to be tolerated equally and radical liberation relativizes all comprehensive commitments but those that equalize power relations. This leaves many yearning for precisely those visions of the good life—Taylor (1989) calls them sources of the modern self—on which their difference is founded.

Another source of the disappointment with secular disenchantment, in addition to the hesitance to embrace comprehensive goods, can be found in an exclusivist conception of truth grounded in hard naturalism—scientific or logical positivism in the rational liberal view, economic materialism in critical social theory. This hard naturalism allows ontological and epistemic standing only to categories that withstand the test of a one or another sort of skepticism. Liberalism grounds skepticism in hypothetical deductive reasoning tied to a sense of objectivity, whereas critical social theory bases it in conflictual analysis connected to discrepancies of power. The two traditions differ as to the ontological substance of what should count as natural but agree that it should be hard—leading to a critical stance according to one or another use of the term, the very aim of which is to disenchant.

The difficulty with these assumptions is that they do not actually deliver the philosophical goods to support the epistemological preference upon which disenchantment is said to rest. Hypothetical deductive reasoning cannot withstand criticism according to its own standards, since it is impossible to offer an account of why one should privilege critical rationality without assuming in advance the very priority granted reasons that it is being called into question. This entails the fallacy of presuming the consequent and applies to the whole of the autonomy liberal tradition from Locke and Kant though Rawls. The postmodern critique of Marxism and neo-Marxism similarly reveals the weakness of social criticism by arguing that liberation is essentially impossible. Every critical perspective entails its own forms of oppression of which we should also be skeptical, which yields the paradoxical result that even this very postmodern critique involves unequal power relations which should be challenged. This leaves one in a quandary as to whether it is ever legitimate to commit to anything at all, even postmodern skepticism itself. Even Habermas's theory of communicative action does not escape this problem since intersubjective consensus can itself become an oppressive ideology especially to those who would choose not to join the consensus.

The idea that there are those who would choose to eschew Habermas's intersubjective consensus, or insist on grounding their own proposals for public policy in a particular comprehensive good rather than Rawls's public reason, draws attention to yet a third source of discontent with secular disenchantment. As mentioned above, in addition to the Hegelian attempt to reconceive reason within history, as opposed to its a priori status in the Kantian account, counter-Enlightenment thought entailed another strand that strived to overcome, not reconstruct, reason by subjecting it to hard criticism from the non-rational perspective of human existence itself, with all of its highs and lows, joys and sorrows, trials and tribulations. We have already noted one trend in this strand of counter-Enlightenment thought—the postmodern critique of the Hegelian utopianism, both left and right, grounded in dialectical reason. There is no account of rationality according to this critique, no meta-narrative that can sort out the oppressive muddle inherent in all human relations.

The postmodern critique has ties to an earlier rejection of rationality by existentialist philosophers, however, who can also be divided into two camps. Some existentialists, Jean-Paul Sartre (1993) and Albert Camus (2004), for example, who are perhaps most closely tied to postmodernists such as Foucault, Derrida, and Lyotard, rejected reason as part of an anti-religious secularism that grounded human existence in absolute, but arbitrary, human choice. But others, such as Soren Kierkegaard (1986; 1992) and Martin Buber (1996), with roots reaching back to Friedrich Schleiermacher (1996), understood the limits of reason as leaving room in human existence for feelings grounded in non-rational, even heteronymous, sources. One example of such feelings can be seen in the willingness to make room for another within one's own subjectivity by way of relations untainted by the interest to dominate or control—Buber (1996) called them I-Thou relations—both among human beings and between humans and the divine.

This attests to the existence of numerous approaches to religion and spirituality grounded in emotion and tradition rather than reason that have long sought expression in the public domain alongside Enlightenment and counter-Enlightenment rationalism. These include orthodox perspectives which may have hardened into various forms of fundamentalism as a consequence, at least in part, of their exclusion from civic life to more dialectical theologies that seek to negotiate tensions between faith and reason, romanticism and rationalism, tradition and modernity, such as Dietrich Bonhoeffer (1995), Reinhold Niebuhr (2013), and Paul Tillich (1986) among Christians and Joseph Soloveitchik (2006), Abraham Joshua Heschel (1955), and Eugene Borowitz (1996) among Jews. In this regard, post-secularism understood in the critical as opposed to the chronological sense is not a new phenomenon, Habermas's recent awakening to the contrary notwithstanding. This kind of counter-consciousness has accompanied secular disenchantment almost since its inception.

The disaffection with secular disenchantment is not merely a consequence of militant liberalism or radical multiculturalism, therefore, such that dialogue could ease the tension between them in such a way as to address the issues that post-secular consciousness brings to the fore. Rather, this disillusionment can be traced to difficulties within the very conceptions of critique that lie at the heart of each of these perspectives even in their more moderate formulations, which make it difficult to commit to or educate in any particular comprehensive good altogether. In a situation of this kind, where there appears to be no objective or intersubjective view upon which to base a common denominator, without a deeper understanding of how to ground positive commitments on the one hand and to hold them accountable to some critical standard on the other, it is hard to imagine what a dialogue between these views might involve, let alone whether it could address difficulties as profound as these.

Reimagining Liberalism for Post-Secular Consciousness

It is here that an alternative account of liberalism comes to the fore along with its consequences for education. To effectively respond to this disappointment with secular disenchantment, it seems to me, such an account needs to meet at least two requirements. First, it must allow for individuals to define themselves within the context of particular comprehensive goods that are sufficiently robust and meaningful as to overcome the discontent with secular disenchantment. Second, it needs to provide a mechanism for people to live together in peaceful coexistence across the deep differences that may divide their distinct ways of life. The first requirement is met, I think, in a liberal reading of communitarianism and the second in Berlin's value pluralism.

Overcoming the disillusionment with secular disenchantment requires enabling comprehensive goods that can provide purpose or meaning to one's life. At least three communitarian ideas are particularly germane to this task: First, Sandel (1998) argues that people do not define themselves in isolation from one another as portrayed by the autonomy liberals, but in the midst of communities in which they are born, raised, and nurtured, whether they embrace, reconceive, or reject the traditions through which those communities define themselves. Second, Walzer (1985) contends that these communities entail local moral inheritances embedded in thick webs of language, history, and culture, not merely thin universal values. Finally, Taylor (1985: 15–44) suggests that these inheritances contain strong values on the basis of which we make crucial choices about the people we choose to be, not only weak preferences relating to how we feel at any given moment. These self-defining people are not the subjective life worlds Habermas describes in his search for intersubjective consensus. Like the unencumbered selves of autonomy liberalism, Habermas's subjective life worlds tend to be too disconnected from their local contexts to nourish identity. Rather, the self-defining people that emerge from the communitarian critique are richly textured selves, rooted in dynamic dialogue with the heritages to which they are heir, which can be embraced, refined, or abandoned to meet their own felt needs.

However, if people so encumbered in community or tradition are to live with others whose commitments may be in conflict with their own they need to remain open to dialogue with people who follow alternative life paths and to create a common life across difference with those who adhere to divergent orientations. It is the focus on meaning and purpose as defined by the individual within the context of and in dialogue with, but not determined by, community, and the insistence on living together with others who may find meaning and purpose in alternative comprehensive goods that leaves this interpretation of communitarianism in the liberal camp with an emphasis on diversity over autonomy. But how is this possible?

Here is where Berlin's value pluralism comes into play. It is well known that Berlin criticized both right and left Hegelians by way of his distinction between two sorts of intellectual types on the one hand and between two concepts of liberty on the other. Following the ancient Greek poet Archilochus, Berlin explained that:

> A great chasm exists between those, on one side, who relate everything to a single central vision, one system less or more coherent or articulate, in terms of which they understand, think and feel—a single, universal, organizing principle in terms of which alone all that they are and say has significance—and, on the other side, those who pursue many ends, often unrelated and even contradictory, connected, if at all, only in some *de facto* way, for some psychological or physiological cause, related by no moral or aesthetic principle. These last lead lives, perform acts, and entertain ideas that are centrifugal rather than centripetal, their thought is scattered or diffused, moving on many levels, seizing upon the essence of a vast variety of experiences and objects for what they are in themselves, without consciously or unconsciously, seeking to fit them into, or exclude them from, any one unchanging, all-embracing, sometimes self-contradictory and incomplete, at times fanatical, unitary inner vision. The first kind of intellectual and artistic personality belongs to the hedgehogs, the second to the foxes. (Berlin, 1953: 3)

Whereas hedgehogs assign privilege to those who follow one particular path to human fulfillment, societies conceived by foxes encourage citizens to choose among competing paths, provided they respect the choices of others. Hedgehogs are attracted to Berlin's positive concept of liberty, the idea of self-mastery, or self-definition, or control of one's destiny; foxes are drawn to negative freedom, the absence of constraints on, or interference with, a person's actions ((Berlin, 1969: 122–135).

Berlin had deep reservations about positive accounts of liberty untempered by interaction with their negative counterparts. Those who advance these extreme approaches often distinguish between a person's actual self and some occult entity referred to as a "true," "real," or "higher" self, of which a person might not be fully aware. Although one's empirical self may indeed feel free, it is argued, one's true self may actually be enslaved. Once I take this view, according to Berlin, I can ignore peoples' actual wishes, to bully, oppress, or torture them in the name of their "real" selves, in the secure knowledge the true goal of existence—happiness, duty, wisdom, justice, or self-fulfillment—is identical with the free choice of their "true," albeit submerged and inarticulate, selves (Berlin, 1969: 133).

Without insisting on a rigid classification, Berlin (1997, 1–24) counted many counter-Enlightenment romantics as hedgehogs, especially those associated with Hegel (1967) and his right- and left-leaning descendants. He criticized the authoritarianism inherent in their views for a tendency toward positive liberty. It may be surprising to learn, however, that he understood Enlightenment liberals to be hedgehogs as well, headstrong about the capacity of hypothetical-deductive reason, grounded in Kant's rational structure of mind, to negotiate competing ways of life. Hence, Berlin's reservations about the excesses of positive liberty extended no less to the monist moral and political theories of Kant and Locke than to the Hegelians. Classical liberalism is often associated with an account of pluralism grounded in prioritizing the right to choose a comprehensive good over any particular good one may choose. This assumes that one can pick freely based on relevant reasons and engage in reasonable deliberation to adjudicate disagreements. However, Berlin held that choices are not always as free nor deliberations as reasonable as they might appear, since the very idea of rational evaluation is historically situated; and though preferring negative freedom, he recognized it too as an historical achievement which tends towards its positive counterpart when transformed into a comprehensive doctrine.

As heirs to these Enlightenment and counter-Enlightenment trends, this analysis applies no less to Rawls and Habermas than to their intellectual ancestors. Both sought to impose a positive concept of liberty on diverse particular heritages, one through public reason and the burdens of judgment and the other through intersubjective consensus. Human societies are comprised of multiple incommensurable cultures and traditions, according to Berlin, but in a weaker sense than that rightly criticized by Habermas in his assessment of the strong relativism inherent in radical multiculturalism.

With its stronger counterpart, weak relativism holds that (a) truth and goodness are products of framework—social, historical, cultural, moral, religious, conceptual, etc. This is sometimes called the thesis of relativism. It is in this weak sense that Berlin's doctrine of value pluralism holds many traditions to be incommensurable. They have distinct origins, concepts, values, and customs that do not easily translate into other idioms and may even be at logger heads with rival perspectives, since we can only see the world through our own eyes and understand it based on our own experience as interpreted through those eyes. This said communication among them nonetheless remains possible. Relativism in the strong sense, on the other hand, also holds that it follows from the thesis of relativism that (b) it is impossible or illegitimate to critique one framework on the basis of another. This presupposes among other assumptions a total isolation of one way of life from another, according to which, communication among frameworks is impossible. I have called this the critical immunity thesis (Alexander, 2001: 94–107).

It is in this strong sense that Habermas critiques radical multiculturalism, and rightly so, because critical immunity simply does not follow from the thesis of relativism. The fact that we see the world only through our own eyes and interpret it based on our own experience does not preclude the possibility that we may see the same world as others, or experience that world in similar ways, such that we can communicate across worldviews, discourses, and conceptual frames. To avoid incommensurability in this strong sense, enabled by what they both describe as a *mere* modus vivendi or thin common life, Rawls and Habermas seek to guarantee communication among diverse cultures by insisting upon a robust civic community grounded in overlapping or intersubjective consensus. But such a commons cannot be foisted on individuals who adhere to their own beliefs, values, and customs without doing violence to the inheritances of which those beliefs, values, and customs are comprised or the choices people may make to uphold, modify, or reject them.

Fortunately, as Berlin points out, it is also unnecessary, since incommensurability in the weak sense entails only that intercultural communication can be extraordinarily difficult not that it is impossible. What is required, according to this view, is a modus vivendi sufficiently robust for peaceful coexistence across difference, crafted out of genuine and ongoing dialogue among rival traditions and cultures, but not so robust as to totally dampen large areas of disagreement or leave particular comprehensive conceptions of the good out of the public square altogether. To accomplish this, an ongoing conversation among citizens adhering to diverse, even rival, viewpoints, is needed, in order to construct a common life across difference from within these very perspectives, one that celebrates rather than dampens distinctiveness.

Criticism is possible, in this view, by learning to view one's own perspective from that of another, not by way of the a priori or dialectical reasoning of classical liberalism and social criticism, or the public reason or intersubjective discourse of Rawls and Habermas. To view another's position from the perspective of one's own, however, one must have a point of view – to hold that something is sacred which can both serve as a basis for assessing rival viewpoints and be assessed by them. In a circumstance in which there is no view from nowhere, even one constructed out of intersubjective consensus, one needs to embrace a view from somewhere. The task of education, according to this perspective, is not merely to inculcate a critical attitude but also to initiate into a concept of the sacred on the basis of which such a critical attitude is possible by means of which to evaluate and be evaluated by alternative positions.

Resanctifying Pedagogy

I have called the search for a vision of the good life that meets the demands articulated here "intelligent spirituality," the education that initiates one into such a life "pedagogy of the sacred," and the process that provides the values and capacities to engage in the sort of dialogue it requires "pedagogy of difference."

"Intelligent spirituality" involves the quest to define oneself in the context of a learning community with a vision of a higher good, "learning" in the sense that a community is prepared to adjust beliefs and customs according to engagement with alternative views and changing circumstances, and "higher," not highest, because transcendent ideals are subject to revision on the basis of that which is learned from experience. Hence, although higher goods are holistic in that they offer comprehensive visions of how one should live, they are also dynamic and evolving, not dogmatic and resistant to change. These are ethical visions in the classical sense that envisages goods associated with life's purposes and meanings rather than in the modern sense that focuses primarily on the analysis and justification of individual rights and duties (Williams 1985: 6–7). They consequently meet three standards that make it possible to engage in normative discourse altogether: that people have the freedom to choose a life path within reasonable limits, the intelligence to tell the difference between right and wrong according to such a path, and the capacity to err in the choices that they make according to the life they have chosen. These visions are also pragmatic in that they address concrete examples of how to live in the context of particular communities, not merely abstract principles and rules. And they are synthetic in that they are open to dialogue with other visions that also meet the conditions of ethical discourse and willing to adapt based on what they learn from such a dialogue (Alexander, 2001: 139–70; 2015: 139–96).

"Pedagogy of the sacred" is concerned with the values and capabilities to engage in a dialogue between identities of primary association and alternative viewpoints in such a way that strengthens, rather than weakening, each orientation through a process that includes both criticizing one from the perspective of the other as well as mutual learning from one another. This entails initiation into a comprehensive concept of the good that forms the basis of primary association, its languages and history; stories, songs, and dances; customs and ceremonies; beliefs, values, and practices. It is from this perspective that a person can learn to participate in deliberation and debate in the public square. It is in this sense that I refer to resanctification of pedagogy. Ethics, in this view, is tied to teleological and theological concepts that give voice to our most cherished ideals in which lesser purposes serve greater ones. I use the term "sanctification" to capture concepts and practices such as holiness and ritual that point beyond our current circumscribed circumstances and not in a parochial, doctrinal, or confessional sense. This is sometimes called natural, as opposed to revealed, theology (Alexander, 2001: 5). Others distinguish between spirituality and religion, the former being more universal and the latter more particular. John Dewey (1976: 1–28) tried to capture a similar distinction, I think, in his use of the term "religiosity" rather than "religion" (Alexander and Ben Peretz, 2001).

Resanctification in this sense responds to disappointment with secular disenchantment because, as Thomas Green (1999) put it:

> In a world where nothing is sacred, moral education is impossible. To think of the absence of the sacred, that is its total absence, is to conceive a condition in which noting excites horror. And in such a world, it is impossible for moral education to gain a foothold. The possibility of moral horror signals not only the presence of the sacred, but an essential prerequisite for moral education itself ... The aim of moral education is that beyond good reasons we have good conduct and good character, that our conduct comes to be governed by moral norms. For that to occur, it must be possible to arouse moral horror, excite awe, provoke reverence. (112–115)

Of course neither classical liberalism nor critical social theory, in all of their varieties, endorses a condition in which nothing excites horror, at least not intentionally. But if, as I have argued, the critical foundation of each tradition cannot itself withstand criticism according to its own standards, not to mention the critique that can be levied against each on the basis of the other, this raises important questions as to whether, under conditions of secular disenchantment, it is at all possible for education of any kind, moral, ethical, political, religious, spiritual, or other—following Green's felicitous phrase—to gain a foothold. Education in this critical sense requires a normative tradition in possession of a higher good that can serve as a standard against which to judge beliefs, values, and behaviors. "Anyone who stands within a moral tradition," Green continues, "respects...boundaries marking off the domain of the sacred precisely because they mark off boundaries of the sacred and not because they accord with reason" (117). However, deep convictions of this kind about what counts as sacred—Taylor (1985: 15–44) called them strong values—are not transmitted by a path of intentional education. Rather, this requires initiation into what Michael Oakeshott (1962) called a "tradition of practice," which in contrast to the "technical knowledge" inherent in deductive, inductive, or dialectical reason is embedded in the histories, languages, and cultures of communities of meaning that share common narratives, values, beliefs, and customs.

But how is it possible to challenge sacred perspectives of this kind which are grounded in particular traditions of practice given that there is no objective or intersubjective view upon which to base this sort of inquiry? One answer involves learning to view one orientation from the perspective of another. This is where "pedagogy of difference" comes into play. It presupposes that an education worthy of the name must not only initiate into a concept of the sacred according to one tradition of practice or another but also to offer exposure to alternative perspectives which can be judged according to the standards of a tradition of primary identity, but also judged by alternative viewpoints. One learns to critique not only according to the internal standards of a tradition to which one is heir or with which one has chosen to affiliate but also according to the criteria of at least one alternative, if not more. Dialogue across difference is integral to pedagogy of this kind which generates the possibility of education in a critical viewpoint consistent with post-secular consciousness (Alexander, 2015: 87–138).

Conclusion

The post-secular condition, then, is a product of neither militant secularism nor radical multiculturalism—at least not entirely. The dissatisfaction with secular disenchantment has accompanied secularism almost from the start as a result of weaknesses with conceptions of criticism that lie at the very heart of both Enlightenment and counter-Enlightenment political theory which are also found in their more moderate intellectual descendants—Rawls's autonomy liberalism and Habermas's liberal multiculturalism. Hence, an education that addresses this dissatisfaction cannot be found in dialogue between extreme or even moderate interpretations of these perspectives—at least not exclusively. Rather, an education that responds to post-secular disappointment with secular disenchantment requires a non-neutral conception of criticism embedded in initiation into an intelligent concept of the sacred prepared to engage in dialogue with alternative perspectives across difference. Among other consequences, it follows that educational research, curriculum planning, and pedagogic practice all need to be carried out within the context of articulate and defensible higher goods that can define sacred boundaries to serve as standards for assessment of beliefs, values, and practices on the one hand, and that are open to dialogue with alternative perspectives on the other.

References

Alexander, H. A. (2001) *Reclaiming Goodness: Education and the Spiritual Quest.* Notre Dame, IN: University of Notre Dame Press.

Alexander, H. A. (2015) *Reimagining Liberal Education: Affiliation and Inquiry in Democratic Schooling.* London: Bloomsbury.

Alexander, H. A., and M. Ben Peretz (2001) Toward a pedagogy of the sacred: Transcendence, ethics, and the curriculum. In J. Erricker, C. Ota and C. Erricker, eds. *Spiritual Education, Cultural, Religious, and Social Differences: New Perspectives for the 21ˢᵗ Century.* Brighton: Sussex Academic Press, pp. 34–47.

Bacon, F. (2002) *The New Organon,* edited by L. Jardine and M. Silverthorne. Cambridge, UK: Cambridge University Press.

Berlin, I. (1953) *The Hedgehog and the Fox: An Essay on Tolstoy's View of History.* New York: Simon and Schuster.

Berlin, I. (1969) *Four Essays on Liberty.* Oxford, UK: Oxford University Press.

Berlin, I. (1976) *Vico and Herder: Two Studies in the History of Ideas.* London, UK: Hogarth Press.

Berlin, I. (1997) *Against the Current: Essays in the History of Ideas.* Princeton, NJ: Princeton University Press.

Bonhoeffer, D. (1995) *Ethics.* New York: Touchstone.

Borowitz, E. (1996) *Renewing the Covenant: A Theology for the Postmodern Jew.* Philadelphia, PA: The Jewish Publication Society of America.

Buber, M. (1996) *I and Thou.* New York: Touchstone.

Camus, A. (2004) *The Plague, the Fall, Exile and the Kingdom, and Other Essays.* New York: Random House, Everyman's Library.

Comte, A. (1988) *Introduction to Positive Philosophy.* London, UK: Hackett.

Derrida, J. (1998) *Of Grammatology.* G. C. Spivak, trans. Baltimore, MD: Johns Hopkins University Press.

Descartes, R. (1996) *Meditations on First Philosophy.* J. Cottingham, trans. Cambridge, UK: Cambridge University Press.

Descartes, R. (1999) *Discourse on Method and Related Writings.* D. M. Clark, trans. London, UK: Penguin.

Dewey, J. (1976) *A Common Faith.* New Haven, CT: Yale University Press.

Fanon, F. (2005) *The Wretched of the Earth.* R. Philcox, trans. New York: Grove Press.

Foucault, M. (1982) *The Archaeology of Knowledge and Discourse on Language.* London, UK: Pantheon.

Foucault, M. (2001) *The Order of Things: An Archaeology of the Human Sciences.* New York: Routledge.

Galston, W. A. (1991) *Liberal Purposes: Goods, Virtues, and Diversity in the Liberal State.* Cambridge, UK: Cambridge University Press.

Galston, W. A. (2002) *Liberal Pluralism: The Implications of Value Pluralism for Political Theory and Practice.* Cambridge, UK: Cambridge University Press.

Gray, J. (1996) *Post-Liberalism: Studies in Political Thought.* London, UK: Routledge.

Gray, J. (2002) *The Two Faces of Liberalism.* London, UK: New Press.

Green, T. F. (1999) *Voices: The Educational Formation of Conscience.* Notre Dame, IN: University of Notre Dame Press.

Habermas, J. (1985) *A Theory of Communicative Action, Vol. I and II,* T. McCarthy, trans. Boston: Beacon Press.

Habermas, J. (1991) *The Structural Transformation of the Public Sphere: An Inquiry into a Category of Bourgeois Society.* Cambridge, MA: MIT Press.

Habermas, J. (1993) *Justification and Application: Remarks on Discourse Ethics.* Cambridge, MA: MIT Press.

Habermas, J. (2008) Notes on a post-secular society, *New Perspectives Quarterly,* 25, 4, pp. 17–29.

Hegel, G. W. F. (1953) *Reason in History.* R. S. Hartman, trans. Minneapolis, MN: Bobbs-Merrill.

Hegel, G. W. F. (1967) *Philosophy of Right.* Oxford: Oxford University Press.

Hegel, G. W. F. (1978) *The Phenomenology of Spirit.* A. V. Miller, trans. Oxford: Clarendon Press.

Heschel, A. J. (1955) *God in Search of Man.* New York: Farrar, Straus and Cudahy.

Hobbes, T. (2002) *Leviathan.* Peterborough, ON: Broadview Press.

Horkheimer, M., and T. Adorno (2007) *Dialectic of Enlightenment.* Palo Alto, CA: Stanford University Press.

Hume, D. (1953) *An Enquiry Concerning the Principles of Morals.* La Salle, IL: Open Court.

Hume, D. (2007) *An Enquiry Concerning Human Understanding.* Oxford, UK: Oxford University Press.

Kant, I. (1960) *Religion within the Limits of Reason Alone.* New York: Harper Torchbook.

Kant, I. (1970) *Critique of Pure Reason* New York: Macmillan.

Kant, I. (1997) *Critique of Practical Reason.* M. Gregor, trans. Cambridge, UK: Cambridge University. Press.

Kant, I. (2002) *Groundwork for the Metaphysics of Morals.* A. Zweig, trans. Oxford, UK: Oxford University Press.

Kant, I. (2004) *Prolegomena to Any Future Metaphysics.* G. Hatfield, trans. Cambridge, UK: Cambridge University Press.

Kierkegaard, S. (1986) *Fear and Trembling.* A. Hannay, trans. London, UK: Penguin.

Kierkegaard, S. (1992) *Either/Or: A Fragment of Life.* A. Hannay, trans. London, UK: Penguin.

Locke, J. (2003) *Two Treaties of Government and a Letter Concerning Toleration.* New Haven, CT: Yale University Press.

Lyotard, J. F. (1979) *The Postmodern Condition*. Minneapolis: University of Minnesota Press.

MacIntyre, A. (1984) *After Virtue: A Study in Moral Theory*. Notre Dame, IN: Univ. of Notre Dame Press.

MacIntyre, A. (1989) *Whose Justice, Which Rationality?* Notre Dame, IN: Univ. of Notre Dame Press.

Marx, K. (1970) *Critique of Hegel's Philosophy of Right*. Cambridge, UK: Cambridge University Press.

Marx, K., and F. Engels (1998) *The German Ideology*. New York: Prometheus.

Niebuhr, R. (2013) *Moral Man and Immoral Society: A Study in Politics and Ethics*. Louisville, KY: Westminster John Knox Press.

Nietzsche, F. (2001) *The Birth of Tragedy, The Gay Science, Thus Spoke Zarathustra, and On the Genealogy of Morals*. D. B. Allison, ed. Lanham, MD: Rowman and Littlefield.

Oakeshott, M. (1962) *Rationalism in Politics and Other Essays*. London: Methuen.

Rawls, J. (1971) *A Theory of Justice*. Cambridge, MA: Harvard University Press.

Rawls, J. (1993) *Political Liberalism*. New York: Columbia University Press.

Said, E. (1979) *Orientalism*. New York: Vintage Books.

Sandel, M., ed. (1984) *Liberalism and its Critics* Oxford, UK: Basil Blackwell.

Sandel, M. (1998) *Liberalism and the Limits of Justice*. Cambridge, UK: Cambridge University Press.

Sartre, J. P. (1993) *Being and Nothingness*. H. E. Barnes, trans. New York: Washington Square Press.

Schleiermacher, F. (1996) *On Religion: Speeches to Its Cultural Despisers*. Cambridge, UK: Cambridge University Press.

Snook, I. A. (1972) *Indoctrination and Education*. London, UK: Routledge and Kegan Paul.

Soloveitchik, J. (2006) *The Lonely Man of Faith*. Rochester, NY: Image Press.

Taylor, C. (1985) *Human Agency and Language*. Cambridge, UK: Cambridge University Press.

Taylor, C. (1989) *Sources of the Self: The Making of Modern Identity*. Cambridge, MA: Harvard University Press.

Taylor, C. (1991) *The Ethics of Authenticity*. Cambridge, MA: Harvard University Press.

Tillich, P. (1986) *The Dynamics of Faith*. New York: Harper Collins.

Walzer, M. (1985) *Thick and Thin: Moral Argument at Home and Abroad*. Notre Dame, IN: University of Notre Dame Press.

Williams, B. (1985) *Ethics and the Limits of Philosophy*. Cambridge, MA: Harvard University Press.

Part II

Historical and Comparative Studies in Education, Religion and Society

3. On the Teachings of George Grant

WILLIAM F. PINAR

[T]he [contemporary] purpose of education is to gain knowledge which
issues in the mastery of human and non-human nature.
—George Grant (1969, 118)

One of Canada's greatest public intellectuals (Potter, 2005, ix; Lathangue,
1998, vii; Lipset, 1990, 36), George Grant (1918–1988), was born on
November 13, 1918. Like his father, he studied history, winning the history medal at Queen's University where, William Christian (2001 [1995],
ix) tells us, "he was drawn to grand themes, rather than to the minutiae of
historical research." That same disposition surfaced later at Oxford,
where he had gone on a Rhodes scholarship to study law (Christian, 2001
[1995], ix). After service as an Air Raid Precautions warden during the
German bombing of London, Grant returned to Canada in February 1942.
Returning to Oxford after the war he left law to study theology, earning
extra money by writing historical articles on Canada for Chambers' *En-
cyclopedia*. "Before I became a philosopher," he reflected years later, "I
studied history and still think very much as an historian" (Christian, 2001
[1995], x).

The history, to which Grant was increasingly drawn, was that of modernity and its "realization of the technological dream," e.g., "universal-
ization and homogenization" (Grant, 2005 [1970], lxxii). Associated with
modernity itself, and with the United States specifically as modernity's most
"expressive manifestation," (Emberley, 2005 [1994], lxxx) technology
had become not just one optional *mode d'être*, but the only way of life on
earth. Technology had become, in Emberley's (2005 [1994], lxxx) succinct
summary of Grant's understanding of the term, "a philosophy of reason as

domination over nature, a politics of imperial, bureaucratic administration, a public discourse of efficiency, and a sociology of adjustment and equilibrium." This contemporary conception of history was for Grant very different from the ancient one, wherein time had been regarded as the "moving image of eternity." (Christian, 2001 [1995], xiv). In the West, Grant concluded, there had been a "close relation" between technology and political liberalism, by which he meant the "belief that man's essence is his freedom" (Grant, 1966, iv).

How did this happen? How did the local become subsumed in the global, and how has the global become technological? Grant addressed these questions through critiques of instrumentalization as he testified to the disappearance of questions of meaning and significance in modern thought and education. To live through modernity he reintroduced a relationship between freedom and transcendence, philosophy and theology, piety and education. In doing so Grant anticipated the post secular movement in Education. As does Philip Wexler (2013, 6), George Grant provides "a particular opening toward half-forgotten languages…that can be rethought and redirected toward the project of social understanding."

Reactivating the Past in the Present

If one denies the possibility of any returning to the past,
and yet does not believe in the assumptions of the modern
experiment, what then is the task of thought?
(Grant, 1969, 36)

The past is a foreign country (Grant, 2001 [1969], 65). Grant journeys to ancient Greece, asking us to join him, "to think with" Plato and Aristotle, to discern "their vision of human nature and destiny."[1] In so doing, he imagines that "we come to see our own" (Grant, 1966 [1959], 26). Through remembrance we might peer through the "principles" of the technological sensorium.

Can there be another life than this one, focused on the screen, accumulating information rather than seeking knowledge and the wisdom (Grant, 1966 [1959], 26) it can confer? Can we find passage to life not structured by the corporate triumvirate—calculation-competition-cooperation—not focused on others as means to our ends but as intrinsically important relationships that render the present meaningful? Could "travel" to the "foreign country" that is the past relocate the present as past? "To put the matter historically," Grant wrote, too panoramically, "from the dawn of western civilization until the nineteenth century the consensus was that piety was necessary to the public good." Piety is less a set of observable behaviors than a state of mind, in educational terms a devotion to study, humbling oneself before the mystery of the world, seeking understanding.[2]

Revelation, not discovery, represents the results of such research. Engagement, not instrumentality, characterizes its mode d'etre. It is spiritual—in contrast to Grant I shed supernaturalism—but less transcendent than immanent, immersed in the moment that is simultaneously eternal and contingent, following from what preceded it, anticipating what is now to come. Grant historicizes what we have lost:

> To repeat, Western Europe had inherited that contemplation in its use of it theologically, that is, under the magistery of revelation. Within that revelation charity was the height and therefore contemplation was finally a means to that obedient giving oneself away. (Grant, 1969, 50)

Charity is not a voluntaristic act of generosity that leaves the structure of subjectivity untouched. When we reactivate the past we are tourists no longer, still lodged within the present. Returning to the past we are "going native," not as escapism or amnesia but in order to dwell within the world as if our lives depended upon it (Grant, 1969, 35). Such virtue is no ornament but recasts one's character. Educationally, it testifies to the openness to alterity that sustained study instantiates.

Such openness implies attentiveness but not the instrumental observation scientific experimentation ritualizes. We are not testing hypotheses to produce outcomes as much as we are discerning what is at stake in the situation that construes us. We are not only trying to solve a problem as much as resolve what remains so we can move on. Discernment reveals resolution; calculation reproduces the problem if in different forms, perhaps as collateral damage or unintended effects, variables (not yet) controlled whose movements perhaps cannot be predicted. Productivity is no working through the injustice of the past that structures the present.

"[T]here were in the pre-progressive societies," Grant remembers, "those complicated systems of education wherein the truth of justice was made central to education." The problem of the present, in this view, requires fewer calculations concerning the claims of conflicting constituencies than it does the wisdom of judgment informed by love. Knowledge, Grant suggests, depends on it: "The close connection between Socrates and Christ lies in the fact that Socrates is the primal philosophic teacher of the dependence of what we know on what we love" (Grant, 1986, 57). Love alerts us to passages from the present, not escape routes but reconstructions—transmutations—of what has been bequeathed us. "Paul's hymn to love," Grant reminds us, "uses the word agape which is best translated as charity; Plato's symposium is concerned with eros which is best translated as desire" (Grant, 1986, 72). The reconstruction of private desire into public service is the calling of a cosmopolitan education.

Charity condensed to kindness obscures its educational potential. One learns from others as one engages with the situation intersubjective presence reveals. No longer contracted—or minimalized in Lasch's (1984) spatialized depiction of our withdrawal from the public sphere—we enlarge our domain of experience as we decline to declinate human relationality to contractual obligations. Openness to what is—willingness to allow reality to speak through us, as we are its mediation—becomes the prerequisite of knowledge. "[F]or Plato," Grant reminds, "the opposite of knowledge is not ignorance, but madness, and the nearest he can come to an example of complete madness is the tyrant, because in that case otherness has disappeared as much as can be imagined" (Grant, 1986, 73). It is the apprehension of alterity—its recognition as difference and shared as resonance—not its obfuscation in narcissism that the adjudication of justice demands.

Such adjudication is institutional and social, but it is also subjective and cultural, all informed historically: what does the present moment require? Alas, the throughline through this ever-shifting simultaneity of domain, scale, and time is not reparation but the triumph of technology. "I cannot describe here," Grant admits, "the complex history of how the progressive hope in American education was gradually emptied of all content except means to technological regulation and expansion" (Grant, 1986, 73). His reconstruction of this devolution of charity into calculations of productivity focuses on the faculty of will. It is the elevation of will—achieved through its detachment from agape, from community, from the humility alterity insinuates—into the arrogant idolatry of science, an institutionalization not of charity but conquest, that propels us into a present shorn of ethics and education. How could this have happened? As Grant acknowledges above, the history is too "complex" to know, but he isolates education as one narrative trail to follow.

Grant appreciates the democratization of knowledge that progressives embraced, their commitment to cut learning free from the confinement of elitism. "Men such as Dewey," Grant notes, "had been profoundly influenced by Rousseau and his desire to give educational content to the life of equal citizens" (Grant, 1969, 130). But its "elitism" remained, if taking different forms, reformulated not as the preservation of privilege but the privileging of reason as an instrument of engineering, in stipulating justice as equality. "[U]nlike Rousseau," Grant continues, the progressives had "an unlimited faith in the conquest of nature as the means to a more formal equality" (Grant, 1969, 130). Science would bring progress to society. That "dream of modern liberalism"—"equality"—would become a nightmare of social conformity and political manipulation as, Grant knew, the "mastery once thought of as a means becomes increasingly the public end" (Grant, 1969, 130). Discovery becomes an unquestioned end in itself, requiring sacrifice of animals—including humanity—as the will is unleashed, authorized to do whatever it can imagine. Humanity becomes means to unspecified ends, no longer "equality" but always punctuated by "productivity," proliferating profits and bankruptcies of virtue.

We cannot undo what is done. We cannot return to the past nor recast its injustices as new and restorative forces. "Socrates' prayer for the unity of the inward and the outward was spoken in an antique world," Grant acknowledges, "the context of which it could not be our historical business to recreate" (Grant, 1969, 130). In one sense we need not, as the past is not past: "Yet the fact begins to appear through the modernity which has denied it: human excellence cannot be appropriated by those who think of it as sustained simply in the human will." (Grant, 1969, 133). Isolated, unrestrained, authorized by its institutionalization, the will—as the scientific method, as the capitalist compulsion for profit, in education as social engineering (Grant, 1969, 133)—mutilates as it manipulates what is. Only when it is embedded in the inheritance we inhabit but cannot control can "will" strive for human excellence, an aspiration undertaken by "those who have glimpsed that it is sustained by all that is" (Grant, 1969, 133). This glimpse is located not in the view from "nowhere," not in the omniscience religion reserves for God, nor in the certainty of progress, historical inevitability guaranteed by the outcomes of scientific discovery with its spectator concept of knowledge (Grant, 1969, 133). Indeed, such a "glimpse" may not be ocular at all but an auditory—discernment not determination. Perhaps such "sustainment cannot be adequately thought by us," Grant wonders, perhaps can never be so thought, in part due to "the fragmentation and complexity of our historical inheritance" (Pinar, 2012, 235). Haunted by what we cannot think through but are obligated to try, our "will" returns from our head to inside, enfeebled but befriending so that we might remain "open to all those occasions in which the reality of that sustaining makes itself present to us" (Grant, 1969, 133). That reality is simultaneously historical and timeless, and its revelation requires contemplation, self-critique, and social engagement.

These modes of being-in-the-world typified George Grant's life, intensified by his courageous charity in London during the 1940 bombings. That experience broke as it healed him, confining him to bed during a year of recovery back in Toronto. His first foray into the world was working with the Canadian Association of Adult Education (CAAE), a challenge he accepted in February 1943. "He had no inkling," Christian tells us, "how much the next two years would affect his mature views of politics and education" (Christian, 1996, 96). Working with Jean Morrison, a permanent CAAE employee, Grant undertook an experiment in public broadcasting: the Citizens' Forum. In my terms, this was curriculum development dedicated to the social and subjective reconstruction of the public sphere. Before each program, listeners, who had assembled in church halls, friends' living-rooms or wherever a radio could be shared, had perused a study guide prepared each week by Morrison and Grant. After the broadcast, discussion followed, perhaps prompted by ques tions in the guide. At the end of the event, each group's secretary submitted a report to the provincial secretary who in turn sent a summary to Grant. He studied the national results and composed a report for a subsequent broadcast (Christian, 1996, 96). Without employing these terms, George Grant was undertaking a complicated conversation with Canadians that would continue until his death in 1988.

It was a national conversation, as Grant managed to visit all nine provinces. By the end of his first term as national secretary, some 1,215 groups had registered to participate. Most adult educators were on the political left, sharing the progressive faith that, unless the postwar period was informed by a vigorous and critical public, Canadians could be manipulated.[3] Many intellectuals and political activists of the 1930s and 1940s appreciated that education was central to citizenship; being informed was the prerequisite for citizens' civic engagement in a democratic society.[4] Like many progressives in the United States, many Canadians thought the appropriate way to educate the adult citizenry was through small groups. On this point Grant agreed. The Citizens' Forum was an exercise in small groups: study, deliberation, communication, action (Christian, 1996, 100).

The CAAE was, then, engaged in the education of the public for the sake of a more just social order. It organized a nation-wide conference in Montreal for September 1943 to coordinate various interested groups. When the Liberal government noticed, it tried to intervene: the parliamentary secretary to the Prime Minister (Brooke Claxton) tried to block the broadcasts at the highest levels of the Canadian Broadcasting System (CBC). Although opposed to ideologues who would propagandize—in the U.S. George Counts[5]—Grant "staunchly defended the [Citizens'] Forum's right to free speech against government pressure" (Christian, 1996, 97). While he defended their right to free speech, Grant could not embrace his colleagues' faith in progressive education. While education for the sake of democracy was a compelling concept, Grant concluded, it risked ruining education, which mattered in its own right (Christian, 1996, 104). By early 1945 he had come to realize: "I had to spend my life thinking out what were the consequences of not thinking progressive liberalism" (Christian, 1996, 104).

Indirectly testifying to his conversion, Grant invoked the Christian conviction that a person is a "free, rational being whose destiny is to live in the light of God." For Grant, such "light" was not doctrinal conformity but, referencing Plato, freeing humanity from "finite chains to the love of the infinite" (quoted in Christian, 1996, 164). He did not claim to comprehend the relationship between freedom and transcendence—it would preoccupy him for the remainder of the decade (Christian, 1996, 177)—but he felt sure it could not be grasped by those "swept away by the new worship of technique and self-expression, prosperity and power, which exalted usefulness above truth, and convenience and worldly success above knowledge." "Time was short," Grant warned, "but it was still possible to preserve the wisest and best from the ancient spiritual tradition" (quoted in Christian, 1996, 164). In a series of articles written for *Food for Thought*, the journal of the CAAE, Grant pursued this possibility. In his 1953 "Philosophy and Education," Grant defined education as "any means that brings the human spirit to self-consciousness"; he cited Socrates as a "saint in whom knowledge of his own mind led to the presence of absolute mind, in other words to God" (quoted in Christian, 1996, 164). The distractions of the present age would lead to cynicism and despair, he predicted, and it was the calling of adult education to offer an alternative:

> When men encounter nothingness they are at last driven to seek reality. As in the pointless universe the days are spent in the beauty parlors…or in the search to prolong a dying virility, in the days when there is always economic plenty and even cruelty has become tedious, then, will be the moment to speak of education, of the journey of their minds to liberation. (Christian, 1996, 165)

Despair demands reflection, study, thinking: the processes of education. But the "liberation" he has in mind is not the secular assurance of social improvement through reconstruction. Grant's rejection of progressive education was now complete (Christian, 1996, 176).

What is at stake

> [I]f we are to live in the modern university as free men, we
> must make judgments about the essence of the
> university—its curriculum.
> (Grant, 1969, 127)

"The curriculum is the essence of any university," Grant appreciated (Grant, 1969, 113). The curriculum is the essence of any educational institution. "It determines the character of the university far more than any structure of government, methods of teaching, or social organization," Grant (1969, 113) asserted, contra the assumptions animating one hundred years of educational research in North America. For Grant, moreover, governance, instruction, and organization were "largely shaped by what is studied and why it is studied" (Grant, 1969, 113). Here he simply inverts organizationalism, casting the curriculum as determinative. However appealing theoretically, it is inaccurate, as Grant knew. Indeed, the quotidian exerts its force relentlessly as the power Grant confers upon the curriculum is inflated, on occasion dissolving into its determination by capital: "The curriculum is itself chiefly determined by what the dominant classes of the society consider important to be known" (Grant, 1969, 113). Here is reproduction theory avant la lettre. Grant resented the rich businessmen[6] who served on the governing boards of the universities he knew—he found them overbearing, always steering the institution toward vocationalism—but accounts of his own teaching belie the assertion of determination.

A teacher's son, Christian (1996, 134) reminds, George Grant was devoted to teaching. Teaching mattered, and not only due to filial fidelity. Grant considered teaching—not research and the specialization it required[7]—as the central mission of the university. Teaching is ethical engagement in complicated conversation. Unless one is subjectively engaged in that simultaneously academically informed interpersonal conversation, teaching can become technical and formulaic, entertainment not education. "For most people still teach philosophy," Grant wrote in a letter, "as if there were still a civilization in North America, instead of teaching it as if the old traditions were completely finished and one had to build new ones" (Christian, 1996, 143). Yet the present moment was no empty space waiting to be filled with new ideas; it was a wasteland piled high with wreckage in the wake of science.

Business does not operate by itself of course, but through technology and the sciences that support both. The crisis of modernity crystallized the crucial questions of the curriculum, questions that came to consume Grant, especially after leaving Dalhousie for McMaster University in 1961. At McMaster Grant settled into that university's new department of religion. In a sermon to students on October 6, 1961, Grant invoked the scene between Jesus and Pilate to dramatize the role of religious studies in a secular university. Grant asserted that McMaster's new Department of Religion should imitate this conversation, this dialogue between the transcendent truth of the soul and the wisdom of the world [that] has gone on in Western society from that day to this. It is the tension in their meeting which has more than anything else given Western society its greatness and only insofar as western society keeps that tension has it anything valuable in it (Christian, 1996, 221). To engage in this dialogue meant confronting the secularization of the contemporary curriculum, and this, Grant knew, would be contentious, as "the curriculum as it is based in our modern secular universities is radically at odds with Christianity" (Christian, 1996, 221).

Grant knew, Christian emphasizes, what was at stake. Given the pervasiveness of the "now-dominant faith of objectivity and progress," the department must proceed cautiously, avoiding the extreme of scientistic positivism on the one hand and of religious proselytizing on the other (Christian, 1996, 221). "The curriculum," in Christian's words, "must take religion seriously without forcing students to accept a position in which they did not genuinely believe" (Christian, 1996, 221). The core of the departmental curriculum, Grant argued, should be a clear, factual knowledge of Christianity—that is, a knowledge of Judaism and the New Testament. Subsidiary to this there must be some factual knowledge of the Mediterranean civilization and its traditions (other than the Semitic) which were brought under Christ by the Fathers. Obviously, also, in a later year when the student has some knowledge of Western religion, he must look at the other religions of the world (Christian, 1996, 221). Because Buddhism was being popularized in North America at this time, Grant thought that tradition must be included.[8]

More contentious was Grant's insistence that new faculty live within the religious traditions they were being hired to teach. What can appear to be doctrinal conformity instead derived, Christian (1996, 222) points out, from St. Anselm's celebrated formula: *Credo, ut intelligam*: understanding arises from belief. Prerequisite to understanding Christianity, Grant was sure, was the Greek philosophical tradition. These convictions came from Grant's ongoing engagement with the historical moment. At this time, in this place, to what could the curriculum testify? Despite the power of the present, Grant knew that "at all times and in all places it always matters what we do" (Christian, 1996, 265). Ethics, not politics, constitutes the core of curriculum.

What knowledge is of most worth is the key curricular question. Because it is an ethical question, it keeps us open: to the subject we study, to the students with whom we are working, to ourselves as we learn anew who we are, to others through dialogical encounter, to the academic knowledge we are laboring together and alone to understand. What knowledge is of most worth invites us to discern what is at stake in the moment at hand, in the place where we are. The canonical curriculum question enacts ongoing openness. "This quality," Grant understood, "is the exact opposite of control or mastery." Mastery tries to shape the objects and people around us into a form which suits us. Openness tries to know what things are in themselves, not to impose our categories upon them. Openness acts on the assumption that other things and people have their own goodness in themselves; control believes that the world is essentially neutral stuff which can only be made good by human effort.

Especially in our time, openness demands exertion; it "requires daily the enormous discipline of dealing with our closed-ness, aggressions and neuroses, be they moral, intellectual or sexual. To be open in an age of tyrannical control will above all require courage" (quoted in Christian, 1996, 265). That courage cannot be innocent, I would add, as tyranny requires that virtue be communicated with caution, especially in public. Within the solitude[9] of ongoing study, openness animates our efforts to understand.

What is the fate of education in this technological era? Teaching devolves into implementation of objectives and professional judgment is replaced by standardized assessment. "At the heart of modern liberal education," Grant knew, "lies the desire to homogenize the world" (Grant, 2005 [1965], 78). Homogenization means the obliteration of difference, including the erasure of that alterity that is the past. In contrast, memory and remembrance mean "[c]ontinually bringing to consciousness all the distortions which are bound to be present from one's individual and social history" (Grant, 1969, 45). Such working through what we have been bequeathed forces to the forefronting of difference the courageous cultivation of openness to what is not obvious, what could become intelligible in a future if we can reactivate the past. George Grant faced the fate of education in a technological era; he taught with courage and conviction to name what imprisons us in the present. In the 20 September 1980 issue of *Today* magazine, George Grant was acknowledged as one of the great teachers in Canada (Christian, 1996, 331). He remains so today.

Notes

1. The nineteenth-century German architect Karl Friedrich Schinkel, Toews (2008, 175) reminds us, was among those who imagined the "past as a foreign country" and one "that could function as a model and norm for the present. But for Schinkel the past lived in the present through all of the historical forms in which its principles had been transfigured and passed on through time. To think historically was not to make an imaginative leap into a past world, but to view oneself within the flow of time in which historical forms were in a constant process of making and remaking." For Schinkel those forms were architectural; I have long argued that they can also be curricular, evident in this current effort to reconstruct the present through "reactivating" the thought of George Grant.
2. See Smith 2014 and Wang 2014. Both summon "wisdom traditions" to recast the present moment.
3. This was Harold Innis' fear. "One of Innis' most bitter memories of the First World War period," Watson (2007, 235) explains, "was the propaganda that had sent idealistic Christian youngsters into the horror of trench warfare. While this had largely been a wartime phenomenon, he now confronted a situation where U.S. propaganda was to be cranked up and continued as a permanent feature of peace under the banner of the Cold War." Now it is rationalized by the so-called "war on terror."

4. In the United States today, businesses brazenly endorse education as job preparation. There is no mention of citizenship in the full-page advertisement in *The New York Times* signed by Alcoa, Bayer, Boeing, BP, Dollar General, Dow Chemical, Dupont, Eli Lilly, Exxon Mobil, GE, General Mills, Harley-Davidson, Intel, ManpowerGroup, McGraw-Hill, Microsoft, National Defense Industrial Association, Northrop Grumman, Raytheon, Rockwell, State Farm Insurance, Taco Bell, Texas Instruments, Time Warner, U.S. Chamber of Commerce, Xerox, and others: "As business leaders, we believe ALL American children have a right to an education that prepares them to be successful in a competitive global economy. We also understand that in order to compete in a knowledge-based, global economy, we must improve the academic performance of our students" (Signatories, 2013, February 12, A7). The Obama administration plans to rank colleges by tuition, graduation rates, debt and earnings of graduates, and use this ranking to influence federal financial aid to students (Stewart, 2013, September 14, B4).

5. On February 18, 1932, George Counts, a Teachers College sociologist, challenged the annual meeting of the Progressive Education Association (PEA) to articulate a critique of the social order so that their students could confront the misery and injustice of Depression-era America. In small groups, those present considered Counts' question—"Dare Progressive Education Be Progressive?"—as other conference presentations were canceled. Later published as an article and expanded into a pamphlet, Counts' speech sparked an ongoing debate regarding the relationship between school and society. Schools inevitably indoctrinate, Counts insisted, and it was essential for educators to counter anti-democratic propaganda (see Perlstein, 2000, 51, 55). Tomkins (1986, 191) reports that "very few Canadian school reformers" advocated Counts' views.

6. At Dalhousie, Christian (1996, 136) tells us, "Colonel Laurie was a powerful figure ... chairman of the [University] board." For Grant, he was the latest of a line of businessmen, despite "benign intentions pushed and pulled, caressed and bullied, to transform the university into an appropriate instrument to serve the needs of the progressive capitalist societies of North America" (Christian, 1996, 136).

7. When Dalhousie's president announced his intention to create a graduate school, especially for the sciences, Grant led the fight against it in the university senate, but the cause was lost, leaving him discouraged: "probably they won't care about real & effective teaching in *Arts*. My department has 30 students with me the only full time teacher & they call that philosophy. The physics department has 8% as much spent on it as on philosophy barring equipment. Dalhousie is going to be a technical college. So there is little hope of getting real philosophy done here. So it makes me want to go" (quoted passages in Christian, 1996, 142). "The affair," Christian (1996, 143) reports, "revealed to him starkly and immediately how powerful were the science departments, especially when they were supported by the businessmen on the board, how they could consume the resources of the university, and how incomparably weaker was a department like philosophy." Now we take that for granted; six decades ago on campuses across North America, today's reality was established.

8. Because it was not at this time compelling in Canada, Islam was not. The cultural significance of Islam to North America—to Canada in particular—has much increased since Grant's death and not only due to increased immigration. Heightened in the years since Grant's death is Benhabib's (2006, 171) concern that the "increasingly hostile security

environment" and the "reality" of "fundamentalist Islamic terrorism" in Europe would mean that "pan-Europeanism may not result in heightened cosmopolitan consciousness but in a new form of chauvinism, heavily interlaced with racist attitudes toward the Muslim world." Never mind that, as John Ralston Saul (2005, 279) observed, "Islam, the religion that most concerns the West these days, is fundamentally open and has a more flexible history than Christianity." That history is obscured by present perceptions that, Butler and Spivak (2007, 99–100) note, "Islam...is contaminated by reactive gender politics and 'terror.'" The former impacts not only women, Ruthven (2009, 54) points out, but contribute to practices not exactly forefronted in popular histories of Islam: boy concubinage and pedophilia. Although *liwat* or *lavat* (sodomy) is condemned in the Qur'an, Ruthven (2009, 54) continues, "homosexual relationships between older men and boys were tolerated, not least because they posed a lesser threat to the patriarchal order than unregulated heterosexual interactions." Would that fact recommend Islam to contemporary religion—or queer studies—curricula?

9. It is not only the acknowledgment of being "behind enemy lines" that requires caution and solitude (Pinar, 2012, 238), it is study—with its traces of a sacred pursuit—itself. After a period of public engagement, Grant himself realized that withdrawal was indicated. In January 1968 he wrote to friends of his need "to be far away within myself...I know that a certain period of my life has come to an end and that I must reform myself to move on—but in doing that I have to retreat away from conversation with people—even those who are most meaningful and most interesting to me" (quoted in Christian, 1996, 267). As the reference to "reform myself" implies, solitude can be an opportunity for subjective reconstruction (Pinar, 2012, 207).

References

Benhabib, Seyla. 2006. *Another Cosmopolitanism*. [With Jeremy Waldron, Bonnie Honig, & Will Kymlicka. Edited by Robert Post.] Oxford: Oxford University Press.

Butler, Judith, and Spivak, Gayatri Chakravorty. 2007. *Who Sings the Nation-State?* London: Seagull.

Christian, William. 1996. *George Grant: A Biography*. Toronto: University of Toronto Press.

Christian, William. 2001 (1995). Editor's Introduction: George Grant's Nietzsche. George Grant's *Time as History* (vii–xli). Toronto: University of Toronto Press.

Emberley, Peter C. 2005 (1994). Foreword to the Carleton Library Edition of *Lament for a Nation* by George Grant (lxxviii–lxxxv). Montreal and Kingston: McGill-Queen's University Press.

Grant, George. 1966 (1959). *Philosophy in the Mass Age*. Toronto: Copp Clark Publishing.

Grant, George. 1966. Introduction to *Philosophy in the Mass Age* (iii–ix). Toronto: Copp Clark Publishing.

Grant, George. 1969. *Technology & Empire*. Toronto: Anansi.

Grant, George. 1986. *Technology and Justice*. Toronto: Anansi.

Grant, George. 2001 (1969). *Time as History*. Toronto: University of Toronto Press.

Grant, George. 2005 (1965). *Lament for a Nation*. [40th anniversary edition] Montreal and Kingston: McGill-Queen's University Press.

Grant, George. 2005 (1970). Introduction to the Carleton Library Edition of *Lament for a Nation* (lxix–lxxvi). Montreal and Kingston: McGill-Queen's University Press.

Lasch, Christopher. 1984. *The Minimal Self: Psychic Survival in Troubled Times.* New York: Norton.

Lathangue, Robin. 1998. Introduction to George Grant *English-Speaking Justice* (vii–xxi). Toronto: Anansi.

Lipset, Seymour Martin. 1990. *Continental Divide: The Values and Institutions of the United States and Canada.* New York: Routledge.

Perlstein, Daniel. 2000. "There is no escape … from the ogre of indoctrination": George Counts and the Civic Dilemmas of Democratic Educators. In *Reconstructing the Common Good in Education: Coping with Intractable Dilemmas*, edited by Larry Cuban and Dorothy Shipps (51–67). Stanford, CA: Stanford University Press.

Pinar, William F. 2012. *What Is Curriculum Theory?* [Second edition.] New York: Routledge.

Potter, Andrew. 2005. Introduction to the 40th Anniversary Edition of George P. Grant's *Lament for a Nation* (ix–lxviii). Montreal and Kingston: McGill-Queen's University Press.

Ruthven, Malise. 2009, July 2. Divided Iran on the Eve. *The New York Review of Books* LVI (11), 53–56.

Saul, John Ralston. 2005. *The Collapse of Globalism: And the Reinvention of the World.* Toronto: Viking Canada.

Signatories. 2013, February 12. Our Collective Support … *The New York Times* Vol. CLXII, No. 56,045, A7.

Smith, David Geoffrey. 2014. Wisdom Responses to Globalization. In the *International Handbook of Curriculum Research* edited by William F. Pinar (45–59). [Second edition.] New York: Routledge.

Stewart, James B. 2013, September 14. New Metric for Colleges: Graduates' Salaries. *The New York Times* CLXII, No. 56,259, B1, A4.

Toews, John. 2008. *Becoming Historical: Cultural Reformation and Public Memory in Early Nineteenth-Century Berlin.* New York: Cambridge University Press.

Tomkins, George S. 1986. *A Common Countenance: Stability and Change in the Canadian Curriculum.* Scarborough, Ontario: Prentice-Hall. [Reprinted in 2008 by Pacific Educational Press.]

Wang, Hongyu. 2014. A Nonviolent Perspective on Internationalizing Curriculum Studies. In the *International Handbook of Curriculum Research*, edited by William F. Pinar (67–76). New York: Routledge.

Watson, Alexander John. 2007. *Marginal Man: The Dark Vision of Harold Innis.* Toronto: University of Toronto Press.

Wexler, Philip. 2013. *Mystical Sociology. Toward Cosmic Social Theory.* New York: Peter Lang.

4. Religion, Education and the Post-Secular Child

ROBERT A. DAVIS

Children—Secular, Sacred, Profane

Children are dumb to say how hot the day is,
How hot the scent is of the summer rose,
How dreadful the black wastes of evening sky
How dreadful the tall soldiers drumming by.

But we have speech, to chill the angry day,
And speech, to dull the rose's cruel scent.
We spell away the overhanging night,
We spell away the soldiers and the fright

—Robert Graves, "The Cool Web"
(Graves, 2003, p. 283)

In "The Cool Web," Robert Graves casts an ironising gaze at the prophylactic properties of language and learning—charged in the literary economy to which the poem alludes with maintaining a fragile and discursive cordon around the segregated sensibilities of adult and child in their contrasting encounters with some of the universals of human vulnerability:

There's a cool web of language winds us in,
Retreat from too much joy or too much fear:
We grow sea-green at last and coldly die
In brininess and volubility.

Graves' clever lyric engages self-consciously with the old Romantic conceit—required to stage several appearances in this brief enquiry into the post-secular child—which associates childhood with artlessness, aphasia, unmediated sensation and a radical subjectivity towards which adults are inclined only in psychologically agitated states such as madness or excessive desire. The scheme of significations arising out of this conceit inevitably encodes intense emotional conditions such as "too much joy or too much fear" as illocutionary realisations from which the educated faculties of rational being, especially language and literacy, are designed to protect us. At one and the same time rehearsing and unravelling the Romantic myth of prelinguistic infantile immediacy, Graves' poem also leads straight back to, yet cunningly interrogates, Rousseau's ambition for a childhood uncontaminated by the intervention of the verbal sign: "What is the use of inscribing in their heads a catalogue of signs, which convey no representation to them? In learning the things, will they not learn the signs?" (Rousseau, 1979, p. 111). The experiences of "dread," "fright," "too much fear" expose the child to an intensity of raw feeling which the Romantic imagination traditionally affirms as a means of maintaining for children access to an otherwise lost or remote source of authenticity embedded in those pristine conditions of nature which, it is supposed, the acquisition and eventual rational mastery of language serves only to obscure and misrepresent.

The "dumbness" of children in the face of primary emotional states such as fear and longing has an historic, religious and educational traction, as well as an imaginary or aesthetic resonance. For in the historical record children are, as Charlotte Hardman (1973) once famously argued, what fieldworkers would call a "muted group," rarely present in their own voices or testimonies and mediated for the most part in the officially sanctioned canons of adult reportage, whether these be the outputs of social science research or the prized artistry of literary memoir and autobiography (Montgomery, 2009, pp. 34–38). Hardman's landmark call for an anthropology of childhood took its cue from the encyclopedic efforts of the celebrated British pioneer ethnographers of children's games and pastimes, Iona and Peter Opie, whose monumental *Lore and Language of Schoolchildren* (1959) appeared to document an astonishingly rich British children's subculture of playground and street imprinted with the hybrid forms of memory, tradition, invention, improvisation and preservation—and promiscuously channelling influences from history, religion, folktale, popular song and mass media into a labile and unpredictable child-centric construction of the world. The Opies' progamme was at once scientific and Romantic: it exoticised and enchanted childhood even as it sought also to listen, attend and classify in accordance with the then newly fashionable observatory styles of the rising sociologies of class, race and gender. Its datazone, indeed, was often the liminal spaces of school *play*grounds, where the looming disciplinary presences of the classroom, the teacher and the curriculum inevitably conditioned and coloured the experi-ence and management of *play* in children's daily lives and recreation.

This putative "liminality" of childhood and its cultural productions has been heavily problematized in the intervening decades, chiefly by the rise of a new sociology of childhood which, when it first appeared in the 1980s and '90s, challenged the quasi-structuralist assumptions of figures such as the Opies and also questioned the presumed impermeability of the mysterious so-cial and epistemological boundaries within which childhood and its cultures were apparently and immovably contained. Investigators such as Alan Prout, Allison James and Chris Jenks (1998) turned their attention to the sites of adult-child *exchange* rather than *separation*—to institutions such as the school, the home, medicine, criminal justice—in order to formulate a new and dy-namic understanding of childhood as a multiple and iterative construction in which recurrent patterns of negotiation, coercion, subversion and accommo-dation undermined essentialised accounts of role and identity and politicised the obvious asymmetries of adult-child relations and conflicts. Strengthened by the advent of an infinitely richer and globalised comparative anthropolo-gy of childhood, which also documented an immensely diverse and crowded spectrum of possible childhoods from across an increasingly interdependent yet economically divided world (Lancy, 2008), the so-called "new paradigm" (Ryan, 2008) seemed to complete what might indeed be termed the "secular-isation" of childhood—banishing forever the lingering and allegedly injurious legacy of Romantic childhood and placing at the heart of scholarly and moral attention a sternly scientific project of understanding, intervention and inclu-sion. In part, the new paradigm was a deeply political undertaking, directly descended from the breakthroughs of feminism and the women's movement; in other key respects it was an intellectual realignment, bent on demystifying the modern Western conception of childhood and purging it of those genea-logical markers such as "innocence," "incapacity," "dependence," "wonder," which, the new paradigm insisted, served only to disguise the gradient of power under which children were comprehensively subjugated. Instead of "play," the new sociology of childhood therefore prioritised "work" as the routine and overlooked demand placed on most children most of the time. Instead of the evasive "innocence," it focused on the complexities of juvenile sexualities and the increasingly visible and shocking narratives of subaltern abuse and heter-onormative exclusion. In place of "dependence," it highlighted "competence" as the centrepiece of a repertoire of capabilities through which children could come swiftly to claim their human rights and entitlements (Oswell, 2013).

If we are to interpret these processes as indeed the expression of a "secu-larisation" of childhood, then it may make good intuitive sense to search out the grounds for a "post-secular" childhood that follows the established trajectory of much recent social theory and philosophy in other, related domains of critical speculation (McLennan, 2010). It is after all in the voices of the abjected, excluded and subordinate that post-secular thought has found many of its most significant and motivating sources of impetus. Children have in the last generation been increasingly enlisted into this alliance of the marginalised by a host of advocates and analysts and now commonly appear in the theoretical literature as very obvious points of reference in charting the seeming exhaustion of the standard technico rationalist managerial models of their liberation, welfare and development. Within the centrally authorised rejections of secularist hegemony from which the post-secular draws inspiration, it is quite possible to locate childhood as a site where the older certitudes of the ideological critique have yielded to sympathetic interest in the place of sincere religious affiliation, identity-formation and the necessary, educative tasks of pluralist engagement with the other in those myriad schools and communities where religious belonging has endured as a recurrent thematic of social being. This perspective largely accords with Habermas's (2008) encouragement of dialogue between "naturalism and religion" as an enabling condition of renovated and religiously-inclusive European liberalism. It is also hospitable, however, to the more challenging, even post-liberal forms of post-secular interrogation, such as Taylor's (2007) vigorous reassertion of the claims of the universal transcendent, or Eagleton's (2009) and Dews' (2008) bold insistence that Western ethics as an educational endeavour remains seriously depleted by its rationalist deafness to the religious registers of conscience, reconciliation, virtue and solidarity by which the human subject is understood to be formed within, for example, the traditions of Judaeo-Christian moral psychology.

The still more provocative analysis advanced by thinkers such as Talal Asad (2003), Jose Casanova (2003) and William Connolly (1999), that secularism has induced in the West a crisis of legitimation—crystalized by the recent botched attempt to comprehend global Islam through the exhausted lexicon of secular multiculturalism, but by no means confined to this egregious error—also holds out the possibility of a refurbished understanding of childhood, because it is consumed by the pursuit of a new religious literacy and by the demand for an enlarged epistemology of the kind young children frequently refract in radical educational and social theory. Asad's searching examination of the angular relationship of secularism to freedom, his insistence that the "straightforward narrative of progress from the religious to the secular is no longer acceptable" (1), underscores the promise of education—and perhaps even religious education—in seeking out and giving pedagogical shape to a much more expansive encounter with the languages of faith, truth and meaning-making (Conroy and Davis, 2008; Watson, 2013). Asad's vision of the post-secular gives back to education a permission it has steadily relinquished: to validate within the practices of collaborative, exploratory learning a critical awareness of the regions of human "spiritual" experience declassified by the same ideological processes which gave birth to modern schooling in the first place.

This basic perception of children and childhood as singular beneficiaries of the post-secular turn, chiefly through the radicalization of their educational entitlements, can perhaps be best understood as a democratic hermeneutic (Fischer et al., 2012). It sees the post-secular as an opportunity to recapture capacities, insights, sensations and resources improperly erased by the march of secular modernity, and by the aggressive assault on religion by the orthodox social sciences, while restoring a richer and more thoroughgoing sensibility to the textured processes of day-to-day learning and teaching. It refreshes the civic task of intercultural (and interfaith) living and it allegedly opens young learners to a much more potent interaction with the visions of morality, celebration and cosmology embedded in the world's major and antique religious traditions. From this fundamentally expanded understanding, the post-secular serves also to question searchingly the often unexamined actuarial architecture of contemporary education itself, amplifying the critical-theoretical denunciation of the occluded workings of the sociobureaucratic state and its performative calculus of educational rationality and output-driven industrial effectiveness. This, of course, includes the dominant and determinant models of the juvenile learner and the battery of metrics within which his "development" and "attainment" are commonly standardized and constrained. It is not simply that the post-secular draws back into the authorized curricular circle regions of human sensibility previously expelled from learning and teaching, restoring the prestige of, for example, the once nugatory claims of faith or the abiding call of the *bildung*. These may be integral features of the alternatives and supplements posited by post-secular education. Much more importantly, however, the daring modalities of thought and apprehension underpinning the post-secular problematize the prevailing classificatory taxonomies through which the hitherto self-evident categories of "learner," "school" and "child" have been sustained and reproduced (Dunne 2005).

This realization postulates the post-secular as a necessary phase in a larger narrative of political and social transformation destined to emancipate the child from every diminished or circumscribed account of his status and possibilities, including those directly emergent from the enlightened mission of popular education itself. Giving something "back" to the child, offering the

child access to a vocabulary of the transcendent, the cosmological, the marvel-
ous; inviting the child to become a protagonist in an enriched appreciation of
his own learning—these are all laudable moral imperatives of the post-secular
tilt in education and they offer huge potential to learning and teaching in,
e.g., the arts and humanities, the early years and infant school curriculum, or
religious education. It remains instructive to consider, however, the extent to
which the central aspiration fueling this movement is nonetheless still grasping
only incompletely the potential of childhood and the palimpsest of story, sym-
bol, faith, myth, tradition and discovery from out of which the conflicted and
protean nature of Western childhood, especially, has been fashioned. It may
well be that in striving to make sense of the "*post*-secular child," and the full-
spectrum education to which he is rightly entitled, we are required to return
to the increasingly forgotten "*pre*-secular child" of the European imaginary,
in order to cure our cultural amnesia and to recognise the extent to which
the symbolic economy of childhood inherited by the West somehow always
already inhabits a space constitutively outside the jurisdiction of the secular. In
the embrace of this possibility we remember that which we have always known
and reconnect with repositories of thought, sensation, belief, longing, affiliation, appetite and wonder which many traditions of faith and wisdom associate uniquely with the volatile yet cherished symbolism of a child-figure often
ecstatically captive to the enchantment of a prodigal world (Thomson, 2013).
These perceptions frequently do materialize around the doctrinal formulations
and liturgical repetitions of the organized religions, to which the post-secular
turn affords a fresh (if critical) hospitality. It can be instructive, however, for
the understanding of the pre-secular, and for the better comprehension of the
child within the patterns of the post-secular, to look to locations other than revealed religion for sight of the nimbus or supplement that clings to the figure
of the child in the European imaginary and which often implicitly reproaches
the grudging and attenuated acknowledgement of childhood difference in the
favoured patterns of contemporary education.

Pedagogies of Fear and Desire

If attention to the pre-secular has anything to teach the post-secular about
childhood and its place in the systematic structures and processes of advanced education, it may be most revealing where it highlights those thresh-
olds where childhood has been, for protracted periods of time, negotiated
and reproduced in culturally enduring yet educationally recalcitrant forms.
The folkloristic and supernatural experiences which figured prominently in
the lives of European children in the past derived chiefly from the treasured

deposits of popular superstition, fairy tales, nursery rhymes, songs and lullabies (Honeyman, 2013). These cultural vehicles remain crucial to an understanding of the theme of transcendence in the lives of children precisely because they have succeeded in retaining a prestige and a currency across several conflicting interpretations of the value and purposes of childhood. Theological, juridical and behaviourally-motivated materials have either in many respects lost their meaning as their supporting pre-modern belief systems have faded, or else they have been deliberately (if misguidedly) suppressed as barbarous in the name of enlightened educational practice—exactly as the secularising paradigm proposed they would be. Folkloristic narratives have, on the other hand, survived sometimes revolutionary secularising shifts in manners and attitudes long enough to lay claim to a distinctive place in the symbolic matrix of adult-child interactions, acquiring a cachet inextricably bound up with the complex emotional and spiritual states they induce and mediate in children. It is indeed sometimes remarkable to observe that in systems of schooling where the religious education curriculum has been thoroughly domesticated and instrumentalised in the name of a progressive rationality quite inimical to the experience of "the religious" itself, the ready embrace by teachers and pupils of storytelling and folklore inadvertently preserves the radiance of the supersensible in the formation and stimulus of children and young people (Phillips, 2011).

This is not to say that the products of folk culture are exempt from the pressures of history. Much interesting scholarship of the past twenty-five years has been devoted precisely to the historicisation of the folk narrative, which has been shown to be far from static or immutable. Documenting the manipulation, the bowdlerising and the censorship of the fairy tale, for example, has brought out the complex interaction within the genre of the spoken and the written, including the appropriation of the dispersed and unstable products of vernacular culture to the centralising moral schemes of the educated polity (Zipes, 2012). Similarly, examination of the conventional sites of adult-child communication has drawn attention to the cultural politics of the folk narrative as it ratifies its originary tableau of transmission and reception: its tacit roles in the creation of gender and class identity, for example, the separation of the spheres, and the construction of a hierarchical subjectivity. Stressing their ultimately educative designs, the feminist critic Maria Tatar (1993) considers fairy tales and traditional stories told to children, throughout their historical evolution from the oral to the textual, to be part of what she terms "the pedagogy of fear" (22). In Tatar's analysis, textualisation may have purged the narratives of many of their original overtly violent and aggressive content, but only to reinscribe a more nuanced moral meaning where the habitual dispositions of childhood are located firmly within an abstract moral code the final guarantor of which is a pseudo-religious mandate vouchsafed by the threat or inducement of *fear*.

Tatar's watchful assessment of the influence of cultural objects the solemnity of which accrues from age, genre and the privileging of speech over writing involves a subtle refinement of the Romantic-sentimentalist view that the folkloristic carries children back unproblematically to a primordial unity with nature and with being validated by the archaic character of the folkloristic forms themselves. The 19th-century recapitulation fallacy infamously argued for the belief that children were destined to an affinity with "primitive" cultural forms because these were the products of the preliterate infancy of the race: cultural ontogeny recapitulating historical phylogeny. In accessing fairy stories, nursery rhymes, folk tales and lullabies, children were thought to be communing with the atavistic sources of human consciousness in actions strongly reminiscent of religious initiation. If, like Tatar, we accept that the only atavism in which these forms participate is disciplinary authority, we are left with a need to explain their continuing hold over the minds of the young when these disciplinary responsibilities have transferred elsewhere or faded away entirely. We are left with the pleasure of the text; the sought-after rewards of scariness and factitious horrors which Tatar and her followers (Purkiss, 2001) ultimately fail to address satisfactorily precisely because the analysis that they advance cannot breach the boundaries of the secular design from which it originated.

Recognising and understanding the stimulus of the pleasure principle in children's experience of fear has been for much of the modern period central to its legitimation, especially within meliorative social practices such as education. The ideological assumptions of contemporary educational practice imply an almost total elimination of this vocabulary from the processes of teaching and learning, except, that is, where it is associated developmentally with that other Romantic configuration with which the fulfilment of the modern child remains inextricably bound up: the imagination. It is, indeed, precisely the Coleridgean emphasis on the imagination's vitally creative power of dissolving and uniting images into new forms, and of reconciling opposed qualities into a new and higher unity, which accords it such unrivalled centrality to the flourishing of young children and which thereby preserves the connection of children with cultural reserves that the secularising impulse would otherwise seriously downgrade or expel. It is the freely creative and transforming properties of the imagination, thus conceived, which justifies its nourishment by aesthetic forms which induce heightened states of sensitivity such as exaltation and disquietude. In her celebrated study of the imagination, Mary Warnock (1976) showed how early formulations of the concept by thinkers such as Schiller and Novalis strongly associated it with health and wellbeing—both individual and collective. Summarising the Romantic position, Warnock argues that the "power in the human mind which is at work in our everyday perception of the world, and…in our thoughts about what is absent" derives its impetus "from the emotions as much as from reason" (196). As R. S. Peters stated in his landmark essay, "The Education of the Emotions" (1972/2009), rather than being a set of "purely automatic" physiological responses to stimuli, the emotional activities of the imagination "are basically forms of cognition" (347), so that what is felt in relation to a particular object or situation is determined by the manner in which it is perceived—i.e., by whether it is felt to be agreeable, disagreeable, reassuring or frightening.

These convictions and the pedigree out of which they descend form the basis of the second great justification of the place of these induced and elevated states of consciousness in the formation of the young: the therapeutic. The therapeutic account of heightened sensation exhibits both a mixed intellectual ancestry and a continuing locus in educational theory. It derives in part from that offshoot of Romantic thinking alluded to previously, which connected childhood to the mentalities of primitive societies. E. B. Tyler's description in *Primitive Culture* of *magic* as an expression of "animistic belief" (1871, p. 453) came to be applied vicariously to the experiences of childhood through the rise of Freudian psychoanalysis with its interest in repressed memories, instinct and dreaming. According to Malinowski, conversely, the "fountainhead of magical belief" is to be found "in those passionate experiences which assail man in the impasses of his instinctive life and of his practical pursuits, in those gaps and breaches left in the ever imperfect wall of culture which he erects between himself and the besetting temptations and dangers of his destiny" (1948, pp. 59–60). Whether the movement is from race to child or from child to race, the academic logic of this analysis is consistent in arguing that the enchanted state is an effect of underdeveloped or even infantile consciousness as it strives for control of an unknown environment, utilising the seemingly miraculous hypothesising resources of the psyche in order to make sense of the mysterious operations of that environment. Whilst not arguing for direct inculcation of "magical thinking" in the minds of the young, the therapeutic model interprets these patterns of perception as pervasive, inevitable and necessary—one of the means, ultimately, for securing the child's achievement of competence in the world exactly as progressive education might champion it. The developmental implications of the model are openly acknowledged by Bruner, Olver and Coreenfield (1967):

> Man seems to have evolved with a unique capacity for helplessness that can be relieved by outside shaping and external devices … The early helplessness of man … seems to be accompanied by a propelling curiosity about the environment and by much self-reinforcing activity seemingly designed to achieve competence

in that environment ... Indeed, the degree to which a supply of stimulation creates a demand for it may be crucial for a species in which morphological adaptation has become so supplemented by technological adaptation—a species that, in
Weston La Barre's striking phrase ... survives by grace of prosthetic devices. (4)

The multiple meetings with the dark, the unknown, the monstrous, the
metamorphic—these are central and primary episodes for the pre-secular
child of story, fable and ritual performance, who can then by his sheer otherness pose impossible problems for the therapeutic model. If, for example, the
fear of these forces is an intentional and contextual state, then the sensation
of the dark menaces the achievement of "competence" by its sheer contex-
tlessness (almost by the absence of difference). Yet the most persuasive and
educationally influential versions of the therapeutic model regard the dark
paradoxically as the major site of illumination because it is the place where the
fictions of the imagination, which trade in the imagery of fright and flight, can
supposedly work their psychic alchemy on the inner lives of the young. For
Bruno Bettelheim—a decisive figure in the rediscovery of the folkloristic by
modern teachers and educators—the language and organisation of fairy stories, folk tales, nursery rhymes and lullabies shared with children in the dimly
lit spaces of the family romance exploit fear as a strategy for the resolution of
Oedipal conflict. Fictive fear here operates as a kind of inoculant, "fortifying"
the child's personality against the "real" fears of growing up by staging the
emotions of the Oedipal drama in a contained and protected theatre of the
mind. For Bettelheim, writes Jacqueline Rose, "The purpose of the fairy tale
is to allow the child that early instability or instance of disruption in order to
ensure that any such instability will, in the last analysis, be more effectively removed" (1984, p. 14). Hence, in the Bettelheimian therapy, there is a strange
complicity between the archaic character of the fictional vehicles of fear and
the notion of the child as the true, unconscious recipient of their meaning.
"The child understands this intuitively," asserts Bettelheim, "though he does
not know it explicitly" (1976, p. 179).

Not all accounts of the therapeutic uses of such emotions need involve
the subordination of children to a regime of what is supposed to be good for
them, to the rehearsal of adulthood. The complicated, layered pleasures of
fear, which the therapeutic model both assumes and explains, can be histor-
icised as well as psychoanalytically validated. This occurs most productively
when the model focuses in on the content, structure and dynamics of the
cultural materials through which heightened awareness of this special kind is
aroused in small children. In her renowned survey of this literature, Marina
Warner (1998) correctly identifies an underlying design recognisable to the
findings of classical structural anthropology. This is the threefold pattern of

naming, transforming and *demarcating*. It resides not merely in the properties of the folk narratives themselves but also in the surrounding relationships that support and communicate the narratives and in the intimations of something approaching "the sublime" that they may sporadically provoke in all concerned with their reproduction.

The *naming* of a danger does not rob it of its anxiety but does mark out the steps towards its containment. The *transformation* of a fear (an essentially Enlightenment task) from the unknown to the known involves the gradual disclosure of its identity and the discovery of the means to combat it. The *demarcation* of a fear brings about the separation of what is to be feared from the community that it menaces. As well as advancing a usable taxonomy of these core sensations, the threefold function can be seen to describe an upswing—from the dark in which the inchoate is shared, to the light in which it is neutralised. Historicising the therapeutic model in this way inevitably also invites consideration of the uses of the functions in specific socialised conjunctures. The folkloristic traditions of fairy tale and lullaby are expressions of particular sets of social relationships and betray the foreboding implicit in these arrangements as well as their reassurances. The functions can be employed, respectively, to terrify, to subordinate, to demonise outsiders. They disclose the innermost workings of domestic stress, parental division, sexual rivalry, intercommunal strife, competition for scarce resources, life-threatening disease and calamity, warfare, the happenstance and provisionality of life. They present in their archetypal content chthonic and horrifying experiences such as cannibalism or child predators in forms which can be simultaneously psychoanalysed and historically corroborated. But they do all this, Warner insists, within a setting of trust and protection which, however externally fragile, is presented to the child as permanent and enduring. They frighten in order to reassure, extending to children a kind of virtual scaring where they can learn what a danger feels like before it is safely taken away. They emphasise the overcoming and defeat of the fear by a renovated human order—even if it is one that is only finally asserted in the warmth of the concluding maternal embrace or Freud's soothing hand in the dark.

Warner provides a highly convincing defence of customary resources of this kind because she locates them in a meaningful historical practice where the initial emotion it excites is not an end in itself but exists as part of a wider recognition of the material and imaginary forces which cultivate the child's receptivity to the authenticity of the marvellous and the extraordinary. This compelling perspective also implies appreciation of the extent to which the folk deposits are also simultaneously an articulation of suppressed *adult* hopes and desires for the recuperation of such capacities in the face of the stifling desacralising discourses through which they are almost everywhere denied and eliminated by the antipathy of a hostile secular liberal order. Drawing attention to the adult side of the equation in the stimulus of children's imaginative capabilities does perhaps call into question the explanatory completeness of the established threefold function. The functions require to be held in tension with a less closed and recuperative theorisation which both confronts the regressive pleasure and enthralment of the sensations involved while engaging with full non-rational supplement that supplies them with their compulsive, often shocking emotional charge. Part of the thrill of the fairytale and lullaby, for example, may lie in the glimpses they provide for adults and for children of a species of unmediated *power*, a potent compound of desire and expiation, where transgressive fantasies can be loosed and dreams of the transcendent valorised. If this is the case, these artefacts are compelling for what they fail to contain as well as for what they successfully organise and assuage. They highlight their own discursive hypertrophy: the excesses of consumption, obliteration, overwhelming might and supernaturally enlarged selfhood. They provide an iconography of interactive motifs unavailable to normal experience, opening a fluent intercourse between human, daemonic and celestial forces. Warner's thesis lays emphasis ultimately upon the healing ceremonial qualities of the storytelling, fairytale pageant or lullaby-crooning scenario, where the sublime is startlingly released only to be regulated and finally rescinded. Attending to the supplement, the excess, in this symbolic economy—to what resists containment and control—extends the possibility of a more radical disclosure, where what is encrypted in the turbulent mythic languages of childhood is the shared pursuit by both child and adult of the transformative magical energy with which the narratives are forever invested and which refuses each and every secular appropriation of them.

Beyond Secular Childhoods

This chapter began with an ironic gesture towards the cluster of Romantic myths within which childhood is customarily seen to be possessed of a radiance or penumbra attached to objects trapped immemorially in the nexus of community and power (Rowland, 2012). There are inflections of this heritage that accord children just those extraordinary and preternatural properties that can be found in the exotic narratives of fairy story and folk tale which are such a prominent aspect of the vernacular or even subversively "unofficial" formation of childhood across the generations. Indeed, it might be argued that the Romantic paradigm in one sense makes children the stars of their own wonder tales, showcasing the prophetic gifts children are themselves believed to harbour in the deepest recesses of their being. The language of such a mode of representation is invariably loaded with a *vitalist* rhetoric: the child is a unique embodiment of the life force, predisposed to an intensity of appetite and apprehension upon which the health of the human imagination (and the human community) depends; an intermediary between lived experience and transcendental influences hovering on the borders of normal perception (Steedman, 1995; Plotz, 2001). In bestowing these characteristics, the legacy of Romantic representation, particularly, renders the child an unparalleled object of desire caught in a fierce dialectic of remoteness and proximity. The child is charged with a numinosity that is quasi-religious in status but which is denied the authority associated with objects of veneration by virtue of its confinement within the ambiguous constructions of adult desire. "For the child," notes Lyotard in his remarkable essay "The Grip," "everything is trauma, the wound of a pleasure that is going to be forbidden and withdrawn." (1993, p. 152).

The language and symbolism which accrue to childhood when it is approached in these terms have significant consequences for an understanding of children, religion and the invitation of the post-secular moment. It is not a coincidence that in the religious movement we call Spiritualism, which flourished in England and America between 1848 and 1890, among the leading mediums of the day were many children. The accentuation of their spiritual qualities in the art and writing of the preceding era created just the right conditions for children to be accepted by the Spiritualist Churches as the obvious intermediaries between the realms of the living and the dead. When the apparitions spoke to Kate and Margaret Fox in New York in 1848, initiating the Spiritualist craze, they were doing no more than sowing ground long prepared by a particular set of juxtapositions of children and specific modes of understanding and communication reserved to them in this potent tradition of thought and belief (Ferguson, 2012). As Coleridge had recognised long before, seeing children in this way was bound "to excite a feeling analogous to the supernatural ..." (1984, p. 314).

When they appeared to traffic between the living and the dead, between reality and the transcendent, children acquired precisely the kind of occult power promised them in the fairy tales and folk deposits into which these capacities had been uneasily exiled by the institutional interests of the secular order. Their voices were listened to and they were accorded authority in their communities. The Romantic myth of the visionary child was momentarily wrested from the dominion of its adult creators and became a way of speaking, resisting and creating—affording children the agency to interact with the expectations of adult desire on their own terms. This turning back by children of the figurations of something as unconditional as the fear of death onto the adults who originate and codify them highlights an infrequently observed thread in the Romantic mythology of childhood—and casts light upon the ambivalence which haunts all attempts to rationalise the "uses of the magic" in the lives of children. When children themselves are seen to be *sources* of this power, rather than the *subjects* of it—whether within the life of the imagination or within the life of the (religious) communities in which they dwell—a point of transition may indeed have been reached. The traditional resources of the fairy tale and the folk narrative cease to ratify a social or affectional bond and instead describe a gulf, an abjection, an essential alienation of the rival subjectivities of adult and child. In such a process of estrangement, innocence and guilt, like ignorance and knowledge, become the mutually-defining signifiers of a shame-culture. Adults and children come to occupy separate dimensions bound together only by the costly combination of anxiety and enthralment with which each perceives the other. In a recent influential and impassioned examination of this impasse as it affects deleteriously the raising and treatment of children in the UK and beyond, the journalist-ethnographer Jay Griffiths (2013) finds herself returning to a redemptive conception of what she terms the "childscape:" the point of convergence between nature, infancy and the adumbration by children of authentically transmundane realities—which is then materialised, she argues, in a symbolic rediscovery and political reclamation of "the outdoors" as the fitting, even Arcadian, setting for the renewal of solidarity between the adult and the child.

The fact that contemporary childhood is now subject to the pernicious conflicting pressures documented by Griffiths and other concerned commentators—and provokes such ambivalence and contradiction—makes it an obvious site for post-secular reappraisal. Unsurprisingly in this context, the greatly enlarged and often deeply unsettling profile of children in popular consciousness and in state activity—and in repeated flurries of newspaper articles and mass media commentaries—has coincided with a new level of academic engagement with childhood as the locus for issues that are as vexing and contested to the era in which we live as they are important to its self-understanding. The new post-secular focus on childhood may of course be seen as reflecting these very particular current circumstances—or alternatively as one strikingly concentrated response to the seismic changes, across social, cultural, economic and political conditions, conveniently labelled "post-modern" in the operation of the social sciences. Yet at the same time there may remain, as this chapter has argued, something *primordial* about childhood, so that *any* society at any time inescapably reveals a great deal about itself—and not least its attitude to the past and future—in and through its ways of envisioning childhood and treating of children. It may be part of the "primordiality" of childhood—in addition to its indisputable universality as a period of initiation or ordeal from which no human being is exempt—that it exercises such a lasting hold on the troubled or even the contented adult mind (Godelier, 2011, pp. 219–229). As evidence of the fascination of childhood as remembered, narrated, imagined or retrospectively imbued with significance, we may consider for instance the popularity of a recent spate of books depicting their childhood by well-known authors or people with unusually lurid or heroic stories to tell (for example, Blake Morrison, Lorna Sage, Frank McCourt, Dave Pelzer). And writing "the childhood"—with all its endemic interpretative ambiguities—has long been an integral element in the art of biography, autobiography and memoir (Coe, 1985). This fascination is surely supercharged in the wake of Freud's presentation of childhood as the crucially determinative chapter of the life-story, the uniquely significant source, for weal or woe, of human character and destiny. And even if Freud's own particular theoretical account and clinical procedure are now contested by a host of successors, the orientation of virtually all contemporary psychotherapies—not least those featuring the attenuated but populist claims of the "the inner child"—remains classically retrospective, finding the source of adult misery or disturbance or possible manumission in the unmet needs and unresolved conflicts of early childhood. But emphasis on the continuing resonance of childhood in adult experience was already—with more stress on its creative potential as the "seed time of the soul'—a key part of Romanticism's shaping influence on modern consciousness. Or much earlier still, in one of the first Western attempts to "gather" a life reflectively in a first-person narrative, the potential significance of childhood intimations and inclinations was incisively scrutinised in the first book of St. Augustine's *Confessions*.

Reference to such precedents is salutary if only to guard against any facile supposition that contemporary and mainstream scholarly preoccupations with childhood are unique. Much of this "orthodox" scholarship is, like the new sociologies discussed above, permeated by a radical historicism that is eager to overthrow older or received conceptions (Jones, 2009). It frames childhood not as a natural life-phase but as a social and cultural fabrication, inscribed in ideological discourses and regulated by disciplinary regimes of surveillance and control. A hermeneutic of suspicion, directed especially against any commitments to "naturalism" or "essentialism," exposes childhood as the product of shifting interactions of economic forces, technological advances, and bureaucratic administrations of education and welfare (Meyer, 2007). Heightened attention to the relativity of significant sites where childhood is constructed is then taken stipulatively to undermine all "universalist" claims

(Levander, 2009). Foundations for any normative judgements with respect to childhood—for example, in terms of the kind of desirable formation recommended in traditions of *Bildung*, or of unique capacities and gifts posited by Romanticism, or of ineluctable needs uncovered by psychoanalysis—are then deemed to be almost entirely unavailable to educators or parents.

These deconstructive designs on childhood of course find a place within wider debates about modernity. Childhood is often now seen as a characteristically modern invention, a key phase in the self-narration of the modern subject—an episode whether of vulnerability and dependency to be overcome, lost grace to be treasured and lamented, or secret longings to be always lived with but never finally appeased. With its defining drive for autonomy and authenticity, the modern subject is the target of much recent critique across a range of disciplines: the kind of continuity, coherence and centredness that it previously seemed to assume—if only as a regulative ideal—is forfeit to the fragmentation, dissemination and decentredness proclaimed by post-modernist critique. Inevitably, as an integral moment in the genealogy of modern subjectivity, childhood falls within the sights of this same critique: its very survival may be doubted, indeed, in an anti-narrative often unabashedly presented as a voiding of the whole humanist project (Baker, 2001).

The post-secular seeks to intervene in these debates over the implications of modernity by reopening the question of childhood from quite different terms of reference. It contests the assumption that older figurations of childhood are now irretrievably derelict, if not outrightly damaging (Alderson, 2013). Some of these figurations, especially the Romantic one invoked throughout this essay, are certainly legacies of high modernity. But an important effect of the post-secular is to show that they are more differentiated, more complexly related to pre-modern intuitions, and more resistant to post-modernist scepticism, than is now often suggested. Academic campaigners such as Rosi Braidotti (2008) or William Connolly (2009), without invoking as much as perhaps they ought to the potential of childhood and its locus in a reformed conception of education and society, seek nonetheless to recover the neo-vitalist strain of the post-secular as the basis for (in Connolly's memorable phrasing) a "metaphysics of the supersensible" (24), an "impious reverence for life" (54) which, in its extravagant release of the "protean energies" (88) of desire and hope, reproaches the cognitive and rationalist hegemony of the secular and repudiates the political and philosophical exclusion of the irrational, the religious, the magical from civic and educational attention. While therefore never ignoring what is to be learned from the myriad critiques advanced by the postmodern or new historicist perspective on the experiences of children and the complex, diverse histories of childhood attendant on these, the post-secular also seeks to take their measure by confronting them with concepts and images of childhood recuperated from diverse layers of earlier traditions, customs and culture. In doing this, its aim is not only to recover lost intimations of childhood but also to test their continuing viability—in conditions increasingly haunted by the spectre of "the post-human"—in supporting the permanent and inescapable task of understanding and caring for the young.

Bibliography

Alderson, P. (2013). *Childhoods Real and Imagined: Volume 1: An Introduction to Critical Realism and Childhood Studies (Ontological Explorations)*. London: Routledge.

Asad, T. (2003). *Formations of the Secular: Christianity, Islam, Modernity*. Palo Alto, CA: Stanford University Press.

Baker, B. (2001). *In Perpetual Motion: Theories of Power, Educational History and the Child*. New York: Peter Lang.

Bettelheim, B. (1976). *The Uses of Enchantment*. Harmondsworth: Penguin.

Braidotti, R. (2008). In Spite of the Times: The Postsecular Turn in Feminism. *Theory, Culture & Society*, 25.1: 1–24.

Bruner, J. S., Olver, R. R., Setampersand Greenfield, P. M. (1967). *Studies in cognitive growth: A collaboration at the Center for Cognitive Studies*. Harvard University. Center for Cognitive Studies.

Casanova, J. (2003). Beyond European and American Exceptionalisms: Towards a Global Perspective. In G. Davie, P. Heelas, and L. Woodhead (Eds.), *Predicting Religion*. Aldershot: Ashgate, 17–29.

Coe, R. N. (1985) *When the Grass Was Taller: Autobiography and the Experience of Childhood*. New Haven, CT: Yale University Press.

Coleridge, S. T. (1984/1817). *Biographia Literaria*. Princeton, NJ: Princeton University Press.

Connolly, W. E. (1999). *Why I Am Not a Secularist*. Minneapolis: University of Minnesota Press.

Conroy, J., & Davis, R. (2008). Citizenship, Education and the Claims of Religious Literacy. In M. Peters, A. Britton, & H. Blee, (Eds.) *Global Citizenship Education: Philosophy, Theory and Pedagogy*. Rotterdam: Sense, 187–203.

Dews, P. (2008). *The Idea of Evil*. Oxford: Blackwell.

Dunne, J. (2005). An Intricate Fabric: Understanding the Rationality of Practice. *Pedagogy, Culture and Society*, 13.3, 367–390.

Eagleton, T. (2009). *Trouble with Strangers: A Study of Ethics*. Chichester: Wiley-Blackwell.

Ferguson, C. (2012). Recent Studies in Nineteenth-Century Spiritualism. *Literature Compass*, 9.6, 431–440.

Fischer, S., Hotam, Y., & Wexler, P. (2012) Democracy and Education in Postsecular Society. *Review of Research in Education, 36*, 261–281.

Godelier, M. (2011). *The Metamorphoses of Kinship*. Nora Scott, trans. London: Verso.

Graves, R. (2003). *The Complete Poems*. Harmondsworth: Penguin.

Griffiths, J. (2013). *Kith: The Riddle of the Childscape*. London: Hamish Hamilton.

Habermas, J. (2008). *Beyond Naturalism and Religion*. Cambridge: Polity Press.

Hardman, C. (1973). Can There Be an Anthropology of Childhood? *Journal of the Anthropological Society of Oxford, 4*, 85–99.

Honeyman, S. (2013) *Consuming Agency in Fairy Tales, Childlore, and Folkliterature*. London: Routledge.

Jones, P. (2009). *Rethinking Childhood. Attitudes in Contemporary Society.* London: Continuum.

Lancy, D. F. (2008). *The Anthropology of Childhood: Cherubs, Chattel, Changelings*. Cambridge: Cambridge University Press.

Levander, C. F. (2009). Innocence, Childhood. In R. A. Shweder (Ed.) *The Child: An Encyclopedic Companion*. Chicago, IL: University of Chicago Press, 501–503.

Lyotard, J. F. (1993). The Grip (*mainmise*). In B. Readings & K. P. Geiman (Ed. and Trans.) *Political Writings*. Minneapolis: University of Minnesota Press, 148–153.

Malinowski, B. (1948). *Magic, Science and Religion and Other Essays*. Boston: Beacon Press.

McLennan, G. (2010). The Postsecular Turn. *Theory, Culture and Society, 27*.3, 3–20.

Meyer, A. (2007). The Moral Rhetoric of Childhood, *Childhood, 14*.1, 85–104.

Montgomery, H. (2009). *An Introduction to Childhood: Anthropological Perspectives on Children's Lives*. Oxford: Wiley-Blackwell.

Opie, I., & Opie, P. (1959). *Lore and Language of Schoolchildren*. Oxford: Clarendon Press.

Oswell, D. (2013). *The Agency of Children: From Family to Global Human Rights*. Cambridge: Cambridge University Press.

Peters, R. S. (1972/2009). The Education of the Emotions. In R. F. Dearden, P. H. Hirst, & R. S. Peters (Eds.), *Education and the Development of Reason*. London: Routledge, 466–483.

Phillips, A. (2011). *The Faith of Girls: Children's Spirituality and Transition to Adulthood*. London: Ashgate.

Plotz, J. (2001). *Romanticism and the Vocation of Childhood*. London: Palgrave.

Prout, A., James, A., & Jenks, C. (1998) *Theorizing Childhood*. London: Polity Press.

Purkiss, D. (2001). *Troublesome Things: A History of Fairies and Fairy Stories*. London: Penguin.

Rose, J. (1984). *The Case of Peter Pan, Or, The Impossibility of Children's Fiction*. Philadelphia University of Pennsylvania Press.

Rousseau, J.-J. (1979) *Emile*. A. Bloom, (Ed. and Trans). New York: Basic Books.

Rowland, A. W. (2012). *Romanticism and Childhood: The Infantilization of British Literary Culture*. Cambridge: Cambridge University Press.

Ryan, P. J. (2008). How New Is the "New" Social Study of Childhood? The Myth of a Paradigm Shift. *Journal of Interdisciplinary History*, XXXVIII. 4, 553–576.

Steedman, C. (1995). *Strange Dislocations: Childhood and the Idea of Human Interiority, 1780–1930*. Cambridge, MA: Harvard University Press.

Tatar, M. (1993). *Off with Their Heads!: Fairy Tales and the Culture of Childhood*. Princeton, NJ: Princeton University Press.

Taylor, C. (2007). *A Secular Age*. Cambridge, MA: Harvard University/Belknap Press.

Thomson, M. (2013). *Lost Freedom: The Landscape of the Child and the British Post-War Settlement*. Oxford: Oxford University Press.

Tylor, E. B. (1871). *Primitive Culture*. London: John Murray.

Warner, M. (1998). *No Go the Bogeyman: Scaring, Lulling and Making Mock*. London: Chatto and Windus.

Warnock, M. (1976). *Imagination*. Berkeley: University of California Press.

Watson, J. E. (2013). Post-Secular Schooling: Freedom Through Faith or Diversity in Community. *Cambridge Journal of Education, 43*.2, 147–162.

Zipes, J. (2012). *The Irresistible Fairy Tale: The Cultural and Social History of a Genre*. Princeton, NJ: Princeton University Press.

.

5. Pedagogy, Spirituality, and Curricular Design in Waldorf Education

Yotam Hotam

Since its foundation in 1919, Waldorf education has become a well-established and recognized pedagogical alternative adopted by a wide range of schools, educational institutes, and organizations around the world, "from Germany, Scandinavia, and the United States to Brazil, Argentina, Japan and India" (Uhrmacher, 1995: 381–406). In some places—such as Germany—it even constitutes the second largest independent schooling system after the church-sponsored system (Zander, 2008: 1). It began as Rudolf Steiner's enthusiastic response to a request to open a school in a Stuttgart Waldorf-Astoria cigarette factory run by a German industrialist by the name of Emil Malt, in which 256 students—primarily children of the factory workers—were enrolled in eight grades. Its educational ideology was a direct outcome of Steiner's philosophy, to which he gave the name Anthroposophy and regarded as a form of spiritual science. Being specifically devised to reflect its founder's unembarrassed spiritual predisposition, it integrated explicitly religious dimensions into theories of human development and pedagogy. One of the most prominent expressions of this direction was its emphasis upon artistic expression—drawing, singing, playing, and dancing—as ways of promoting spiritual growth.

Given its strong spiritual overtones, it comes as little surprise that Waldorf education remains a controversial type of schooling. The community of educators as a whole, in fact, appears to be largely ignorant of the method (Uhrmacher, 1995: 381–382; Zander, 2008: 1–8, 11–72; Woods, Ashley, and Woods, 2005: 1–10). This circumstance may reflect the fact that Steiner's radical educational ideas are considered highly problematic if not downright bizarre, its whiff of religious fundamentalism also possibly evoking pedagogical mistrust—undoubtedly fuelled by the racist and anti-Semitic overtones attributed to Steiner's philosophy (Staudenmaier, 2005).

The rapid growth and spread of the movement, especially within the context of today's "return of the religious," nonetheless call for a critical examination of its pedagogical aims, methods, and contents. This paper investigates an "understanding" (Pinar, Reynolds, Slattery, & Taubman, 1995) of the Waldorf curricular design—i.e., the structuring of its study program—from a philosophical and historical perspective in order to demonstrate the amalgam of spiritual and rational ideals in Steiner's pedagogy. I wish to argue that its optimistic entwining of spiritual notions with a belief in human reason and rationality reflects Steiner's commitment—rather than renunciation—of the ideals of the enlightenment. In this sense, his spiritual quest may be regarded as a late but influential agent of the "religious enlightenment" (Sorkin, 2008) which views a human rational understanding of the world as being not only compatible with but also conducive to the divine and spiritual world.

My launching point is Steiner's explicit desire to find a way to bridge the dichotomy between human beings and transcendent, divine, and "concealed" reality—a project exemplified in restoring the profound and the profane, the sacred and the secular, reason and faith to a harmonious relationship. I seek to contextualize this pedagogic pursuit within the *Kulturkrise* that engulfed central Europe in the late nineteenth and early twentieth century, suggesting that it forms a specific example of the post-Nietzschean, radical, antimodern *Lebensphilosophie* or "Life Philosophy" movement prevalent amongst German intellectuals and the cultural milieu of the time (Aschheim, 1992; Hotam, 2013).

In integrating theoretical and historical perspectives, I hope to offer a fresh insight into the Waldorf curriculum without seeking any ideological promotion of Steiner's spiritual approach, engaging in esotericism, or succumbing to mysticism (Faivre & Voss, 1995). My contextualization of Steiner's pedagogy diverges slightly from the common scholarly trend, which focuses upon Steiner's engagement with Goethe's romantic science of nature, Plato's philosophy, and early commitment to "Theosophy" (Zander, 2008: 907–909, 1395).

Such an investigation is particularly significant for the field of curriculum studies, which is currently experiencing a sharp increase in scholarly interest in the relationship between spirituality, religion, and education (Henderson & Slattery, 2005; Stambach, 2011; Wexler, 2013). It also resonates with contemporary challenges to the "great divide" between reason and religiosity

(Wexler, 2013) or science and spirit (Reynolds, 2007) so embedded in scholarly circles. In its unequivocal emphasis on the arts, the Waldorf curriculum may join contemporary calls for the arts to become the center of school life in order to counter the so-called "drill-and-kill" pedagogy and "teacher-proof" curricula (Rabkin, 2010; Stanley, 2009; Pinar, 2004). On this reading, we are invited to regard Waldorf education as forming part of the "historical memory" (Morris, 2009) of curriculum studies that is an integral part of the past controversies in the field.

In the first section, I shall discusses Steiner's Anthroposophy in the light of its quest to overcome dualism. In the second, I shall review the Waldorf curricular design as proposing a solution to the faith/reason dichotomy and examine its religious implications.

Anthroposophy as Life Philosophy

Anthroposophy as a spiritual science

Steiner's pedagogic worldview being articulated within the framework of what he termed Anthroposophy, my first task is clarifying this concept. There are two main points to note. First, Steiner himself defined Anthroposophy as a type of spiritual science (Zander, 2008: 163–169) that, viewing reality as a transcendent spiritual realm that lies beyond the world as we experience it through our senses, seeks to acquire a systematic knowledge of that reality (Steiner, 1952: 7). In more than 600 essays and lectures written and delivered between 1912 and 1925, Steiner repeatedly argued for the existence of a hidden spiritual reality beyond our sense data that can nonetheless be grasped by human powers. This belief reflects the influence of Plato's system of Ideas on Steiner: "Anthroposophy does not wish to be a matter of amateurish talk but a path of knowledge along which the higher, supersensible worlds are approached with the same scientific exactitude, the same methodical and disciplined thought with which natural science has for so long approached the laws of nature" (Steiner, 1947a: 4).

Second, Anthroposophy developed as a direct counter-theory to the occult spiritualism promoted by the Theosophic society. Founded in 1875 in New York by Helena Petrovna Blavatsky (1831–1891), Henry Steel Olcott (1832–1907), and others, the latter movement maintained that hidden divine forces exist in the world about which human beings can learn via a form of occult science—Theosophy. Being based on the common spiritual denominators within all religions, its founders hoped that it would promote a universal brotherhood of humanity (Prothero, 1993; Zander, 2008). Although Steiner joined the World Theosophic Society in 1901, becoming one of its most prominent European members, his well-documented break with its members led him to found the Anthroposophic Society in December 1912 (Ahlstorm, 1972; Moore, 1977; Braude, 1989; Zander, 2008). As the wide range of his publications—such as *Theosophie* (Steiner, 1962; originally published 1904), *On the Reality of Higher Worlds* (Steiner 1947a; originally published 1904), *An Outline of Occult Science* (Steiner, 1972; originally published 1910)— indicate, he had constantly—at times even compulsively—been engaged in refining his own independent spiritual approach.

One of the unique features of Steiner's views was his attraction to Christian symbolism (Steiner, 1962)—which led him, for example, to define education in terms of a quest for the restoration of "Pauline spiritualism" (Steiner, 1947b: 121). This proclivity separated him from other Theosophists, tending in general to espouse eastern rather than Christian traditions of religiosity and symbolism (Ellwood, 1979: 104–135; Jackson, 1981: 157–177; Prothero, 1993: 197–199; Zander, 2008: 91). At one point, his insistence on employing explicitly christological terminology impelled Anny Besant—the then charismatic leader of the Theosophic movement—to formally demand that he cease using the word "Christ" (Zander, 2008: 167).

In characterizing Anthroposophy as a type of "spiritual science," Steiner demonstrates his diverse, rather eclectic, philosophical background—which, as we have noted, evinces signs of Platonic, Theosophic, and Christian ideas. The term also reflects his embrace of the nineteenth-century central-European Romantic tradition and radical critique of rationality (Steiner, 1977). Under the influence of Goethe's "science of nature," for example, Steiner produced his own definition of the "etheric body" as a non-material entity that endows the body with "life" and teleological purpose as well as determining its shape and appearance.

While scholars such as Zander (2008), Uhrmacher (1995), and Staudenmaier (2005) have discussed Steiner's writings and viewpoint and their importance for our understanding of his philosophy—and pedagogy—in light of these sources, they have failed to contextualize them within the milieu of the late nineteenth and early twentieth centuries in central Europe. The significance of Steiner's work can only be fully grasped if we read it against this historical background—especially in relation to the *Kulturekrise* and the emergence of Life Philosophy.

The historical background

As a growing body of historical research indicates, the end of the nineteenth century and the first decades of the twentieth century were characterized by a feeling of *Kulturkrise* or "cultural crisis" (Ringer, 1969; Stern, 1965; Koselleck, 1988; Nipperdey, 1990; Eley, 1996; Hotam, 2013). At the core of this cultural and intellectual discomfort lay the sense that rationality could no longer be presupposed to form the sole basis for understanding the physical world and human social and political reality. In the wake of a growing disillusionment, alienation from the world, and genuine existential perplexity, many scholars and intellectuals experienced a sense of imminent doom. Such figures as Henri Bergson, Georg Simmel, and Oswald Spengler—*inter alia*—reacted, each in his own way, to the rapid growth of the modern, industrial, and technological mass culture by publishing accounts of alienation, distress, and a feeling of being lost.

Prominent amongst these was what came to be known as Life Philosophy (Hotam, 2013; Schmidt, 2000). There are three points to note regarding this type of thought. First, Life Philosophy was a dualist ontological speculation concerning reality that held to an alleged dichotomy between the false world which we sense around us and the real world that lies beyond it. In Life Philosophy, the rather vague term "life" (*Leben*) represents this reality *per se* (*Wahrheit an sich*), Being (*Sein*), and truth (*Wahrheit*) (Fellmann, 1993: 1–8; Hotam, 2013: 3–7). While we find our way in the world around us on the basis of our sense perception, the world we see and feel is a false representation, dissociated from what is real and true. The real/true world remains hidden and concealed from our consciousness.

Second, and in following this last point, Life Philosophy, also opposes the faculty of human rationality because reality should be amenable to intimate experience alone, not rational analysis. Herein, Life Philosophy constitutes a broad anti-rational or counter-rational worldview rather than a distinct philosophical school, responsible for influencing a wide range of intellectuals, thinkers, writers, artists, scientists, and even political and cultural events (Hotam, 2013). Its traces are evident in a wide-ranging gamut of thought— from Hugo Ball's notion of subjectivity, Lukacs' Marxism, Walter Benjamin's early writings, Wilhelm Dilthey's philosophy, Max Scheler's and Georg Simmel's sociology, and Heidegger's philosophy (Krell, 1992; Jay, 1973). The conflict between rational control and "authentic" passion was also expressed by such preeminent writers as Thomas Mann.

Third, many of the scholars attracted to Life Philosophy (Bergson, 1921; Dilthey, 1883; Simmel, 1918; Spengler, 1920; Klages, 1929/1931; Lessing, 1924) based their radical socio-cultural, educational, or political vision on the antithesis between true and monistic essence and false and deceptive rationality. Adopting Nietzsche's cultural critique, many espoused a radical, anti-rational— or, more accurately, counter-rational—social and political agenda (Aschheim, 1992: 10–15; Rabinbach, 1997: 45–50). Contending that alienation leads human beings to become more and more estranged from the essence of life, they stigmatized modernity and its belief in progress through science and technology as an era of oppression of life and decline that was threatening to plunge the world into an acute state of emergency (Ringer, 1969).

Anthroposophy and Life Philosophy

To some extent Anthroposophy is a type of Life Philosophy. Consider for example Anthroposophy's dualism between reality and the world which we perceive through our senses, which echoes the dichotomy Life Philosophy makes between the false/real world, reason/life, and the rational/natural. As Steiner himself noted (1959), because Anthroposophy maintains that true reality is the transcendent spiritual world that lies beyond the world we experience via our senses, it pits two types of reality against one another. Steiner also argues that human essence is transcendent and alienated from the world: "The human being stands on Earth and has in the back of his mind the feeling: I do not belong to this world" (1959: 16). In his idiosyncratic terminology (1947a: 24, 30), the "astral body" or the "divine spirit within us" represents the "eternal core of our being." The human task is to acquire "knowledge of the higher worlds," beginning with knowledge of our own human reality. Calling this "the path of veneration" or "imaginative thinking" (Steiner, 1947a; 1952), Steiner envisions this as a type of scientific exploration—quite different from mysticism, which he regarded as representing a dive "into the depths of the life of the soul" devoid of scientific "inwardly disciplined, systematic meditation" (1947a: 6–7). It also diverges, however, from the knowledge acquired via empirical science, which denies the existence of the spiritual transcendent world.

In correlation with this, Steiner clearly recognized the transcendent realm as a life force—a crucial point for understanding his spiritualism. The hidden natural force (*verborgene Natur*) being equivalent to the transcendent world that lies beyond our knowledge, it constitutes the force that endows the world with meaning (Steiner, 1912: 1–2). Steiner's stress that "life," the "life force" (*Lebenskraft*), or the "principles of life" (*Lebensprinzip*) that form the "hidden nature" of the world and human beings further confirms his affinity with Life Philosophy. It is thus important to understand that he employs the terminology of Life Philosophy that refers to vivid forces of nature in speaking of the "transcendent" spiritual realm of reality and truth. Ultimately, what transcends the false world are the hidden forces of life. Steiner thus integrates the concept of life with that of a transcendent divine force that lies beyond the world as we know it as much as it slumbers within the human soul.

It is of no surprise then that Steiner also adopted Life Philosophy's dichotomous terms in his critique of the "crisis" of the modern era. As he pointed out in a lecture in Dornach on June 30, 1923, the problem of modernity derived from its reliance on scientific rationalism. This confidence is accompanied according to Steiner by a rejection of a different kind of knowledge which aims at the hidden forces of life (Steiner, 1947b: 100–103). In endorsing this split, modern culture has "gradually lost true knowledge of the human being" (Steiner, 1996: 132), which is "rooted solely in the true knowledge of life" (*Lebenserkenntnis*) (Steiner, 1961b: 11). This type of knowledge encompassing all the emotional, cognitive, and practical aspects of human behavior, understanding human growth, social conduct, affectivity, or psychology must start with experiencing the hidden forces of life which lie beyond the grasp of the empirical sciences.

Anthroposophy thus champions emancipation from rationality and the rediscovery of life (Steiner, 1952: 1–17; Zander, 2008: 122; Ahem, 1985: 10–11), ultimately seeking—as we shall see below—the reconstruction of rationality and thus also its redemption. By using such vocabulary as the "astral body," the "etheric body," and the "world beyond the senses" (Steiner, 1947b: 94–95; 1959: 126–135), Steiner clearly sought to articulate some of the notions propounded by the Life Philosophers—many of which were pervaded by anti-Semitic overtones that also colored Steiner's cultural critique (Staudenmaier, 2005; Hotam, 2013). In its dichotomy between life and reason, cultural critique, and underscoring of life as a hidden natural and yet transcendent force, Steiner's Anthroposophy preeminently represents a form of Life Philosophy.

The Waldorf Curricular Design

In order to examine how the Waldorf curriculum realizes Steiner's spiritual quest of overcoming the antithesis between life and reason we must review two of the essential elements of Waldorf training as he articulated it. The first relates to his definition of schooling as a form of art, the second to the three-phase model of human physical and spiritual growth.

The role of art

According to Steiner, teaching "cannot be a science, it must be an art" (1996: 4). This statement reflects Steiner's belief that the task of this new form of schooling was to help "re-harmonize" the spiritual and the physical spheres within children (Steiner, 1947b: 30). Although both realms are intrinsically interconnected in children, traditional forms of education violently sever this primal connection by systematically separating subjects such as art and physical education from science. Regarding such rigorous curricular divisions as reflecting the dominant social paradigms of knowledge classifications and hierarchies, Steiner sought to develop a pedagogy that would break down the dichotomies between "nerves" (physical) and "blood" (spiritual), "antipathy" and "sympathy," the "awakened consciousness" and the "reality of dreams" by ensuring their pedagogic integration (Steiner, 1947b: 49).

Thus, for example, Eurythmy—an Anthroposophic dance art in which mental dispositions are expressed through movement—was introduced to all classes and ages as part of their daily activity in order to promote the harmonization of the "human organism." The primary curricular method of removing the dichotomous system, however, lay in celebrating artistic expression, leading pedagogical theory to directly underpin daily practice. The Waldorf curriculum was oriented towards a wide range of artistic expression—drawing, singing, playing, and dancing—all of which were thought to unite body and soul. Writing was taught, for example, "when allowing letters to develop from pictures" (Steiner, 1996: 137; 1961b: 26–27). Steiner viewing "art" as free artistic expression of true emotions and authentic feelings rather than the learning of a skill, technique, or craft, not only constituted the focus of the curriculum but, in a more profound sense, comprised a cross-curricular or interdisciplinary pattern of learning.

The three-phase model of human growth

As part of his understanding of education as art, Steiner argued that human physical and spiritual growth develops in three stages of seven years each. In the first (ages 1–7—or until the "growth of teeth" [*Zahnwechsel*]), children learn through "instruction in painting and drawing." This discovering of the "curriculum in each child" (Steiner, 1996: 37) begins with simple imitation (*Nachahmung*) of the teacher. This meant, however, a physical act or mechanical replication devoid of any examination, observation, imagination, and understanding. The children simply imitate the teacher, and in this respect he/she serves as a model (*Vorbild*) of behavior.

The second phase (ages 7–14—or from the "growth of teeth until puberty") focuses on "moral education" or socialization. The curriculum is designed to shape the behavioral, social, and ethical aspects of children's lives—good vs. bad behavior, just vs. unjust conduct, and reasonable vs. unreasonable social performance. Such schooling is also achieved primarily through the appeal "to the artistic aspect in children" (Steiner, 1996: 136). Imagination and fantasy forming the principal tools of education, Steiner explicitly asks teachers to devote the opening session of each day to storytelling. Each of the eight elementary classes goes through its own storytelling cycle during the year, Grade 1 pupils listening to fairy tales, Grade 2 to animal allegories such as Aesop's fables, Grade 3 to Bible stories, etc. (Finser, 1995; Petrash, 2002; Nicol, 2007). Significantly, this daily "fantasy" hour is also used to convey historical knowledge. As Nicholson (2000) demonstrates, during a lesson block in a Waldorf Grade 6 class he delivered historical content via oral storytelling, creative writing, drawing, music, and singing. Children thus grasp history not through a positivistic learning of facts but via their imagination. At this stage, the child's imitation and the teacher's modeling role are replaced by the child's emulation (*Nachfolge*) of the teacher's authority (*Autorität*) (Steiner, 1961a: 27). Thus while during the first phase of human growth "the teacher should be an example," "during the second period the teacher should be an authority in the noblest sense—a natural authority due to the qualities of character" (Steiner, 1961a: 27).

The third phase (ages 14–21) focuses on the perfection of consciousness and rationality. Only at this stage are young people educated via abstract concepts, philosophical knowledge, and ethical ideas, their minds now being sufficiently mature to comprehend on a rational level. The curriculum at this stage is thus oriented towards theoretical and conceptual knowledge in various fields of study—such as natural sciences, geography, and mathematics. This phase resembles the standard schooling of Steiner's own era, the authority of the teacher established in the second stage being maintained but now related to an empirical, practical, formal type of knowledge.

The definition of schooling as a form of art and the three-phase model of human growth constitute the two key elements of Waldorf training as articulated by Steiner. The underlying thread is the pursuit of harmony between the spiritual and physical spheres in the course of children's growth—achieved when technical, routine acts are replaced (supplemented) by the development of an ability to cogently analyze, understand, and evaluate complex abstract issues. This is the focus of every stage of (spiritual) growth, being attached to and evolving from the previous phase. Jejune acts of artistic creativity are thus succeeded by the empowerment of fantasy and imagination in children, followed by development of the faculty to understand complex themes rationally. The teacher starts off as a behavioral and learning model, progresses to representing spiritual authority, and eventually forms the anchor for all forms of knowledge. Steiner does not differentiate between the teacher as an authority of character and an authority of knowledge because these aspects are interrelated in his mind. Finally, as part of his/her practical pedagogical performance, the teacher speaks "as a messenger of the Spirit, a messenger of God, and knows something from the higher worlds" (Steiner, 1961a: 9–11), hereby acting as the ultimate authority of knowledge.

Overcoming dualism

The notion of harmony is central to the Waldorf educational method and directly reflects Steiner's quest to overcome the dualism that lies at the heart of Life Philosophy. This is evident in his depiction of the ideal process of physical and spiritual growth (Steiner, 1947b: 129). According to Steiner, the imitation—i.e., physical routine and mechanical replication—that is characteristic of the first stage of growth reflects the infant's so-called "original" union with the element of life, intertwining mental existence and biological rhythms. The simple physical routines, devoid of any contemplative aspect, serve as a way to immerse the youngster in natural life. The aim being to unite the child with his/her natural existence, reason and rationality play no role during this educational phase. Imitation thus represents the way in which life should remain unscathed by consciousness. On the basis of this harmony, spiritual understanding can gradually evolve during the second and third phases of growth. In line with Life Philosophical concepts, therefore, the acquiring of consciousness should be the outcome of vibrant (*lebendig*) forces. In other words, if consciousness is not gained through such a progression, the child will experience an inner rift between his/her authentic "life" forces and rational grasp of the world.

Although both Steiner and the Life Philosophers adduced this split as lying at the root of the crisis of modernity, Steiner sought to avert it by outlining a pedagogic plan that enabled the pure powers of life to progress into abstract concepts, theoretical knowledge, and rational articulation. This evolution commences with the simple imitation routines of the first educational phase and climaxes with the third educational phase, which promotes the development of the full awakening of reason and consciousness to enable the creation of a mature human (Steiner, 1947b: 163). This path of growth constitutes an uninterrupted evolution of the human being from the "soul" (*Seele*) to the "spirit" (*Geist*) (Steiner, 1947b: 129). In this context, it is important to note that the concepts of "following" and "authority" that belong to the second stage of growth differ from the "imitation" and "modeling" of the previous stage merely according to the level of consciousness they embody. Likewise, the point at which consciousness is slowly cultivated in children interlinks imagination, morality, authority, and divinity via edification, thus merging human nature and a godly existence (Steiner 1947b: 163–177).

Such a process of gaining consciousness is then significant because it actually endowed Steiner with the tools to overcome the alleged dichotomy between life and spirit, which he, as a life philosopher, endorsed. Bluntly put, it enables him to overcome dualism. Although a person becomes more spiritual, s/he nonetheless remains in constant touch with the hidden forces of life—or, more accurately, with the divinity embodied within the forces of life. The fact that this maturation process derives from the natural powers of the human soul rather than being taught externally ensures that rationality is now in harmony with the divine reality of life. Hereby, Steiner redeems rather than rejects reason and rationality, a person being capable of being simultaneously rational and conscious and in harmony with the spiritual world. Waldorf education is thus heavily informed by uniformity and homogeneity. The children experience a systematically designed edification, which limits diversity. The reason, however, lies in Steiner's main concern to eliminate the dualism between life and reason by suggesting a course of growth that ultimately underpins reason as a force of life. The split between the divine essence within human beings and human existence in the world is therefore transcended. In more abstract terms, the Waldorf curricular design can be explained as seeking to transform structure (dualism) into pedagogy (the cultivation of a person during his/her lifetime) or the metamorphosis of an aesthetical form into historical reality. Hereby, modernity can be saved from the crisis it poses to itself, a conclusion that no doubt characterized Steiner's socio-political worldview.

The mixture of sacred and secular aspects within Steiner's curricular design is explained by the fact that he seeks to link reason and faith and harmonize the human being with the cosmos. It does so by helping him/her "find [the] way from the divine world order into the earthly world order" (Steiner, 1947b: 163). The point to note is that the Enlightenment ideals of rational, modern, progressive human society are preserved by the fact that human reason is anchored in the divine order. Divinity—albeit defined via the terminology of Life Philosophy—guarantees a human rational understanding of the world. Both the three- phase model of human growth and the teacher's role are designed to enable the growth of the student from life to reason without cutting the delicate thread between the two entities.

Unsurprisingly, Marie Steiner (Steiner, 1947b: 7) described her father's educational goal as being "sacred religious" in seeking to cultivate the "spiritual godly" (*Göttlich-Geistige*) element within human beings. Cultivating the "spiritual godly" representing the roadmap to the "complete human being" (Steiner, 1961a: 122), the Waldorf curriculum sought the perfection of the "concealed mental and spiritual" essence of the human being (Steiner, 1947b: 14). More profoundly, however, the curriculum was carefully crafted in order to maintain the human being's spiritual unity with the hidden, benevolent (living forces of) divinity while also growing into a rational entity in the most enlightened sense.

How should we then understand this crafting of the curriculum? The answer is that Waldorf education may be seen as a unique example of the "religious enlightened" tradition (Sorkin, 2008; Gottlieb, 2011) that sought to create a synthesis between rationality and spirituality. The Enlightenment, accordingly, "was not only compatible with religious belief but conducive to it" (Sorkin, 2008, 3). Moreover, as Amos Funkenstein (1988) had argued, this is a type of secular-religious attitude that also characterized the inception of modern science in the sixteenth century, which began as a type of "secular theology" (1988: 12–22). Funkenstein's aim was to argue that the origins of science at the threshold of modernity (i.e., the sixteenth century) were based on the entwining of the belief in God with secular interest. Thus, for him, the early modern scientific approach of such central figures as Newton, Leibniz, and Descartes was "secular-theological of sorts," and that in such an approach God was not the enemy of rational understanding of the world but rather the guarantee of such understanding (Funkenstein 1988, 12–22). With this rich historical background in mind, we may then argue that the Waldorf curricular design does not represent occult religiosity in any simple sense as many scholars would argue. Such representation, prevalent, apparently, among adherents and critics of Waldorf alike, bowdlerizes Steiner's complex mission of harmonizing modern secular ideals with religious convictions. This mission resonated with a long history of such modern attempts and was a late, perhaps not last, endeavor to bring the two together.

Conclusion

In defining itself as a form of art and promoting a three-phase model of human growth Waldorf education seeks to transcend dualism. It focused on the re-emergence of the human being—a being who maintains mystical unity with the divine while retaining his rational faculties. This conclusion possesses broad pedagogic implications. It bears—for example—upon current discussions regarding the relationship between education, religion, and spirituality. A wide range of scholars of education oppose the traditional curricular dichotomies between science and spirituality (Reynolds, 2007), reason and faith (Johnson, 2005; Noddings, 2005; Miller 2007; Fischer, Hotam, and Wexler, 2012; Wexler, 2013), logic and imagination (Egan, 1987), learning and artistic expression (Rabkin, 2010).

From a theoretical perspective, Waldorf education presents an early example of how such education can be achieved—taking into consideration its inherent limits and potential dangers (authoritarianism, uniformity, elitism, racism). From an historical perspective, a study of Waldorf education helps us better understand the links between current pedagogic calls and time-honored modern traditions (Pinar et al., 1995). In its attempt to maintain "religiousness" not bound to a particular religious institution, Waldorf education may be regarded as a later example for "secular-religious" tradition of thought and practice—quite possibly explaining why it has continued to exist and spread within the modern Western secular educational arena. Its popularity may well, in fact, be due to the fact that it offers a spiritual confidence to humans who refuse to accept the absence of divinity in a godless universe.

References

Ahern, G. (1985). Gnosis and the Rudolf Steiner Movement (Anthroposophy). *Journal of Contemporary Religion, 2*(2), 10–21.

Ahlstorm, S. E. (1972). *A religious history of the American people.* New Haven, CT: Yale University Press.

Aschheim, S. E. (1992). *The Nietzsche legacy in Germany, 1890–1923.* Berkeley: University of California Press.

Bergson, H. (1921). *Schöpferische Entwicklung.* Jena: Diederich.

Braude, A. (1989). *Radical spirits: Spiritualism and women's rights in nineteenth-century America.* Boston, MA: Beacon Press.

Dilthey, W. (1883). *Einleitung in die Geisteswissenschaften.* Leipzig: B. G. Teubner.

Egan, K. (1997). *The educated mind: How cognitive tools shape our understanding.* Chicago, IL: University of Chicago Press.

Eley, G. (Ed.). (1996). *Society, culture, and the state in Germany, 1870–1930.* Ann Arbor: University of Michigan Press.

Ellwood, R. S. (1979). *Alternative altars: Unconventional and eastern spirituality in America.* Chicago, IL: University of Chicago Press.

Faivre, A., and Voss, K. C. (1995). Western esotericism and the science of religions. *Numen, 42*(1), 60–72.

Fellmann, F. (1993). Lebensphilosophie: Elemente einer Theorie der Selbsterfahrung. Hamburg: Rowohlt.

Finser, T. M. (1995). *School as a journey: The eight-year odyssey of a Waldorf teacher and his class.* Hudson: Anthroposophic Press.

Fischer, S., Hotam, Y., & Wexler, P. (2012). Democracy and education in postsecular society. *Review of Research in Education, 36,* 261–282.

Funkenstein, A. (1986). *Theology and the scientific imagination from the Middle Ages to the seventeenth century.* Princeton, NJ: Princeton University Press.

Gottlieb, M. (2011). *Faith and freedom: Moses Mendelssohn's theological-political thought.* Oxford, England: Oxford University Press.

Henderson J. G., & Slattery, P. (2005). Editors' introduction: Critical issues in curriculum and pedagogy. *Journal of Curriculum and Pedagogy, 2*(2), 1–7.

Hotam, Y. (2013). *Modern gnosis and Zionism: The crisis of culture, Life Philosophy and Jewish national thought*. London, England: Routledge.

Jackson, C. T. (1981). *The Oriental religions and American thought: Nineteenth-century explorations*. Westport, CT: Greenwood Press.

Jay, M. (1973). *The dialectical imagination. A history of the Frankfurt School and the Institute of Social Research 1923–1950*. London, England: Heinemann.

Johnson A. N. (2005). Diverse perspectives on spiritual curriculum and pedagogy. *Journal of Curriculum and Pedagogy, 2*(2), 30–34.

Kerr, S. (1983). *The culture of space and time, 1880–1918*. Cambridge, MA: Harvard University Press.

Klages, L. (1929/1931). *Der Geist als Widersacher der Seele*. Leipzig: J A Barth.

Koselleck, R. (1988). *Critique and crisis: Enlightenment and the pathogenesis of modern society*. Cambridge, MA: Harvard University Press.

Krell, D. F. (1992). *Daimon life: Heidegger and Life-Philosophy*. Bloomington: Indiana University Press.

Lessing, T. (1924). *Untergang der Erde am Geist (Europa und Asien)*. Hannover: W. A. Adam.

Miller, J. P. (Ed.) (2007). *The holistic curriculum*. (2ⁿᵈ ed.). Toronto: OISE Press.

Moore, R. L. (1977). *In search of white crows: Spiritualism, parapsychology and American culture*. New York: Oxford University Press.

Morris, M. (2009). Dare curriculum scholars cultivate historical memory? *Journal of Curriculum and Pedagogy, 6*: 1, 67–74.

Nicholson, D. W. (2000). Layers of experience: Forms of representation in a Waldorf school classroom. *Journal of Curriculum Studies, 32*(4), http://www.informaworld.com/smpp/title~db=all~content=t713741620~tab=issueslist~branches=32 - v32 575–587.

Nicol, J. (2007). *Bringing the Steiner Waldorf approach to your early practice*. London, England: Routledge.

Nipperdey, T. (1990). *Deutsche Geschichte 1866–1918*. München: Beck.

Noddings, N. (2005). Can spiritual/theological discourse guide curriculum and pedagogy? *Journal of Curriculum and Pedagogy, 2*(2), 21–23.

Petrash, J. (2002). *Understanding Waldorf education: Teaching from the inside out*. Lewisville, NC: Gryphon House.

Pinar, W. F. (2004). *What is curriculum theory?* Mahwah, NJ: Lawrence Erlbaum.

Pinar, W., Reynolds, W., Slattery, P., & Taubman, P. (1995). *Understanding curriculum: An introduction to the study of historical and contemporary curriculum discourses*. New York: Peter Lang.

Prothero, S. (1993). From spiritualism to Theosophy: 'Uplifting' a democratic tradition. *Religion and American Culture, 3*(2), 197–199.

Rabinbach, A. (1997). *In the shadow of catastrophe*. Berkeley: University of California Press.

Rabkin, N. (2010): Artists, art teachers, schools, and art: Can they live together? *Journal of Curriculum and Pedagogy, 7*: 1, 43–4.

Reynolds, S. (2007). A Goethean approach to science education. *Journal of Curriculum and Pedagogy, 4*: 1, 160–171.

Ringer, F. (1969). *The decline of the German Mandarins: The German academic community 1890–1933.* Cambridge, MA: Harvard University Press, 1969.

Schmidt, C. (2000). *Der häretische Imperativ: Überlegungen zur theologischen Dialektik der Kulturwissenschaft in Deutschland.* Tübingen: Niemeyer, 2000.

Simmel, G. (1918). *Lebensanschauung: Vier metaphysische Kapitel.* Berlin: Duncker & Humblot.

Sorkin, D. (2008). *The religious enlightenment: Protestants, Jews and Catholics from London to Vienna.* Princeton, NJ: Princeton University Press.

Spengler, O. (1920). *Der Untergang des Abendlandes: Umrisse einer Morphologie der Weltgeschichte.* München: Kindler.

Stambach, A. (2011). Religion and education in secular institutions: A moderated discussion. *Comparative Education Review, 55*(1), 111–142.

Stanley, W. B. (2009). Curriculum theory and education for democracy. *Journal of Curriculum and Pedagogy, 6*(1), 44–56.

Staudenmaier, P. (2005). Rudolf Steiner and the Jewish question. *Leo Baeck Institute Year Book, 50,* 127–147.

Steiner, R. (1912) *Ein Weg zur Selbsterkenntnis des Menschen, in acht Meditationen.* Berlin: Philosophisch-Theosophischer Verlag.

Steiner, R. (1947a). *On the reality of higher worlds.* London: Anthroposophical Publishing.

Steiner, R. (1947b). *Allgemeine Menschenkunde.* Freiburg: Novalis.

Steiner, R. (1952). *Anthroposophie: Ihre Erkenntniswurzeln und Lebensfrüchte.* Dornach: Rudolf Steiner Nachlassverwaltung.

Steiner, R. (1959). *Anthroposophie Eine Enifuehrung in die Anthroposophische Weltanschauung.* Dornach: Verlag der Rudolf Steiner-Nachlassverwaltung.

Steiner, R. (1961a). *Die Erziehung des Kindes/Die Methodik des Lehrens.* Stuttgart: Verlag Freies Geistesleben.

Steiner, R. (1961b). *Methodische Grundlagen der Anthroposophie Gesammelte Aufsaetze 1884–1901.* Dornach: Verlag der Rudolf Steiner-Nachlassverwaltung.

Steiner, R. (1962). *Theosophie: Eniführung in übersinnliche Welterkenntnis und Menschenbestimmung.* Stuttgart: Verlag Freies Geistesleben.

Steiner, R. (1972). *An outline of occult science.* Dornach: Anthroposophic Press.

Steiner, R. (1977). *An autobiography.* New York: Rudolf Steiner Publications.

Steiner, R. (1996). *Waldorf Education and Anthroposophy.* Hudson, NY: Anthroposophic Press.

Stern, F. (1965). *The politics of cultural despair. A study in the rise of the Germanic ideology.* New York: Knopf.

Uhrmacher, B. (1995). Uncommon schooling: A historical look at Rudolf Steiner, Anthroposophy and Waldorf education. *Curriculum Inquiry, 25*(4), 381–406.

Wexler, P. (2013). *Mystical sociology: Toward cosmic social theory.* London, England: Peter Lang.

Woods, P., Ashley, M., & Woods, G. (2005). *Steiner Schools in England.* Bristol: University of West England.

Zander, H. (2008). *Anthroposophie in Deutschland.* Göttingen: Vandenhoeck & Ruprecht.

6. *The Post-Secular Rhetoric of Contemplative Practice in the Public Curriculum*

Oren Ergas

In the past decade a surge of interest in the incorporation of diverse contemplative practices in the curriculum is becoming apparent in primary, secondary, and higher education (Barbezat & Bush, 2014; MLERN, 2012; Todd & Ergas, 2015). This growing movement is supported by various institutions (e.g., Mind and Life, Garrison Institute, Contemplative Mind in Society, the Collaboration of Academic and Social Emotional Learning), a host of networks (e.g., Mindfulness in Education, Mindfulness and Contemplative Education) and is manifest in diverse curricular interventions (e.g., MINDUP, CARE, '.b' curriculum). Yet, the presence of such practices in a contemporary curriculum strongly shaped by economic-rational-secular agendas pointing towards performativity, accountability, and standardization is hardly obvious. Contemplative practices stem from wisdom-traditions that seem to be offering a counter-movement to such narrative by introducing some measure of non-productive-affective-spiritual flavor into the curriculum.

This chapter offers an analysis of a spectrum of rhetoric that undergirds the advocacy and justification of contemplative practices in the curriculum. Its poles are defined by wisdom-traditions on the one hand, offering a non-instrumental educational narrative, and an instrumental scientific educational narrative on the other. The chapter interprets this spectrum as a locus for understanding a "post-secular" society that is reflected in a continuous blurring of dualistic categories (e.g., science/religion, spirituality/secularity, body/mind, self/society). Contemplative practices incorporated in education are interpreted here as bearing the potential of healing these traditional rivalries and hierarchies. Yet, these healing processes bring about novel complexities and tensions described in this chapter.

The chapter begins by offering a theoretical review of the contemporary interest in contemplation in the curriculum. It then analyzes the challenges that such practices pose in the face of the hegemonic economic-rational-secular narrative reflected in the contemporary public curriculum characteristic in many Western industrialized countries. I propose two rhetorical strands that have developed to justify contemplative practices based on wisdom-traditions on the one hand and evidence-based science on the other. The second part of the chapter demonstrates these two strands by interpreting the rhetoric applied within two examples representative of each. The third part concludes by conceptualizing the spectrum marked by these two strands to locate them within an era that may be appropriately termed "post-secular" (Hotam & Wexler, 2014; Taylor, 2006)

Part I: Contemplative Practices as a Challenge to the Contemporary Curriculum Narrative

In the past decade we have witnessed an increasing interest in contemplative practice in the public domain (Heelas & Woodhead, 2005) and across the curriculum within primary, secondary, and tertiary education (Ergas, 2014). Contemplative practices have been defined broadly as: "the many ways human beings have found, across cultures and across time, to concentrate, broaden and deepen conscious awareness" (Roth, 2008, p. 19). Examples include diverse forms of meditation (e.g., mindfulness practice, compassion meditation), body-based contemplative practice (e.g., postural yoga, tai chi, walking/standing meditation), ecological practices (e.g., nature walk), reflective practices, journaling, and many others (Hart, 2004; Lin, Oxford & Brantmeier, 2013). The growing incorporation of contemplative-based curricular interventions is funded and supported by various institutions including Mind and Life, Garrison Institute, Contemplative Mind in Society, the Collaboration of Academic and Social Emotional Learning, and a host of networks. The Garrison Institutes' contemplative education program database,[1] lists dozens of programs that are currently implemented across North America, some of them, such as MINDUP (developed by the Hawn Foundation) and the '.b curriculum' (developed in GB by Richard Burnett and Chris Cullen) are implemented in hundreds of schools in many Western industrialized countries.

Yet, such novel curricular orientation is not obvious. Against the backdrop of an era in which accountability, productivity, standardization, and high-stakes testing seem to capture much of the educational discourse, yogic postures and breathing techniques seem slightly off the mark. Contemplative practices in schools may be introducing a shift in educational practice and concomitantly in its understanding as a whole. Neil Postman (1995) viewed education as inevitably committed to a narrative. Such narrative "tells of origins and envisions a future…constructs ideals, prescribes rules of conduct, provides a source of authority, and above all, gives a sense of continuity and purpose …"; a great narrative is "one that has sufficient credibility, complexity, and symbolic power to enable one to organize one's life around it" (pp. 5–6). Hanan Alexander (2001) similarly proposed that education requires some "vision of the good" around which individuals and societies can organize life within a framework of meaning. While much of school life amounts to the "daily grind" (Jackson, 1968) comprised of all those seemingly benign practices in which teacher and students engage in a specific classroom, all these must somehow be tied to a bigger picture that makes-sense—that has broader *meaning*. Part of the educational process we undergo entails an initiation of a student into what Peters (1966) referred to as "educationally worthwhile activities." An educational narrative thus does not only concern the vision that constitutes the social ethos of education. Rather, as we are initiated into what society deems as meaningful knowledge based on school subject matter, we are concomitantly initiated into the understanding of what pedagogies make sense as teaching such subject matter. Following this logic (or education, if you will), the sight of students reading, writing, or working out a mathematical problem very naturally connotes with "education." However, the sight of students being instructed to perform a yogic posture, count their breaths, close their eyes and extend compassion to a friend in need, or other practices currently introduced to schools, seems like "something else."

The vagueness of the term "something else" is the crux of the matter, for contemplative practices can be interpreted, applied, used, abused, introduced and implemented in diverse ways. For example, mindfulness practice in its diverse forms, currently the most popular contemplative practice incorporated in the curriculum, is rendered as cultivating resilience (Greenberg & Harris, 2012), enhancing executive functions (Flook, Smalley, Kitil, et al., 2010), treating ADHD (Carboni, Roach & Fredrick, 2013), contributing to social-emotional learning (Davidson et al., 2012), fostering self-knowledge (Lin, Oxford & Brantmeier, 2013), and treating teacher burnout (Jennings, Snowberg, Coccia & Greenberg, 2011). At the same time let us not forget the origins of mindfulness: *an ancient Buddhist text*, namely the *Satipatthana Sutta*, in which the Buddha prescribes the practice of *Sati* (trans. as "mindfulness") to his monks. This practice is proposed as the way to overcome *dukkha* (dis-ease, suffering). *Dukkha*, the First of the Four Noble Truths, is the constant feeling of lack that thrusts us mortals to constantly shift between grasping at what we have, wanting what we do not have, or wishing we would not have what we do have (Loy, 1996). Mindfulness is prescribed by the Buddha as no other than the path to *Nirvana*—a realization of the true nature of the insubstantiality of "self," the ephemeral nature of all existence, the pointlessness of grasping, and thus the freedom from all sorrow; for sorrow can emerge solely from grasping at that which is not yet or could have been other than what it actually is.

We can thus see quite a remarkable spectrum of educational, spiritual, psychological, health-related possibilities connoting with "mindfulness," as a representative case of contemplative practices. The association of contemplative practices with the concept and practice of education thus becomes a locus of controversy based on the diverse rhetoric that surrounds it. As the Mind and Life Education Research Network, comprised of leading scholars of contemplation, indeed acknowledge: "Contemplative practices such as meditation and yoga are structured and *socially scaffolded activities* ..." (MLERN, 2012, p. 147, emphasis mine). The "otherness" that contemplative practices bring to the social discourse of education thus needs to be probed more deeply in order for us to make sense of what exactly it is that contemplative practices are "doing" to the curriculum, and, no less, what the curriculum might be "doing" to *them* in the processes involved in their "pitching" to policy makers, principals, and teachers towards their acceptance as legitimate pedagogies alongside math, history, chemistry, etc.

In the following I offer a coarse framework against which to examine the dilemmas that the entrance of contemplative practices into the public curriculum brings. I frame these as challenges to a current predominant educational narrative that I here present based on three "coarse" categories; the word "coarse" indicating that much more analysis is required to further our understanding of this domain. Each of these challenges needs to be addressed somehow by advocates of contemplative practices if they wish to indeed introduce such practices into the curriculum. Failing to do so would mean ignoring foundational premises that guide the current theory and practice of education, resulting in contemplative practices' conception as too alien to be considered within contemporary educational practice. The presentation of all three challenges leads to a general claim that I sum up at the end: the advocacy of contemplative practices in the curriculum has three options: 1) present them as complying with and even enhancing the current educational narrative; 2) present them as proposing an alternative to the current educational narrative; 3) find a middle path of complying with the contemporary narrative yet concomitantly forging a trajectory of educational renewal and improvement.

The first of these three intertwined challenges concerns *contemporary public education's economic-narrative* that is reflected in the fact that "Powerful supranational organizations, such as the OECD and the World Bank, … view education primarily as a tool for improving economic performance" (Gilead, 2012, p. 113). Many countries have been initiating educational reforms that establish a clear link between individual and national economic progress. This trend can be tied directly to the conceptions of standardization, high-stakes testing, efficacy, and grading, as principles that hover above the daily activities performed in school (Apple, 2004). In an instrumentally and narrowly-conceived economic narrative the study of a certain discipline will be "valued only if it enables one to directly or indirectly turn it into profit" (Gilead, 2012, p. 117). There is clearly a long list of critics of this narrative as reifying (Robeyns, 2004), as exacerbating consumerism (Postman, 1995) and other, yet its grip on curriculum thinking is quite steady as manifest in policies such as NCLB. Within a curriculum conceptualized from this perspective, the sight of students closing their eyes and "doing nothing" or engaged idly in "some yogic posture" when there seems to be so much to do and learn would strike the outsider as requiring some serious explanation. Common sense would propose that if we want productive students we would need pedagogies that yield "products" that are relevant to the job market. These products need not be directly material, yet they would be conceived as lending themselves to future production. At least judged by their outer appearance many contemplative practices fail to comply with such conception. Following the three options listed above, advocates of contemplative practices in the curriculum facing the economic challenge framed within productivity seem to have these three options: a) play the game, and show how contemplative practices can actually contribute to productivity; b) challenge the economical narrative and suggest that education is not about economic productivity; c) find a rhetoric that walks between these two poles.

The second challenge concerns *the reason-based narrative* that takes us to the foundations of Western culture within the co-ordinates of Plato, Descartes, Kant and others as establishing the hegemony of reason, with the latter two edifying modern science (Eisner, 1996). Educational practice has been grounded in this ethos in a most substantial way. As Wexler (2008) writes, "In educational practice cognitivism continues the seventeenth-century cultural regime of decontextualizing knowledge and separating epistemology from ontology and cosmology" (p. 193). We see this as we trace early 20th-century conceptions of the curriculum that intentionally attempted to emulate the scientific model (Bobbitt, 1918), and we witness this contemporarily reflected in calls for treating education as a science (MLERN, 2012). Much curricular theory and practice is dedicated to improving "how we think" mostly in rational ways as expressed in the writings of Dewey and many of his followers (Ergas, 2013). The model of the "educated person" following upon this conception of schooling is one of a Cartesian "thinking thing," far more than as a "feeling," "emoting" and spontaneous being. Many critics have been pointing to this as a delimiting and deadening narrative (Eisner, 1996; Kincheloe & Steinberg, 1993). Much of this critique revolves around a difficulty that is accentuated when attempting to introduce contemplative practices into the curriculum. An understanding of the curriculum as a locus of reason is based on a dualistic conception in which emotions, feelings, and the body as a whole are either irrelevant or in fact get in the way of proper education. Recent neuroscientific evidence of a clear link between cognition and affect (Damasio, 1994; Davidson, 2012), and growing interest in social-emotional-learning (SEL) (Durlak, Weissberg, Dymnicki, et al., 2011) reveal the buds of a paradigm shift. Still, many of us are very much schooled in the conception that allocating most (if not all) curricular time to reason-based activities makes the most sense. In the face of such deep-seated conception it is hard to understand how practices such as observing one's breath or sitting still and scanning bodily sensations can find a respectable place in the curriculum alongside working out mathematical problems, conducting an experiment in the chemistry lab, or even studying Hamlet. Contemplative practices may simply feel too "weird" to be considered as activities that belong in a place in which thinking beings are educated to think rationally. They hold the lure of East-Asian "enlightenment," mysticism, and religion which I soon develop as a third challenge. Within the context of a reason-based curriculum these notions seem out of place, for their very essence points to that which is beyond reason. Advocates of contemplative practice in the curriculum are thus compelled to offer an appropriate response that may take the following forms: 1) suggest that contemplative practices can contribute to rational thinking; 2) propose that the reason-based narrative is too limited, and the curriculum must be extended to treat the "whole person" including emotional, spiritual, aesthetic and other aspects of his being; 3) find the middle ground—cater to rational thinking while pointing beyond it.

The third challenge concerns *the secular narrative*—Contemplative practices have stemmed from Western philosophical schools of thought, monotheistic religions, East-Asian wisdom traditions (Roth, 2008), and from more contemporary worldviews such as Rudolph Steiner's Anthroposophy (explored by Yotam Hotam in the previous chapter). They thus come with a "baggage," and that "baggage" is in many cases interpreted as associated with spirituality, religion, and mysticism. In fact, sociologists identify the contemporary interest in such practices as signifying a turn to a "mystical society"

(Wexler, 2000) or "a spiritual revolution" (Heelas & Woodhead, 2005). Currently, many of the practices advocated across school ages and higher education are rooted mostly (but not only) in different schools of Buddhism (Hyland, 2014; Simmer-Brown, 2009; Todd & Ergas, 2015). These include diverse ways of practicing mindfulness, compassion meditation (Grace, 2011), and loving-kindness meditation (Hinsdale, 2012). While the relation of Buddhism with Western conceptions of "religion" is contested by scholars (Hyland, 2014), the incorporation of contemplative practices in school is constantly accompanied by concerns as to the danger of proselytizing and an ethos of "secularity" as an interpretation (or misinterpretation) of the First Amendment. Scholars have been careful to emphasize that the First Amendment is by no means a call for secularization but rather an advocacy of freedom and a warning against proselytizing (Speck, 2005). However, proselytizing is exactly what many fear as exemplified in cases such as parents recently filing a lawsuit against California's Encinitas County because it incorporated yoga lessons as part of its schools day.[2] The secular narrative poses a serious rhetorical and pedagogical dilemma that seems to offer the following alternatives for those wishing to incorporate contemplative practices in the curriculum: 1) "secularize" contemplative practices to comply with the current narrative; 2) resacralize education as an alternative narrative; 3) walk the thin line "in-between."

To sum the three challenges described, if allowed a metaphorical explanation, we may think of the situation as follows: the current economical-rational-secular educational narrative guiding the social ethos of education can be considered as a framework that determines the legitimacy of practices that make their way into the *box* of the curriculum. Contemplative practices seem to propose an *out-of-the-box-ness*. Applying Kuhn's sociology of science (1962) to education, if the curricular *box* is a paradigm, contemplative practices seem to offer a paradigm shift. In Postman's (1995) terms—they offer a different narrative; one that conflates with different aspects of our current hegemonic educational narrative.

In the next part of this chapter I suggest that a rhetorical spectrum has been developing to address the dilemma of either squeezing contemplative practices so that they fit the box, or reconceptualizing the box to accommodate for contemplative practices. This rhetorical spectrum emerges from two "camps" that have hardly been bedfellows in the past centuries: science and religion. Within this rhetorical spectrum the scientific evidence-based approach speaks from within the box. It justifies contemplative practices based on conceptualizing the intentions behind their incorporation in the curriculum through a rhetoric that caters to the ear of contemporary policy-makers. The "religious" or "pure" approach, however, re-conceptualizes the educational box as it emerges based on the foundations of wisdom-traditions. The following part will exemplify this claim by interpreting the rhetoric applied by representative scholars of both sides of the spectrum. I will begin by exploring the rhetoric that relies on contemplative practice's origins and then elaborate the rhetoric emerging from the contemporary scientific evidence-based approach. Later on I will reveal this spectrum as the makings of a "post-secular" age as it is reflected in and reflects on contemporary education.

Part II: A Rhetorical Spectrum Between Wisdom Traditions and Science

Reconceptualizing the curricular box through wisdom-traditions

Whether we turn to Taoism and Buddhism, to the monotheistic religion, to Native American wisdom-traditions, or even to Greek philosophy, these wisdom-traditions entail theories (whether oral or written) alongside practices many of which comply with Roth's (2008) earlier-mentioned definition of contemplation. It is to these roots that some educational theorists and practitioners turn to reconceptualize education as exemplified in Robert Hattam's (2004) conception of Buddhism as a source for critical theory and pedagogy, in Eppert and Wang's (2008) edited anthologies of East/West cross-cultural curricular studies, in Roth's (2008) and Todd and Ergas's (2015) conceptualization of the contemplative initiative at Brown University, etc. By elucidating foundational concepts within wisdom-traditions these scholars have been offering a critique and rethinking of our current educational narrative to forge a deductive justification for the inclusion of contemplative practices in the curriculum. These accounts propose alternative principles, terms, and virtues over which our curriculum ought to be established. In the following I focus on two examples, Bai, Scott, and Donald (2009) and Miller (2000), to demonstrate the rhetoric of this strand.

Bai, Scott, and Donald (2009) propose an educational theory that is based on Taoism, Buddhism, and Raja yoga. The educated person they seek is one that is grounded in, "*the way* that cannot be discursively codified; in generosity of heart and spirit that manifest as boundless love and compassion (characteristics of the *bodhichitta*, enlightened heartmind)..." (p. 323). They view the goal of education as targeting three levels of bifurcation that emerge as a foundational teaching of contemporary curriculum: the somatic (body/mind), the perceptual ("self"/"world"), and the intersubjective ("self"/"other"). Healing these splits is an education in "being interbeing" that points to the integration of body-mind-soul, "self"-world, and "self"-other. In order to foster such being-knowing they propose a contemplative pedagogical orientation referred to as "indwelling" that entails "the capacity for knowing through silence, looking inward, pondering deeply, beholding, witnessing the contents of our consciousness, and so on" (p. 327).

John Miller's (2000) *Education and the Soul* is an invitation to the concept and practice of soul in the classroom. It is proposed as a remedy to the economic educational narrative that tells us constantly "that the purpose of schooling is to prepare our children to compete in a global economy" (p. 2). The second chapter of the book explores the concept of soul based on diverse examples from East Asian, monotheistic religions, and Greek philosophy as well as contemporary views of the soul. Miller defines soul as "A vital, mysterious energy that can give meaning and purpose to our lives" (p. 5). An educational appeal to this non-linear locus becomes a pedagogical task that requires means that transcend and overcome an objectifying, rationalistic, and instrumental narrative that contemporary educational practices bring forth. The pedagogical turn suggested, then, is again a contemplative one:

> Contemplation, which is the soul's main form of learning and knowing, is hardly ever encouraged in education. Instead we are taught to find the right answer or develop the right argument. By ignoring or denying contemplation the soul is also denied. The soul hides while our minds analyze, memorize, and categorize. (p. 39)

Bai, et al. (2009) and Miller (2000) propose an educational narrative that reconceptualizes the curricular *box*. Their rationale can be located within a twofold typology offered by Wexler (2008) that suggests a distinction between "informationalism" and "in-formationalism." The former would be associated with the current economic-rational-secular narrative that associates education with a subjugation of "self" to a world residing *out there*. Knowing the economic social order and conception of this world and performing within it constitutes a primary concern within such a model. The latter, "in-formation," however, shifts the axis to target the knowing and forming of "self," or perhaps, in light of East Asian traditions, transcending a misperceived false "self" grounded in a day-to-day ego-based consciousness. We find this typology in Bai, et al. (2009) as they state, "the kind of education focused on knowledge/information and technical skill acquisition, as in K-12 and post-secondary schooling, shapes and entrenches an alienated or objectified consciousness" (p. 324). Conversely they seek to encourage students to inhabit deeply and continuously their body, sense, feeling, and thought. We thus see here a substantial shift of the axis of education from a content-based curriculum to a model that is concerned with "the shape of the container" (p. 327).

Similarly we find in Miller's (2000) appeal to wisdom-traditions a counter-reaction to the misconception of many educators of learning as "adding or accumulating knowledge" (p. 3). The alternative Miller proposes is "timeless learning" that he characterizes as connected to emotions, body, and soul. Miller develops the concept of "Timeless learning" as transgressing the linearity we associate with the accumulation of "information." It is summoned through contemplative ways that can be solitary-based or socially-based as well as in Csikszentmihalyi's famous concept of "flow." Both Miller's and Bai, Scott, and Donald's conception of education thus entails invoking certain states of consciousness that connote with Wexler's "in-formation" rather than with "informing" students of a world conceived as residing apart from them. This concept of "timeless learning" resonates well with the way Wexler (2008) frames in-formational education as concerned with topics such as, "consciousness, embodiment, emotions, and transcendence as altered states, the senses, energy, and complex transformations across lived worlds of *timeless time* that reframe consciousness and experienced embodiment." (p. 193, emphasis mine)

The examples brought above reveal one strand of justifying contemplative practices in the curriculum through a reconsideration of what education in fact *is*. These scholars suggest that education can be founded on a different set of suppositions that they derive from diverse wisdom-traditions. Once these are established, the contemplative practices proposed by these wisdom-traditions emanate naturally from this theoretical grounding to curricular practice. The narrative emerging from such work is one that substantially questions the validity of the economic-rational-secular triad. It rejects education as an economic instrument, challenges the hegemony of the rational by appealing to the non-rational and soulful domains, and perhaps targets an over-secularized approach by seeking anchor in wisdom-traditions that set forth "soul" and "being interbeing" at their core.

The rhetoric found in this strand that certainly has other representatives (Eppert & Wang, 2008; Hattam, 2004; Palmer, 1983) can be conceived in Weberian terms as one of re-enchantment. The sources for re-enchanting education are found by these scholars in reconvening the wisdom-traditions from which we have gradually departed according to the Weberian "disenchantment" narrative into contemporary educational discourse. Yet, a critical question lurks behind this rhetoric; Would policy-makers, school principals, and educators heed this rhetoric if their own conception of "good" education has long been shaped by the economic-rational-secular narrative in which they themselves have been initiated? They are themselves judged by the economical practices of assessment (e.g. accountability, tests, poles, GNP, etc.) typical in a social setting that reproduces such narrative. Those favoring an economic-rational-secular narrative, even in a mild version, might find concepts such as "being interbeing" and "timeless learning" as detached from the "reality of life." Even if some might be lured by them, the idea of advocating them seriously might seem too risky in terms of their own career-future.

Changing the curriculum box from within through an evidence-based approach

A different rhetoric emerges from evidence-based research that proves contemplative practices' contribution to human traits that can be rendered as supportive of the current educational narrative while perhaps even pushing its envelope. There is still a significant change involved in introducing contemplative practices in the curriculum, even when they are appropriated to serve an economic-rational-secular narrative. Yet, the rhetoric involved here, quite interestingly, attempts to sneak these practices in by rendering their application as "common-sense." Kabat-Zinn (2011) expresses the ethos behind this path in describing his own journey of establishing mindfulness practice as a therapeutic intervention. He sought "to present it as commonsensical, evidence-based, and ordinary, and ultimately a legitimate element of mainstream medical care" (p. 282).

In cases representative of this strategy the origins of contemplative practices (e.g., Buddhism, Taoism) may be hidden, marginalized, or stated directly, but they will not serve as justification for inclusion of contemplative practices in the curriculum. The strategy of justifying the incorporation of contemplative practices into the curriculum is treated here as no different than the one that guides the introduction of, say, new pedagogies for teaching algebra, history, or any other school discipline. Hard evidence is garnered in order to cater to the ear of those policy makers and education practitioners that are swayed by science and numbers far more than by the lure of wisdom-traditions. As Zins, Bloodworth, Weissberg, and Walberg et al. (2007) attest, in an atmosphere imbued by accountability and standards-based education school principals are reluctant to incorporate novel curricular interventions unless empirical evidence of their efficacy is provided. This orientation implies that the educational narrative offered at this end of the spectrum will be confined to what science has so far uncovered (or is in the process of uncovering) in regards to contemplative practices' association with standard educational goals commensurable with the current educational narrative. The rhetoric thus required in order to sway policy makers to include such interventions in the curriculum will associate contemplative practices with quicker understanding of subject matter or acquisition of skills, storing information for longer periods of time, sharper thinking, enhanced problem-solving skills, higher academic achievements, and perhaps even higher rates of immersion in the job-market. The change introduced here will have less to do with challenging the goals of education, *per se*, and more to do with *which* educational practices make for "effective pedagogies" within a current understanding of "education." Examples of this rhetoric can be found in an exponentially growing body of research studying the effects of meditation, mindfulness, tai chi, for example, on diverse aspects of education. Following the structure of the previous section I analyze two recent examples: MLERN (2012) and Greenberg and Harris (2012). Both offer state-of-the-art reviews of scientific research on contemplation and education involving some of the leading scholars in the field.

MLERN (2012) offer an account of scientific evidence of contemplative practice's contribution to a host of psychological functions including stress-reduction, executive functions, attention, emotional regulation, and more. The sources of contemplative practices are mentioned yet quickly abandoned in favor of the rhetoric of science:

> By contemplative practices, we refer to a wide variety of strategies and methods originally *rooted in contemplative traditions such as Buddhism. In modern scientific terms*, these practices are forms of mental and behavioral training that are intended to produce alterations in basic cognitive and emotional processes, such as attention and the regulation of certain forms of negative affect, and to enhance particular character traits that are considered virtuous, such as honesty and kindness". (p. 147, emphasis mine)

The mentioning of "Buddhism" is quite interesting, given that the first sentence might have worked just fine with a more neutral term such as "wisdom-traditions." My interpretation suggests that there is an agenda at stake here that some might miss if not aware of the biographies of some of the authors of this paper. Neuroscientist Richard Davidson, himself a long-time meditator as disclosed in his recent book (2012), serves on the board of directors of the Mind and Life institute (MLI). MLI was initiated by the Dalai Lama, Adam Engler, and the late cognitive scientist Francisco Varela for the purpose of exploring the intersection of science and Buddhist contemplative practices. As Davidson attests he has made a promise to the Dalai Lama to conduct research that will explore the effects of meditation on the brain, and this has been a focal aspect of his career for almost two decades. Thus, there is no coincidence in the specific mentioning of "Buddhism" in the first sentence.

However, Davidson is a rigorous scientist speaking the language of a neuro-scientific community that might not have much tolerance for Buddhist lure. He quickly shifts to "scientific terms" following a clear reasoning that guides the Mind and Life institute in pragmatically choosing science as the most effective vehicle towards educating society as to the potential contribution of contemplation to human flourishing.[3] The goal of contemplative practices as rendered in this paper is thus concerned with handling cognitive-affective processes and the cultivation of virtues. These educational goals are arranged in their paper around three domains that corroborate the effect of contemplation on neural substrates, psychological functions, and behavioral outcomes. This methodological structure is nested within an educational narrative that can be found in the opening lines of the paper:

> Current global conditions, including increasing economic interdependence, widespread intercultural contact, and the emergence of knowledge-based societies, require new forms of education…schools play a major role in cultivating the kinds of mental skills and socioemotional dispositions that young people will need to realize productive, satisfying, and meaningful lives in the 21st century. (p. 146)

In this sentence we find three terms that clearly represent the economic-rational narrative: economy, knowledge-based societies, and production (and perhaps even satisfaction, if economy is associated with the satisfaction of needs as some economic views might suggest). At the same time, two decades ago the term "socioemotional dispositions" that follows the first sentence would perhaps not appear in conjunction with the latter economic-rational terms listed. The "new forms of education," to which the authors of the paper refer, are thus found mostly in subtle language that transgresses customary dualisms. With the expression of "socioemotional dispositions" we find cognition and affect somewhat dissolved and self and society abridged. There is certainly novelty in such expression yet this novelty is not proposed as a reconceptualization of what education is *about* in the same way that we would find in Bai et al.'s and Miller's work.

The idea reflected in this paper is that the economic knowledge-based narrative is served by means that we have not tended to consider and perhaps were not sufficiently studied by science. The paper thus could be interpreted as advocating two agendas, one more conventional and the other pushing the envelope of contemporary understanding of contemporary curriculum thought. The former reviews the diverse contributions of contemplative practices to cognitive skills that scaffold conventional learning (e.g., executive functions, attention). The latter, however, resides both in venturing toward the affective domain and pointing to the clear relations between cognition and affect as they emerge from contemporary cognitive and neuroscientific studies (Damasio, 1994; Davidson, 2012). Within this we find a challenge to the rationalistic tendency described earlier as characteristic of the contemporary narrative.

Greenberg and Harris (2012) similarly offer a review of research in the field, although their tone is slightly more reserved for the field suffers from lack of rigorousness and a need for higher sophistication in research methodologies. The framing of contemplative practices in this case appears as follows: "Recent years have witnessed an explosion of interest in secular mindfulness strategies (including meditation, attention training, yoga, and other techniques) as methods to support wellness" (p. 161). The concept of "wellness" is interpreted as concerned with mental and physical health that reflect on diverse aspects including "academic performance, substance use, violence, and obesity...habits of mind, and resilience" (p. 161). Overall, in this paper the economic narrative is less prominent, however, cognition and affect are again tied together to challenge a strictly rational narrative. Describing contemplative practices Greenberg and Harris write:

> Although different techniques have different goals, they share a focus on sharpening concentration or attention, building emotion regulation skills to effectively manage stress, and gaining self-knowledge. Some practices consciously focus on building empathy and compassion. (p. 162)

At some point, hints of the more profound educational narrative proposed by contemplative practices, such as described by Bai, Scott and Donald (2009), Miller (2000) and others, lurks behind as Greenberg and Harris add:

> these practices involve a relational context with other children and a teacher who is likely to emphasize values of personal growth and ethics. Thus, contemplative practices often feature a "world view" including social or moral values. (p. 162)

One certainly wishes to learn more about this "world view," for there lays the crux of the matter. A "world view" underlying mindfulness practice, for example, is linked to Buddhism, and from there it is not too long an excursion to the Buddha's Four Noble Truths along with uncanny *nirvana* and the possibility of no-self. Thus a thin line is treaded here, quite similar to the brief mentioning of "Buddhism" in the previous paper (MLERN, 2012), albeit even more vaguely.

MLERN (2012) seem to have avoided the relation between contemplation and religion, or spirituality. There may be a rhetorical strategy there as well—as that which is not spoken of may not exist. Greenberg and Harris, however, respond to the secular narrative and seem to be tailoring their claim so it suits the contemporary "curricular box" in claiming that there is "some concern regarding the spiritual or religious origin of some practices" (p. 161). They mention Transcendental meditation's use of mantra for example as suggestive of religiosity which may imply a violation of the separation of Church and State. Their paper thus deliberately focuses on what they refer to as "*secularized contemplative practices* that generally fall under the labels of mindfulness, meditation, and yoga" (p. 162, emphasis mine). It is the ambiguity of the emphasized term that leads me to the final part of this chapter that explores the rhetorical spectrum so far described that I interpret as (un) defining "a post-secular age."

Part III: Contemplative Practices as an Exemplary Arena of a Post-Secular Age

As suggested, we can locate the attempts to justify contemplative practice in the curriculum as emerging from a spectrum between two broad (perhaps outdated) categories: science and wisdom-traditions.[4] The rhetoric surrounding the justification for contemplative practice in education, as I claim, creates a novel situation in which science and wisdom-traditions (connoting with religion and spirituality), those notorious historical rivals, find themselves peculiarly collaborating. While each pole seems to be drawing on different sources of justification, both can be seen as working towards a shared "mission" of rejuvenating education. This part of the chapter sheds more light on the spectrum that runs between these two orientations as a curricular locus that is increasingly conquering an influential position within contemporary educational discourse. Within this process, science and wisdom-traditions are drawn closer together in what some have appropriately termed "post-secularity," with education as the social arena in which this takes place.

One way of locating the tensions that wisdom-traditions and science bring to the question of contemplative practice and education can be explored based on Weber's twofold typology of education: "Historically, the two polar opposites in the field of education ends are: to awaken charisma, that is heroic qualities or magical gifts; and, to impart specialized expert training" (in Gerth & Mills, 1969, p. 426). Weber identified these two ideal types as pulling in opposite directions. The former, "charismatic education," represents an appeal to the irrational and spontaneous qualities of being to resist institutionalization. The latter can be viewed as "professional education" that represents rationalization, order, and bureaucratization. According to Weber's "disenchantment narrative," modernization is a process that erodes "charisma." It is a process that leads notoriously to the "iron cage" of "specialists without spirit." Yet, both Wexler (2000) and Huss (2014) have been contesting the validity of Weber's "disenchantment" prophecy. Wexler claimed that a mystical society is edified as we witness a substantial movement of individuals and groups that are seeking antidotes to alienation within practices, defined in this chapter as contemplative. Huss (2014) argued that the, "divide between religion and the secular becomes less compelling in contemporary Western societies" (p. 55). These are dated categories that are the heritage of modernism that fail to capture the complexity of contemporary times. This manifests, according to Huss, in people's shunning rigid identities as they engage in what Hanegraff referred to as "secular spiritualities" (1998, p. 152). Perhaps this is what Greenberg and Harris (2012) mean by confining their research to those earlier-mentioned "secularized contemplative practices" (p. 162)? These somewhat oxymoronic terms "secular spirituality," "spiritual but not religious," "secularized yoga," may be descriptive of an age that is characterized by the eschewing of rigid identities, and the embrace of a more open space for the experiment of life. Following Taylor (2006), Hotam & Wexler (2014), and others I suggest that these are characteristics of a "post-secular age" reflected in:

> A meltdown between the religious and the modern, the secular and the theological…a breakdown of the core separation that starkly informed the secular (as much as the religious) master narrative. (Fisher, Hotam & Wexler 2012. p. 263)

According to these views, what Weber would have viewed as practices that seek to awaken "charisma," namely contemplative practices, are certainly not abandoned. They are rather molded to suit a complex reality the understanding of which has outgrown neat dualisms. Disenchantment may have indeed been enacted, but it is not some linear trajectory as Weber envisioned but rather a pendulum swing towards the rational that when accentuated begs an opposition and leads to a dialectical movement. Very much as Hotam and Wexler (2014) suggested, "It is not a binary, but a dynamic, dialectical complexity which defines relations between the sacred and profane in the modern/secular world" (p. 3). In somewhat of a Hegelian move society might be playing out a broader narrative in which the poles of rationalization and "charisma" are seeking balance or perhaps even the buildup of a pendulum swing in the other direction?—Or is it a new trajectory?—The rhetoric involved in justifying contemplative practices in the curriculum results as an interesting social locus in which to ponder such claims and quandaries.

As outlined in the first part of this chapter, the economic-rational-secular narrative certainly manifests Weber's disenchantment narrative and a departing from charisma. Yet, the growing incorporation of contemplative practices in the curriculum is perhaps the most apparent rejection to the full enactment of this prophecy. Contemplative practices, at least in their "purer" rhetoric represented here by Bai, Scott and Donald (2009) and Miller (2000), bring with them non-rationality, spirituality, non-instrumentalism, perhaps "other-worldliness," and a resistance to the institution of a current social-economical order. They thus seem to be offering a "charismatic narrative" that pulls a contemporary economic-social-rational narrative from heading undisturbed in its Weberian "fixed destination." Yet, such process is by no means obvious, for educational policy makers are a product of a social order that is reproduced as schools comply with the economic-rational-secular narrative. The conviction that contemplative practices may have a place in the curriculum requires more than an appeal to wisdom-traditions. That is where the tremendous rhetorical power of science comes into play within education as a social arena. As Simon (2008) writes:

> As a society, we value what we can count. Without qualitative proof that a system or practice offers benefits, it's an uphill battle toward social acceptance. We need scientific evidence of the results of spiritual practice so that experts in such fields as education, healthcare and medicine, psychology and psychiatry, can seriously consider the inclusion and integration of spiritual approaches in their work. (p. 10)

The predominant ways in which contemplative practices are making their way into the curriculum have less to do with "charisma" and wisdom-traditions. They have more to do with the rhetoric of science as a demythologizing force that curves the religious, non-rational, non-instrumental edges of contemplative practices so that they cater to the economic-rational-secular ear and fit the curricular *box*. As Hyland (2014) rightly claimed:

> Contemporary therapeutic applications of mindfulness in mind–body medicine, psychotherapy and education…are unequivocally secular in all senses of the term in that their aims are essentially pragmatic and make little or no reference to the spiritual traditions in which mindfulness originated. (p. 9)

Interestingly, however, this very approach is supported by the Dalai Lama and Thich Nhat Hanh, perhaps the most renowned Buddhist world leaders. Hanh, for example, writes, "…spiritual life should be based on evidence, which can be verified, not on esoteric beliefs which cannot be tested" (2012, p. 82). The Dalai Lama, as mentioned, is one of the initiators of the Mind and Life Institute that purposefully promotes the mutual dialogue between science and contemplation towards the dissemination of contemplative practices in the curriculum. Both of these leaders reveal a very down-to-earth rhetoric that appeals to the minds that are very much accustomed to an economic-rational-secular narrative.

It seems that the curricular *box* is thus being reshaped from within, more than it is shaped from without. What this implies is that contemplative practices are being molded to the native language of the economical-rational-secular narrative. The extent to which they are allowed to bring the native narrative of their origins is limited. How much of wisdom-tradition lure can the contemporary curricular *box* withhold without eschewing it all together, or collapsing? How much can we mold contemplative practices so that they suit this narrative, and still consider them to be contemplative practices, and not simply ways of serving the very same narrative that perhaps had sent us searching for alternatives? There are certainly risks involved in this carpentry work of negotiating the curricular *box*. These risks have to do with the scientific method itself and a culture that is so well-practiced in commodifying that it is quick to commodify even what might seem the uncommodifiable meditative experience.

Critique along these lines is not uncommon. Both Nelson (2012) and Rosch (2007) showed that scientific research is limited to the measurable aspects of mindfulness. Their claim suggests that the narrative with which the scientific inquiry of mindfulness provides education is far narrower than the one offered by wisdom-traditions. Other critics have pointed to the problem of disengaging the practice from its theoretical-ethical context and its commodification (Purser & Loy, 2013). Incorporating yoga or mindfulness towards reducing stress, enhancement of executive functions, etc., all geared towards increased work-place productivity or boosting academic achievements, might not be too far-fetched in our contemporary climate. There are quite substantial differences involved in the intentions of practicing mindfulness as a means for productivity, versus viewing it as part of the eight-fold Buddhist path. These claims should be well taken, however they do not change the sociological phenomenon identified here: *the economic-rational-secular narrative is making room for practices that emerge from wisdom-traditions through the language of science.*

From a Weberian perspective there is certainly a dis-enchanting aspect to the scientification, economization and even rationalization of contemplative practice, yet just as the dualism of religion vs. secularity may be contested as capturing the understanding of contemporary society, enchantment or disenchantment are by no means discrete categories. There may be a narrative far more open-ended at play here in which science is being re-enchanted through its engagement with the study of contemplative practices—a notion that would have been unheard of some decades ago (Ergas, 2014). What we are witnessing is a complex arena in which scientists, spiritually-oriented curriculum theorists, Buddhism scholars, Contemplative leaders, and even politicians such as US Congressman Tim Ryan (2012) involved in the advocacy of mindfulness practice, are opening a rhetorical spectrum in which the argument transgresses the traditional debate between faith and reason or science and religion. It is rather an expression of different rhetorics involved in justifying the place of practices that originated in wisdom traditions and are now entering public schools. The spectrum created between the rhetoric of science and of wisdom-traditions as sources for justification of contemplative practices in the curriculum proposes poles that run between instrumentalism and non-instrumentalism, evidence and faith, secularity and profanity, rationalism and non-rationalism, yet they nevertheless emerge from pedagogies grounded in wisdom traditions. It is in between these poles that human action takes place in a locus that is appropriately termed "post-secular"—a definition that suggests more of what this is not than what this is. It is not secular, nor is it exactly religious, or non-religious, certainly not in the familiar ways we have been accustomed to understand these terms. Interestingly this very rhetoric undergirds Advaita Vedanta and Buddhism in many incidences with the Sanskrit words—*neti, neti*—not this, nor that, as indicating the nature of *Brahman* (ultimate reality) or the idea of non-self (Loy, 1996). It is a complex social arena in which presumably an economic-rational-secular narrative gives birth to the need for a return to religiosity (Hotam & Wexler, 2014, p. 1), yet this religiosity is engulfed by a scientific rhetoric that attenuates its full claim. Wexler suggests that the work lying ahead is the creation of

> a social vision from the mediating revitalization practices by a shared rediscovery of redemptive traditions, both in a study of the traditional texts and in an active renewal of the ancient techniques of self-realization. A prophetic mysticism, even in deformed expressions of closed-eyed irrationalism, already hovers about the cognitive schoolhouse. (2008, p. 195)

What may be added to this is that this "closed-eyed irrationalism" is paradoxically supported by the very rational rigorousness of scientific inquiry that has opened its eyes to study the closed-eyed practice of meditation. We witness these processes and can only hope that education, society, you, and I will reap the fruits of these processes.

Notes

1. http://www.garrisoninstitute.org/contemplation-and-education/contemplative-education-program-database
2. http://www.10news.com/news/ruling-on-yoga-instruction-at-encinitas-union-school-district-070113
3. Refer to MLI's website. https://www.mindandlife.org/about/mission/
4. In this chapter I refrain from distinguishing between the two.

References

Alexander, H. A. (2001). *Reclaiming goodness.* Notre Dame, IN: University of Notre Dame Press.

Apple, M. (2004). Creating difference: Neo-Liberalism, neo-conservatism and the politics of educational reform. *Educational Policy, 18*(1), 12–44.

Bai, H., Scott, C., & Donald, B. (2009). Contemplative pedagogy and revitalization of teacher education. *Alberta Journal of Educational Research 55*(3), 319–334.

Barbezat, D., & Bush, M. (2014). *Contemplative practices in higher education.* San Francisco: Jossey-Bass.

Bobbitt, F. (1918). Scientific method in curriculum-making. In D. J. Flinders & S. J. Thornton (Eds.), *The curriculum studies reader.* New York: Routledge.

Carboni, J. A., Roach A. T., & Fredrick, L. D. (2013). Impact of Mindfulness Training on the behavior of elementary students with attention-deficit/hyperactive disorder. *Research in Human Development, 10*(3), 234–251.

Damasio, A. (1994). *Descartes' error.* New York: Penguin.

Davidson, R. J. (2012). *The emotional life of your brain.* New York: Penguin.

Durlak, J. A., Weissberg, R. P., Dymnicki, A. B., Taylor, R. D., & Schellinger, K. B. (2011). The impact of enhancing students' social and emotional learning: A meta-analysis of school-based universal interventions. *Child Development, 82*(1), 405–432.

Eisner, E. W., (1996). *Cognition and curriculum reconsidered.* London: Paul Chaoman Publishing.

Eppert, C., & Wang, H. (2008). *Cross-cultural studies in curriculum: Eastern thought, educational insights.* Mahwah, NJ: Lawrence Erlbaum Associates.

Ergas, O. (2013). To think or not to think. Contemplative practice and education. *Journal of Transformative Education 11*(4), 275–296.

Ergas, O. (2014). Mindfulness in education at the intersection of science, religion and healing. *Critical Studies in Education, 55*(1), 58–72.

Fisher, S., Hotam, Y., & Wexler, P. (2012). Democracy and education in postsecular society. *Review of Educational Research, 36*, 261–281.

Flook, L., Smalley, S. L., Kitil, M. J., Kaiser-Greenland, S., Locke, J., Ishijima, E., & Kasari, C. (2010). Effects of Mindful Awareness practices on executive functions in elementary school children. *Journal of Applied School Psychology, 26*, pp. 70–95.

Gerth, H., & Mills, C. W. (1969). *From Max Weber.* New York: Oxford University Press.

Gilead, T. (2012). Education and the logic of economic progress. *The Journal of Philosophy of Education, 46*(1), 113–131.

Grace, F. (2011). Learning as a path, not a goal: Contemplative pedagogy—Its principles and practices. *Teaching Theology and Religion 14*(2), 99–124.

Greenberg, M. T., & Harris A. R. (2012). Nurturing mindfulness in children and youth: Current state of research. *Child Development Perspectives 6*(2), 161–166.

Hanegraaff, W. J. (1998). *New age religion and western culture: Esotericism in the mirror of secular thought.* Albany, NY: SUNY Press.

Hanh, T. N. (2012). Science and the Buddha: 21-day retreat, Jun 1–21, 2012. Thenac: Plum Village Practice Centre.

Hart, T. (2004). Opening the contemplative mind in the classroom. *Journal of Transformative Education, 2*(1), 28–46.

Hattam, R. (2004). *Awakening struggle—Towards a Buddhist critical social theory.* Flaxton: Post Pressed.

Heelas, P., & Woodhead, L. (2005). *The spiritual revolution.* Oxford: Blackwell Publishing.

Hinsdale, M. J. (2012). Choosing to love. *Paideusis (20)*2, 36–45.

Hotam, Y., & Wexler, P. (2014). Education in post-secular society. *Critical Studies in Education, 55*(1), 1–7.

Huss, B. (2014). Spirituality: The emergence of a new cultural category and its challenge to the religious and the secular. *Journal of Contemporary Religion, 29*(1), 47–60.

Hyland, T. (2014). Buddhist practice and educational endeavour: In search of a secular spirituality for state-funded education in England. *Ethics and Education,* 1–12.

Jackson, P. (1968). *Life in classrooms.* New York: Teachers College Press.

Jennings, P. A., Snowberg, K. E., Coccia, A., & Greenberg, M. T. (2011). Improving classroom learning environments by cultivating awareness and resilience in education (CARE): Results of two pilot studies. *Journal of Classroom Interaction, 46*(1), 37–48.

Kabat-Zinn, J. (2011). Some reflections on the origins of MBSR, skillful means, and the trouble with maps. *Contemporary Buddhism, 12*(1), 281–306.

Kincheloe, J., & Steinberg, S. R. (1993). A tentative description of post-formal thinking: The critical confrontation with cognitive theory. *Harvard Educational Review, 63*(3), 296–321.

Kuhn, T. (1962). *The structure of scientific revolutions.* London: New American Library.

Lin, J., Oxford, R., & Brantmeier, S. (eds.) (2013). *Re-envisioning higher education.* Charlotte: IAP.

Loy, D. (1996). *Lack and transcendence.* Atlantic Highlands, NJ: Humanities Press.

Miller, J. (2000). *Education and the soul.* New York: SUNY Press.

MLERN: Davidson, R. J., Dunne, J., Eccles, J. S., Engle, A., Greenberg, M., Jennings, P.,...Vago, D. (2012). Contemplative practices and mental training: Prospects for American education. *Child Development Perspectives, 6*(2), 146–153.

Nelson, D. L. (2012). Implementing mindfulness: Practice as the home of understanding. *Paideusis, 20*(2), 4–14.

Palmer, P. (1983) *To know as we are known: Education as a spiritual journey.* New York: Harper Collins.

Peters, R. S. (1966). *Ethics and education.* London: Allen & Unwin.

Postman, N. (1995). The end of education. *Psychological Inquiry, 4*(18), 258–264.

Purser, R., & Loy, D. (2013) http://www.huffingtonpost.com/ron-purser/beyond-mc-mindfulness_b_3519289.html

Robeyns, I. (2004). Three models of educational rights, capabilities, and human capital. *Theory and Research in Education, 4*(1), 69–84.

Rosch, E. (2007). More than mindfulness: When you have a tiger by the tail, let it eat you. *Psychological Inquiry, 18*(4), 258–264.

Roth, H. D. (2008). Against cognitive imperialism. *Religion East & West 8*, 1–26.

Ryan, T. (2012). *A mindful nation*. Carlsbad, CA: Hay House Inc.

Simmer-Brown, J. (2009). The question is the answer: Naropa University's contemplative pedagogy. *Religion and Education 36*(2), 89–101.

Simon, T. (Ed.). (2008). Measuring the immeasurable. Boulder, CO: Sounds True.

Speck, B. (2005). What is spirituality? *New Directions for Teaching and Learning. 104*, 3–13.

Taylor, C. (2006). *A secular age*. Cambridge, MA: Harvard University Press.

Todd, S., & Ergas, O. (2015). Introduction. to special issue: Philosophy East/West: Exploring intersections between educational and contemplative practice. *Journal of Philosophy of Education.*

Wexler, P. (2000). *The mystical society*. Boulder, CC: Westview press.

Wexler, P. (2008). *Symbolic movement*. Rotterdam: Sense.

Zins, J. E., Bloodworth, M. R., Weissberg, R. P., & Walberg, H. J. (2007). The scientific base linking social and emotional learning to school success. *Journal of Educational and Psychological Consultation 17*(2–3), 191–210.

Part III

Case Studies in Palestine and Israel

7. Demarcating the Secular: Education Policy in Mandate Palestine

SUZANNE SCHNEIDER

Surely the church is a place where one day's truce ought to be allowed to the dissensions and animosities of mankind.[1]

In an important study published in 2003, which has subsequently become required reading for those interested in the critique of secularism, Talal Asad outlined two essential tasks for the scholarly community: First, to ask "how, when, and by whom are the categories of religion and the secular defined," and second, to ask "what assumptions are presupposed in the acts that define them?" (p. 201). Notwithstanding recent calls for a theory of the "post-secular" that recognizes that "the European development, whose Occidental rationalism was once supposed to serve as a model for the rest of the world, is actually the exception rather than the norm" (Habermas, 2008), I would like to suggest that historians of the modern Middle East must, with good reason, dwell for some time on Asad's challenge to understand the history of secularism in the societies they study.

The reason for this is, briefly stated, as follows. To recognize the deeply Protestant roots of secularism—with its Pauline equation of "religion" with faith and corresponding construction of the private individual and the public citizen—is to confront a historical trajectory that could have no easy equivalent within juridical traditions like Islam for whom *sola fide* was an inadequate basis for producing a moral social order. Yet, one still finds countless studies of the modern Middle East in which leaders and movements are uncritically described as "secular" or "religious" with little theoretical engagement as to what exactly such labels might mean in non-Christian settings. The post-secular turn may have drawn needed attention to the historical contingency of secularism, but that still does not explain how such a worldview migrated to colonial settings, the intellectual re-orientations it engendered, or how they differed from the experience of Christian Europe. Consequently, it would seem that scholars of the Middle East must first wade through these historical and intellectual legacies of secularism before turning toward the post-secular embrace.

By looking at the education system developed during the period of British Mandatory rule in Palestine (1917–1948), and using its curricula as an analytic lens, this chapter will shed light on just what was at stake in the process of demarcating "secular" and "religious" forms of knowledge in one colonial context. The central argument is that the government of Palestine promoted a view of religious education as a locus of "universal" values that could transcend national turmoil and disavowed any notion of religion tied to mass politics.[2] Understanding this educational program requires a direct confrontation with the fundamental assumptions upon which the government's policy was based: namely, that of education as a practice distinct from, and indeed outside of, the political realm; and that of religion as inherently, or at least ideally, apolitical. The seepage of political concerns into the schoolroom therefore constituted nothing less than an *intrusion* that compromised the nature of education itself. Thus while Arabic was the language of instruction and the curriculum even devoted some attention to the Arab Enlightenment movements (*al-nahḍa al-ʿarabiya*), administrators aimed at "the formation of individual character" rather than the cultivation of "an artificial and hysterical racial pride" (Farrell, 1946, Sec. 21). Thus "politics" figures in the writings of British officials as a transgressive force that upsets the educational equilibrium rather than as an inevitable component of modern national schooling under centralized state supervision.

On the other hand, educators assigned a monumental task to religious education. This amounted to nothing less than instilling in children a "universal" moral system that was presumably shared by Palestine's three major monotheistic religions—and yet bore a striking resemblance to a particular form of British Protestantism. Moreover, it was through the cultivation of religious education that children could presumably be shielded from the destructive pull of mass politics. As such, religious education represented a lynchpin in the effort to maintain the "traditional" order in which rule through religious authorities was thought to offer an antidote to popular mobilization.[3]

In sum, we confront in Mandatory Palestine the peculiar intersection of the secular and the sectarian. On one hand, secularism—defined as the removal of religion from the public sphere and the creation of administrative structures distinct from religious authorities—was not a political order that British administrators promoted. And yet, in their approach to public education, government officials nonetheless carried with them secular assumptions regarding the universal and apolitical nature of religious values. Looking at education as a concrete case study can help demonstrate these dynamics and suggest that, for the Mandatory government, the secular and the sectarian were in fact two sides of the same coin.

Foundations of British Education Policy in Palestine

Before diving into this analysis, some general remarks are required to elucidate the nature of education in Palestine following the First World War. The Allies conquered Palestine in December 1917 and established an interim military administration that assumed direct control over the former Ottoman public schools and nominal control over a plethora of private schools—ranging from missionary schools to *ḥederim*, *katātīb*, and the approximately 40 schools that formed the nucleus of the Zionist school system (Department of Education [DoE], 1929).[4] Authority was transferred to a civil administration in July 1920, and in 1922, Palestine was recognized by the League of Nations as a Class A Mandate under British control. In general terms, what occurred over the three decades of British rule was the large-scale transformation of education from a decentralized practice managed largely by religious communities into formalized systems centrally managed by state or quasi-state institutions.[5]

Apart from various private institutions, the Mandate government recognized two distinct public school systems, the Hebrew and Arab Public Systems, "classified according to the principal language of instruction" (Government of Palestine, 1933, Part I).[6] The former was maintained and supervised by the Education Department of the Jewish Agency and, after 1932, the Va'ad Leumi. The extension of a large block grant beginning in 1927, tied to the proportion of Jews in the population, in theory subjected the Hebrew Public System to closer government supervision. In practice, the Department of Education never posed a serious threat to the autonomy of Zionist schools (Reshef, 1999, p. 153). Conversely, the Arab Public System—which was composed of former Ottoman public schools, village *katātīb* that were incorporated through grants-in-aid, and a number of new schools opened during the early years of British rule—was placed under the direct supervision of a British Director of Education. Despite Palestinians' demands for greater local participation in the management of the schools, as was occurring in other

Class A Mandates, the British continually rejected these overtures, as implementing the Jewish National Home project against the wishes of the majority clearly foreclosed any possibility of indirect colonial rule.

As Education Director, the Colonial Office appointed Humphrey Bowman, a product of Eton and Oxford, who previously served in the education departments of Egypt and Iraq. Bowman never tired of stressing the importance of education as a means to inculcate a sense of public service and civic engagement among Palestine's youth; similarly he led the country's Baden Powell scouts and shared in contemporary views that saw scouting as an important exercise in character formation. Yet Bowman distinguished absolutely between "healthy" forms of civic responsibility and political activism on the national scale and, indeed, looked upon the latter as a deadly virus that threatened to undermine his efforts. Education officials therefore viewed the entrance of national politics into the classroom with great anxiety. This unease peaked at times of domestic upheaval, such as the school strikes that accompanied Lord Balfour's 1925 visit, and during the riots in 1929.[7] In Bowman's words (1942), "As the political situation gradually worsened, we were faced by another danger. This was the effect of politics on teachers and pupils. In the neighboring Egypt, school strikes and demonstrations had had a disastrous effect on discipline, and had seriously reacted on educational progress. Once this virus entered the schools of Palestine, I knew we were doomed" (p. 310).

In contrast to the dreaded creep of "politics" into the classroom, colonial administrators believed that religious education, if done properly, could form the basis of universal moral principles that stood aloof from political affairs. In the words of Jerome Farrell (1946), the Director of Education for the second half of the Mandate period, "Religion is a full subject in the curriculum and thus the ultimate basis of ethical values in the Government schools is common to Islam and to Christianity" (Sec. 22). Conversely, the most frequent critique leveled at Zionist schools was that they upset the proper relationship between politics, religion and education. The fact that nearly every Zionist school was administered by one of the three major political parties—Labor, "General" Zionists and the Orthodox Mizrahi party—represented a direct challenge to the British ideal of education devoid of political influence. Moreover, Farrell's comments reflected the Enlightenment framework that increasingly excluded Jews from "the religious patrimony of Western nations" because the "Hebrews simply could not provide the model of universal humanity that would regulate the new ideology of culture" (Sheehan, 2005, p. xiv):

> Both [Islam and Christianity] accept a theology and moral principles based largely on Greek philosophy, while Islam regards Christ as at least a prophet. But

'unassimilated' Judaism after rejecting successively both Hellenism and Christ is now reducing its own traditional faith, so far as it still survives at all as a religion, from monotheism to the older henotheism which leads to that racial self-worship which Albert Rosenberg borrowed from the Jews for Nordic ends and which Andrew Lang might have called 'a projection of Teutonic barbarism on the mists of the Brocken'. But most Palestine Jews seem now to be atheists and materialistic 'ideologists'. (Farrell, 1946, Sec. 22)

Having turned away from all possible sources of civilization, i.e. Christianity and Hellenism, Zionism was found guilty of transforming the moral core of Judaism into a hollow shell of national chauvinism. Regarding the religious education given in Zionist schools, Farrell pronounced that within the Mizrachi system as "formal and dead, a matter of ritual and obsolete taboos." The General schools hardly fared any better in his estimation, as "the majority [of teachers] seem to have replaced religion by racialism." But worst of all was the situation within Labor schools, which were "in general secularizing and many are actively *anti-religious*" (original emphasis; Farrell, 1946, Sec. 36).

It was not only Zionists who were guilty of trying to turn education into an instrument of political indoctrination, however they were deemed the most successful. In the same memorandum, Farrell continued to state, "the attitude of Palestine Zionists to education is essentially identical not only with that of the Nazis and the Russian Communists but also with that of Jamal Hussaini and other Arab politicians who wish to use the Arab schools to inculcate fanatical anti-Zionism." However, he noted with satisfaction, "the Arab politicians have been less successful and their influence touches in any considerable degree only Moslem private schools.... Thus a large majority of the Moslem and Christian population is still educated in the common principles of conduct which inform Christianity and Islam" (Farrell, 1946, Sec. 6).

As we can see from this brief discussion, British administrators were informed by a clear set of dictates regarding the proper content and role of religious values within an educational framework. If the education imparted by certain communities failed to conform to the vision, the resulting failure was not explained by questioning the absolute separation of "religion" from mass politics, but rather by arguing this education was no longer religious in nature. This prompts us to ask what the "proper" content of religious education consisted of and what subjects were deemed outside of its purview. To answer this question, it is perhaps a useful exercise to look more closely at the syllabus created for the Arab Public System, over which the Government of Palestine exercised complete control.

That Old Time Religion

The official syllabus for town and village schools, based largely on the Egyptian model, was first published in 1921. It included detailed instructions regarding the number of hours devoted to each subject in each grade, the topics to be covered therein, and additional directions to teachers regarding the proper conduct of students. While education administrators often stressed the novelty of this new curriculum, most Arab public schools remained anchored by subjects that were commonly found in the *katātīb* they were meant to supersede: namely, Arabic, religious instruction, and Arithmetic.[8] However, there was much about customary forms of Islamic schooling that was deemed archaic, misdirected or pedagogically unsound. The *katātīb* were therefore a favorite target of colonial administrators and Palestinians alike. The Department of Education Annual Report (1926) characterized these schools as "old-fashioned and often inefficient" institutions in which "the standard [of instruction] remains rather low."[9] Anecdotal evidence suggests that Palestinian Arabs were similarly dissatisfied with the state of rural schooling, and particularly with the village teacher. Even before the First World War, letters in the burgeoning national press lamented that the village teacher was "more ignorant than Hubnaqa" and "the germ of every evil and the source of all corruption" (Beidas, 1911).[10] Rather than preserving the existing systems of Islamic schooling, the goal was to reconstitute older forms of education to accommodate the contradictory demands that schooling both nurture the "traditional" order and support the introduction of new technical skills geared for Palestine's changing economy.

One way of differentiating new village schools from their former selves came in the manner in which "traditional" subjects were taught. The new directives shied away from memorization, which was thought to come at the expense of true comprehension, and instead aimed to develop the child's "facility for and a habit of rapid silent reading" (DoE, 1925, p. 10). Oral recitation and memorization were to be used only sparingly in teaching religious subjects and expunged from all other parts of the new curriculum. Moreover, administrators placed increased emphasis on agricultural and vocational training, as the subjects typically encountered in *katātīb* were seemingly devoid of practical application. Indeed, an over-emphasis on the dreaded "literary education" was thought to produce children who were alienated from the necessities of village life. The Palestinian educator Khalil Totah offered the anecdote of overhearing a peasant exclaim, "What! Do you expect my son to work—he can read!" Echoing the viewpoint of the British administrators, Totah identified this alleged distaste for "practical education" to be at "the crux of the educational problem in the Holy Land, where education, elementary as it is, seems incompatible with manual work" (Totah, 1932, p. 165). Without addressing the agricultural basis of village life, it was argued, the customary curriculum would do nothing to remedy the economic hardship that propelled urban drift. Thus, to the usual subjects were added geography, nature study, history, hygiene, drawing, and gardening and manual work (DoE, 1921, p. 6).[11]

However, the introduction of new subjects into the curriculum was arguably less significant than the divisions created between existing types of knowledge. The syllabus in fact reflected an effort to remove "religion" from sites it formerly seemed to subsume: among them were the Arabic language, the historical record, and the human body. One consequence of this contraction of "religious" topics was that it largely freed religious education from matters concerning material relations or the political order. Such instruction could therefore be reconstituted as the basis of a "universal" code of individual ethics. To understand this shift, and the tensions it generated, we must look not merely at the government curriculum for religious instruction but what was newly *excluded* from the category of religion itself.

The Arabic language, which had historically been a core subject of study within the *kuttāb* and *madrasa* (and indeed, many of the great treatises on the Arabic language were published by Muslim theologians), was now treated as a distinct subject that aimed at the attainment of permanent literacy.[12] Further departing from the traditional order of the *kuttāb*, the 1925 version of the syllabus stated that the aim of Arabic language instruction was to develop interest in classical and modern Arabic literature. Memorization was to be avoided and "vulgarisms and provincialisms in pronunciation, grammar and vocabulary must be carefully eradicated" (DoE, 1925, p. 8–9). Interestingly, memorization was allowed within the context of religious education, but "vulgarisms" were similarly discouraged: thus "the Qur'an should be memorized perfectly and read with the intonation practiced by the early Moslems," a feat which required that "the affected method of reading the Qur'an followed in the old maktabs [*katātīb*] should be discarded" (DoE, 1921, p. 32). In this instance, modernization came to depend precisely on abandoning contemporary practices in favor of reconstructed—and supposedly more authentic—classical models.

Hygiene represents a subject that could have quite easily been subsumed under the category of religious education. Indeed, children did study "practical knowledge of the principles of ablutions" as part of the class dedicated to Islamic religious instruction (DoE, 1925, 72). However, in treating hygiene as a distinct component of the syllabus, the curriculum indicated that these practices were not to be regarded as part of a particular religious ritual but rather as universal norms grounded in scientific objectivity. As Ellen Fleischmann has argued (2003), the inclusion of hygiene as a school subject also reflected the larger trend whereby everyday rural activities were transformed into forms of knowledge that were only acquired by removing the child from the home in which they were usually learned. This was true not merely of hygiene, but also of poultry keeping, agricultural work, or embroidery (in girls' schools)— skills with which no child in rural Palestine was truly unfamiliar. As I have argued elsewhere, the result was an educational paradigm in which corrupt village conditions were thought to necessitate the academic training of children in an idealized "traditional" life.

However noteworthy these curricular innovations, it is by comparing syllabi for Islamic religious instruction on one hand, and history on the other, that the approach to religion as a distinct category of personal experience becomes most apparent. As numerous authors have noted (Tibawi, 1956; Miller, 1985; Khalidi, 2006), the teaching of history and geography in Arab public schools constituted a continual source of tension between the Department of Education and the Palestinian Arab public. Palestinian nationalists regarded the government curriculum as a classic colonial attempt to obviate the identity formation of the Arab child by turning his attention to foreign events while simultaneously neglecting the history of modern Palestine.[13] There is certainly an element of truth to this claim, though it does not fully capture the matrix within which these curricular decisions operated, how the boundaries between sacred and secular events were established, and what significance was attached to each.

The general structure of the new history curriculum narrated a teleological story at whose apex sat European modernity, its commercial triumphs, scientific advancements and political conquests. Thus the child may study figures from the Arab past in classes devoted to ancient or medieval history, but modernity as a historical period was reserved almost exclusively for European (and, to a lesser extent, North American) developments. The second class, for instance, included the following topics under the heading of "modern history": Columbus; Drake and his voyage round the world; Cromwell and the struggle between King and Parliament; Watt Stephenson and the invention of the steam engine; William Wilberforce and the abolition of slavery in British domains; Napoleon; Nelson and the battle of the Nile; Gordon and the suppression of the slave trade in the Sudan (DoE, 1925, p. 37). To the extent that lands outside of the Euro-American context appeared, it was as objects of colonial conquest and, as the Sudanese example above suggests, improvement.

Yet, as indicated above, the curriculum was not totally bereft of Arab historical figures or events. For instance, teachers were given a list of "great men" whose biographies formed the basis of lessons, particularly in the lower grades. They included "the principal characters in Bible history," Socrates, Josephus, the rightly guided Caliphs, 'Abd al-Malik ibn al-Marwan, Harun al-Rashid, Charlemagne, al-Ghazali, Richard the Lionheart, Salah al-Din al-Ayyubi, Christopher Columbus, Napoleon and Ibrahim Pasha, to give only a very small sampling (DoE, 1925, pp. 30–37).[14] There are two questions we must therefore address: first, if Arab history was not actually excluded to the extent that has been suggested, what topics were fit for inclusion and why? Second, how did caliphs and jurists come to be included in "secular" history rather than within religious instruction, and what were the interpretive consequences of this shift?

On one hand, the figures and events deemed worthy of inclusion function as milestones within an unbroken chain of Arab national heritage extending back to pre-Islamic times: the *Jahaliya* poets Hatim al-Ta'i and 'Amr ibn Madi Karib initiate a chronology that includes the rightly guided caliphs, great military heroes (Khalid ibn al-Walid, Tariq ibn Ziyad, Jawhar al-Siqilli, Salah al-Din), renowned artists and scholars (al-Shafi'i, al-Farabi, al-Ghazali, al-Mutanabbi), and culminates in 19th-century reformers (Muhammad 'Ali, Ibrahim Pasha, 'Abd al-Qadir al-Jaza'iri). This was by now a familiar narrative, one that found its first modern articulation in the writings of figures associated with the Arab *nahda* before its adoption by Arab nationalist thinkers. It is therefore not surprising to find a similar version of this chronology within history textbooks written by Palestinian nationalist educators, such as those by Muhammad 'Izzat Darwaza (Darwaza, 1929).

Thus, it is not that Arab history was entirely neglected. On the contrary, figures from the Arab classical heritage commanded a great deal of attention. What was neglected, however, was contemporary Arab history as seen from the perspective of national revival, foreign betrayal and colonial conquest. For instance, while the government syllabus and 'Izzat Darwaza's nationalist textbook both concluded with lessons on "The Great War and its results in the Arab land" ("*al- harb al-kubra wa atharuha fi al-bilād al-'arabiya*" in Darwaza's text, suggesting a rather literal mirroring of the government curriculum), the content of those lessons were quite different. Nonetheless, the topical similarities between these two, allegedly oppositional, history curricula gesture at one of the great tensions of the Mandatory government's educational planning: students were expected to gain the literary skills required to appreciate classical and modern Arabic literature, and to deduce moral lessons from the great military and political heroes of the Arab past, but were to avoid relating to this knowledge as a source of inspiration for their modern political identities.

As indicated by the list of "great men" above, the child's first introduction to history was a mixed one in many ways. It included both Arab and foreign figures, taken from both sacred and secular settings. Here Biblical figures could inhabit the same historical space as al-Shafi'i and King Alfred. It was not merely figures from the Judeo-Christian tradition that found their way into the syllabus, as intermediate classes covered the family of Muhammad, "his mission and life in detail," the spread of Islam and the decay of the Caliphate (DoE, 1925, pp. 40–41). This removal of characters and events from the annals of sacred history can be read as an attempt to naturalize the historical record, wherein the rapid spread of Islam, for example, is attributable to the "organisation of the Arab Empire" and its "fiscal system" rather than divine providence (DoE, 1925, p. 40). Similarly, lessons should stress "the effect of climate, physical conditions means of communications, and environment on the development of the different races" (DoE, 1921, p. 16). What is evident from this example is the fragmentation of Islamic history into discrete ethical and political components, to be dealt with in the contexts of religious instruction and secular history, respectively. As such, the history curriculum posited a new interpretive framework for explaining familiar episodes from the human past. What occurred within the "old-fashioned" *kuttāb*, on the other hand, was not genuine history, perhaps less on account of *what* was studied than because of how the march of time was encountered and explained.

With overtly "religious" leaders relegated to the ancient and medieval periods, and naturalistic explanations provided to explain even the most theologically charged events, historical time is doubly purged of the political-theological mingling that European modernity deemed unacceptable. Following Bruno Latour (1993), we might characterize this as an act of "purification" that distinguishes secular and sacred discourses of the past while, we might suspect, at the same time facilitating the violation of that very same boundary. Yet we should not conflate the creation of this new discursive framework with a broader attempt to promote secularism as an ideological framework. On the contrary, religious institutional networks and interpretive structures still had much work to do in Palestine. A closer look at the syllabus for religious instruction will help illustrate this argument.

Given the popularity of "Protestant" approaches to Islam within reformist circles of the late 19th and early 20th centuries, it should serve as no surprise that the Qur'an served as the center of religious education in government schools. "The Qur'an should be the source of authority in deducing doctrines, ritual, moral axioms, and civil transactions" (DoE, 1921, p. 32). The Qur'an and *sunna* functioned as the vessels for the transmission of these virtues, as it was through the moral exemplars contained therein that the child acquired "fear of his maker in all his religious and worldly (*dunyawiya*) acts" (Government of Egypt, Ministry of Public Education [MoPE], 1920, 15).[15]

Furthermore, the first goal of religious instruction (*al-diyana* or *al-taʿlīm al-dīnī*) was "the propagation of superior moral virtues by means of example and good lesson" (MoPE, 1920, 17). This passage suggests, and the following analysis will substantiate, that Mandatory officials promoted religious education as a means of character formation that was not dissimilar to contemporary British views of education at home. And indeed, taking into consideration Jonathan Sheehan's (2005) excellent study of approaches to the Bible in late 19th-century England, it is not altogether surprising that British administrators in early 20th-century Palestine would regard religious education as a means of diffusing "universal" ethical and civil values rather than an integral component of material life or a means to secure individual salvation.

The syllabus further divided its contents into two segments: "Qur'an" and "Religious Instruction." The former consisted of an ordered timetable for reading the Qur'an in its entirety by the end of the final year of schooling, prescribing which *ajza'* should be read and which committed to memory. The creation of a large network of public schools in which each child learned the same portion of the Qur'an at the same time must itself be appreciated as a novelty. As such, the incorporation of religious education into the school curriculum was not the mere continuation of the past but a significant attempt to create a uniform approach to the Qur'an's teaching and interpretation. In the same vein, the introduction of an official textbook for the upper grades reflected the urge to ensure teachers followed a standardized curriculum. This necessarily stripped the teacher of some of the autonomy he possessed within private *katātīb*, and the development of detailed syllabi and textbooks can in fact be read as an attempt to mitigate the uneven influence of individual teachers. In this, the British did nothing that wasn't already envisioned decades earlier by Muhammad ʿAbduh, who argued that only a unified approach to religious education, purged of its irrational elements, could combat the creep of ignorance (*jahl*) among Ottoman Muslims (ʿAbduh, 1993).

In addition to stipulating which Qur'anic passages the child would read and memorize each year, the syllabus reflected a long-standing European anxiety that the practice of memorization left the child bereft of true comprehension. This concern was not a mere pedagogic one, but rather emerged from the idea that a religious text must contain some ethical core that is distinct from the ritual practices and performances that surround it.[16] This understanding no doubt emerged from approaches to religious education in 19th-century Britain, where reformers insisted that, in the words of Gregory Starrett, "true moral instruction lay in the study and understanding of 'lessons' drawn from Scripture. The text itself, aside from refining literary taste, was secondary to the conveyance of such lessons" (Starrett, 1998, p. 38). Therefore, teachers were to give "the meaning of difficult words and a resume of the general sense" of each *juz'* that was memorized. Furthermore, "the verses selected for the various years of study should be explained so that they may become firmly rooted in the minds of the pupils who should be led to act in keeping with the principles and precepts embodied therein" (DoE, 1921, p. 32). As Brinkley Messick has argued in the context of Yemen (1996), this emphasis on understanding the ethical content of the Qur'an overturned older modes of relating to the text's divinity as something to be embodied through recitation. As such, it was not merely that memorization was deemed pedagogically unsound, but that it compromised the modern project of relating to the Qur'an as a coherent set of dogmas and ethical precepts to be absorbed by the individual conscience.

Under the heading of "Religious Instruction," lower classes focused on the life and attributes of Muhammad, his family, migration to Medina, death, and burial. These were, significantly, all topics that appeared in the history syllabus as well, though here particular stress was paid to the prophet as a moral guide, "his self-abnegation and humility," "his interest in the well-being of children," "his refraining from revenge when revenge lay in his power." Through the incorporation of "moral training"—namely "virtues whose practice is inferred from verses in the Qur'an"—the upper grades combined the earlier emphasis on Muhammad's biography with the reformist stress on the Qur'an as the authoritative source for deducing ethical principles. These included, for instance, "respect due to parents," "obedience due to rulers" and "the etiquette of visiting" (DoE, 1921, pp. 34–35).

On one hand, the emulation of Muhammad's behavior as a means of moral fashioning was as old as Islamic education itself. What is interesting for our purposes is that this emphasis came at the expense of teaching the material, social or political dimensions of Islam. The curriculum thus promoted a view of religion as largely limited to the biography of Muhammad, the text of the Qur'an and the "universal moral values" that were thought to represent an ethical core shared by Christianity and, to a lesser extent, Judaism. In contrast, many Muslim "religious" thinkers and leaders appeared not within the syllabus for religious instruction but within that for Arab history. Thus 'Abu Bakr and al-Ghazali take their place in the curriculum among other heroes of the classical Arabic tradition in much the same way that Socrates and Julius Caesar were used to symbolize the intellectual and political triumphs of the Greco-Roman period.

I would like to suggest that, in this instance, secular history was linked to the nation in a way that religion, imagined as a source of universal values, could not support. Echoing the earlier transformation of the Bible into an ethical text of neo-humanistic heritage, religious education in Palestine was meant to function as a moral common ground that could rise above the political clamor. If any degree of particularism was allowed to creep into the classroom, it was through the historical study of the great men of the past, and hence the heightened level of supervision over schools' history curricula. Prominent Muslim figures could therefore migrate from sacred to secular history as exemplars of the Arab nation, a movement that facilitated the reconstitution of Islam as a defined group of beliefs, ritual practices and ethical norms. Stripped of most of its political leaders and social content, Islamic religious instruction could thereby be reconstituted as part of a universal—or perhaps more to the point, universalizing—moral system that was largely removed from those affairs now claimed by the secular.

Conclusion

In concluding, it is worth restating the tension we highlighted at the outset and ask what, if anything, this case study reveals about the intersection of the secular and the sectarian in Mandate Palestine. As mentioned above, the understanding of religion as a depoliticized entity was directly at odds with the actual administrative structure of Palestine, whose governance through religious units obviated the emergence of what we might term a "secular" public space. More radically, might we suggest that it was precisely *because* religion was conceived of in apolitical terms that the British chose to govern through it, that sectarian rule was facilitated by the epistemic shadow of secularism? However provocative and preliminary, this interpretation would explain why Judaism appears in the reflections of education officials, like Jerome Farrell, as not quite a religion anymore; that is to say, the Jews, as the only community granted recognition as a national entity, gained this status at the expense of their "religious" authenticity. Further investigation may be required to support this premise, though it is hoped that even this brief discussion of public education in Palestine is adequate to convey the need for more critical attention to the trajectories of the secular in colonial settings.

Notes

1. Edmund Burke, *Reflections on the Revolution in France* (Oxford: Oxford University Press, 2009), 12.
2. In the words of Gil Anidjar, "Is it possible not to notice—in spite of Azmi Bishara's tireless efforts to remind us—that American foreign policy, like its British, French, and other seasoned and enduring counterparts, has long been strategically playing Islam against Arab nationalism, ethnicity against religion, and national against religious uni-

ty? Is it possible not to notice that religion and nationalism are strategically divided and must therefore be considered in their joined operations?" (Anidjar, 2006 p. 67).

3. For instance, the creation of institutions such as the Supreme Muslim Council and the later recognition of Knesset Israel as the official representative body of the Jewish community in Palestine reflected a desire to render the religious community the sole unit for making political claims. There are number of works that discuss the development of sectarian rule in the 19th-and 20th-century Middle East, see for example, (Dirks, 2001; Khalidi, 2006, Ch. 1; Makdisi, 2000; Robson, 2011).

4. (Department of Education, 1929) The exact number of schools under Zionist control during this time is subject to some debate. For alternate figures see Bentwich, 1965, pp. 14–15. For greater detail on the early administrative structure of the Zionist schools, see Elboim-Dror, 1986, Vol. 2, Sections 1–2.

5. At the outset of the war, more than half of the Arab children who attended school were in private communal institutions: approximately 8,705 in private Muslim schools and thousands more in Christian (largely missionary) schools, versus 8,248 in the Ottoman public schools. (Tibawi, 1956, p. 20) Within the Jewish community, exact statistics of school enrollment by administrative body are unavailable, but it is unlikely that the number of students in schools managed by the *vaad ha-hinuch* approached the number in private *hederim* and *Talmud-torahs* given the difference in population between the Old Yishuv (66,000) and the New Yishuv (13,900) at the outbreak of the war. (Elboim-Dror, 1986, p. Vol. 2. 21).

6. For an extended discussion of the problems inherent in this system of classification, see (Schneider, 2013).

7. For an extended discussion of school strikes, see Tibawi, 1956, Ch. 7. For a discussion of the 1925 strike within the Government Arab College, see (Davis, 2003).

8. The matter was further complicated by the fact that many "new" public schools were actually *katātīb* that had been absorbed into the Government system through the extension of grants-in-aid (Tibawi, 1956, p. 27).

9. This characterization of *katātīb* remained consistent in the Department of Education's Annual Reports throughout the Mandate period. Compare, for instance, Government of Palestine Department of Education *Annual Report*, 1925–26, 1940–41 and 1945–46.

10. The figure of Hubnaqa is allegedly based on the example of Yazid ben Thurwan and has for centuries served as a model for foolishness and stupidity. The medieval writer Ibn al-Jawzi immortalized the figure of Hubnaqa and his follies by featuring him in his *Akhbar al-hamqa wa al-mughallafin* [Annals of fools and the uncivilized (literally, uncircumcised)].

11. On the mixed record of the DOE in implementing agricultural training in schools, see Miller, 1985, pp. 108–12; Tibawi, 1956, pp. 235–38.

12. The acquisition of permanent literacy was a primary goal of the Department of Education. See, for example, "Testimony of Mr. H. E. Bowman, C. M. G., C. B. E., Director of Education. November 27, 1936."

13. According to Tibawi's account, Arab nationalists never ceased to point out that the History syllabus "insisted in its content and tone on the international rather than the national character of Palestine" (Tibawi, 1956, p. 88). More recently, Rashid Khalidi has pointed to this fact (and the educational structure as a whole) as being partially responsible for the lack of Palestinian state formation during the Mandate period and in the years following (Khalidi, 2006).

14. As this list suggests, the syllabus was entirely devoid of great women, though this was interestingly not the case in curricular materials prepared by the Palestinian nationalist educator, 'Izzat Darwaza. His Arab history textbook included a discussion of Khula bint al-Azwar, who led a group of women in the battle of Yarmouk, and invited students to compare her heroic deeds with the lowly condition of Muslim women in their day (Darwaza, 1929). Darwaza served as principal of the Najah National School in Nablus from 1922–1927. He was later one of the founding members of the Istiqlal nationalist party. For more on Darwaza's political activities, see Matthews, 2006.
15. Like other curricular and pedagogical materials, this text was borrowed from the Egyptian education system, however it remained in use even after the original Palestinian syllabus (based on the Egyptian model) was revised. Thus the 1925 Elementary School Syllabus specifies, "the teacher of Quran and Moslem Religious Instruction should read carefully pages 15 and 17 of the '*Irshadatu 'l 'Amalieh*' on the teaching of Quran and Moslem Religion" (DoE, 1925, p. 71).
16. For an alternate interpretation of the functional role of memorizing the Qur'an, see Boyle, 2007.

Bibliography

'Abduh, M. (1993). la'iha islah al-ta'lim al-'othmani. In M. 'Imarah (Ed.), *Al-A'mal al-kamila li al-Imam al-Shaykh Muhammad 'Abduh*. Beirut: Dar al-Shuruq.

Anidjar, G. (2006). Secularism. *Critical Inquiry, 33*(1), 52–77.

Asad, T. (2003). *Formations of the secular: Christianity, Islam, modernity*. Stanford, CA: Stanford University Press.

Beidas, S. (1911). Al-ta'lim fi al-Qurah, *Filistin*, 16 Tamuz.

Bentwich, J. S. (1965). *Education in Israel*. Philadelphia: The Jewish Publication Society of America.

Bowman, H. (1942). *Middle East Window*. London: Longmans.

Boyle, H. N. (2007). Memorization and Learning in Islamic Schools. In W. K. a. V. Billeh (Ed.), *Islam and education myths and truths* (pp. 172–189). Chicago, IL: University of Chicago Press.

Darwaza, M. 'I. (1929). *Durūs Al-Tārikh Al-'Arabi Min Aqdam Al-Azmina Ila Al-Ān*. Cairo: al-mutba'a al-salfiya.

Davis, R. (2003). Commemorating education: Recollections of the Arab College in Jerusalem, 1918–1948, *Comparative Studies of South Asia, Africa and the Middle East 23*, no. 1–2.

Dirks, N. B. (2001). *Castes of mind: Colonialism and the making of modern India*: Princeton, NJ: Princeton University Press.

Education, M. o. P. (1920). *Irshadat al-'amaliya*. Cairo: Royal Printing Press (al-mutba' al-amiriya).

Elboim-Dror, R. (1986). *ha-Hinukh ha-'Ivri be-Erets-Yisrael*. Yerushalayim: Yad Yitshak Ben-Tsevi.

Farrell, J. (1946). *Notes on Jewish Education and the McNair Report*. November 30, 1946. TNA (The National Archive of the UK), CO/733/476/2.

Fitzgerald, T. (2000). *The ideology of religious studies*. Oxford: Oxford University Press.

Fleischmann, E. (2003). *The nation and its "new" women: The Palestinian women's movement, 1920–1948*. Berkeley: University of California Press.

Government of Egypt, Ministry of Public Education (1920). "*irshādāt al-'amaliya*." Cairo: Royal Printing Press (al-mutba' al-amiriya).

Government of Palestine, Department of Education. *Annual reports, 1924–25–1945–46*. Jerusalem.

Government of Palestine, Department of Education (1921). *Syllabus for state elementary schools for boys in towns and villages*. Jerusalem.

Government of Palestine, Department of Education (1925). *Elementary school syllabus* (Revised edition). Jerusalem.

Government of Palestine, Department of Education (1929). *Note on education in Palestine 1920–1929*. Jerusalem.

Government of Palestine (1933). Education ordinance.

Habermas, J. (June 18, 2008). Notes on a post-secular society, *Signandsight.com*. Retrieved from http://www.signandsight.com/features/1714.html

Khalidi, R. (2006). *The iron cage: The story of the Palestinian struggle for statehood* (1st ed.). Boston: Beacon Press.

Latour, B. (1993). *We have never been modern*. Cambridge, MA: Harvard University Press.

Makdisi, U. S. (2000). *The culture of sectarianism: Community, history, and violence in nineteenth-century Ottoman Lebanon*. Berkeley: University of California Press.

Matthews, W. C. (2006). *Confronting an empire, constructing a nation: Arab nationalists and popular politics in Mandate Palestine*. London and New York: I. B. Tauris.

Messick, B. (1996). *Calligraphic state*. Berkeley: University of California Press.

Miller, Y. N. (1985). *Government and society in rural palestine 1920–1948*, Modern Middle East Series. Austin: University of Texas Press.

Reshef, S. D. Y. (1999). *ha-Hinukh ha-`Ivri bi-yeme ha-bayit ha-leumi, 1919–1948*. Yerushalayim: Mosad Byalik.

Robson, L. (2011). *Colonialism and Christianity in Mandate Palestine* (1st ed.). Austin: University of Texas Press.

Schneider, S. (2013). Monolingualism and education in Mandate Palestine. *Jerusalem Quarterly*, Winter (52), 68–74.

Sheehan, J. (2005). *The Enlightenment bible*. Princeton, NJ: Princeton University Press.

Starrett, G. (1998). *Putting Islam to work*. Berkeley: University of California Press.

Testimony of Mr. H. E. Bowman, C. M. G., C. B. E., Director of Education. November 27, 1936. (1937) *Palestine Royal Commission minutes of evidence heard at public sessions*. London: His Majesty's Stationery Office.

Tibawi, A. L. (1956). *Arab education in Mandatory Palestine: A study of three decades of British administration*. London: Luzac.

Totah, K. (Nov. 1932). Education in Palestine. *Annals of the American Academy of Political and Social Science, 164, Palestine. A Decade of Development*, 156–166.

8. Palestinian Secular and Muslim Organizations' Educational Activism in Israel: Without, Within and Against

AYMAN K. AGBARIA & MUHANAD MUSTAFA

This chapter attempts to provide a comparative micro-level analysis of the involvement of two Palestinian civil society organizations in the field of education in the State of Israel, focusing on their ideology and practice vis-à-vis the State. Specifically, the chapter presents two instrumental case studies (Stake, 2000; Yin, 2003): The Follow-Up Committee on Arab Education (FUCAE)—a secular organization that operates under the auspices of the National Committee for Arab Mayors and aspires to represent Arab society as a whole—and Eqraa, the Association for the Promotion of Education in the Arab sector (Eqraa), a faith-based organization that is controlled by the Islamic Movement in Israel.

Specifically, the article compares the two organizations in terms of their ideological and functional differentiation, by juxtaposing their goals, strategies, arenas of action, and funding sources. For the most part, our goal is to illustrate the centrality of the dynamics of the presence and the absence of the State in the analysis of the engagement of the two organizations vis-à-vis the State in education. Most importantly, the article underscores the importance of Islamic religious ideals and rationales in generating collective action in the public sphere in Israel and highlights the role of Islamic perceptions of "civil society" and its links vis-à-vis the State in carving an alternative sub-State at the local community level and transnational at the global level, spaces, and routes for political mobilization, and educational activism. Moreover, as

Palestinian civil society organizations in Israel are often approached mono-lithically and with little scholarly attention to faith-based organizations (e.g., Haklai, 2011; Jamal, 2008; Payes, 2005), it is critical to recognize similarities and differences between secular and faith-based organizations.

The rest of the chapter is divided into three main sections. The first pro-vides the theoretical framework within which we will first explore the nexus between Islam and "civil society" and, second, clarify the background of the educational activism of Palestinian civil society in Israel. The second section introduces and compares FUCAE and Eqraa. Finally, in the third section, we present and discuss insights and conclusions that are derived from the com-parison between the two organizations.

Part 1: Theoretical Framework

Islam and civil society

Debates about religion's place within the public sphere and whether it indeed merits one, have become cross-disciplinary phenomena attracting the atten-tion of researchers from a variety of disciplines. The trend for a long time has been to uphold as normative the dichotomy pitting "religious/traditional" and "secular/modern" against one another, ignoring the historical and cul-tural specificity of secularism, religion, tradition, and modernity (Kaplan, 2005: 668) while simultaneously equating the notion of modernity with that of secularity—the disengagement and segregation of religion from the public sphere (Friedland, 2001: 127). This equation of secularity and modernity has led to a general belief among scholars in the decline of religion in social life, individual life and religious institutions.

Far from receding from the public sphere, however, as expected by sec-ularization theorists, religious actors and faith-based organizations appear to be gaining more and more salience while revitalizing new discourses of reli-giosity, spirituality and morality in public life and policy (Clarke, 2006; Wald, Silverman, & Fridy 2005). Specifically, since the rise of politicized Christian-ity and Islam in the 1970s (Emerson & Hartman, 2006; Sherkat & Ellison, 1999), it has become increasingly difficult to theorize the complexity of re-ligious phenomena from the lens of secularization theories (Philpott, 2009). It was not until the 1980s—when scholars such as Rodney Stark and William Sims Bainbridge published their seminal books (1985, 1987) and social move-ment theorists began to engage more robustly with religious movements (see more in Sherkat & Ellison, 1999)—that studies began to re-examine religious ideologies and institutions.

In this regard, a nuanced understanding of the current relationship between religion and the public sphere is delineated by Habermas (2006) who differentiates between what he calls the formal and informal public/political spheres, the former consisting of parliaments, courts and ministries, and the latter as being the appropriate setting for communication between religious and non-religious people. He maintains that although political institutions need to maintain neutrality with respect to religion, discourse between secular and religious citizens as well as those of different religions can and should utilize religious language and argument. Habermas entitled the reentrance of religion into the public square as a shift into what he pronounced a "post-secular age" (Habermas & Reemtsma, 2001 in Gorski & Altinordu, 2008). This was not meant to insinuate that the world was returning to a state where secularism and rationalism did not exist—rather, "one in which religious and secular worldviews could co-exist and even enter into dialogue with one another" (Habermas, 2006; Habermas & Mendieta, 2002 in Gorski & Altinordu, 2008: 56).

At the center of the scholarly attention to the religious actors' rationales and strategies in mobilizing their collective identities, narratives and solidarity is the complex interplay between religion, civil society and the State (Gorski & Altinordu, 2008; Grzymala-Busse, 2012). Notwithstanding the contested meanings of "civil society" (Kumar, 1993), it is safe to argue that civil society is a realm of associational and voluntary activity conducted by both domestic and foreign non-governmental organizations (NGOs). Its various manifestations include workers' unions, domestic and international NGOs, professional guilds, welfare organizations, educational activities, sports associations, etc. An ongoing debate exists within the civil society literature as to whether faith-based actors should be included in the realm of civil society. The until recently dominant liberal school of civil society excludes religious actors from this realm (Fukuyama, 1995). Yet, there is an evolving school of civil society which takes a more communitarian approach and sees civil society as containing non-liberal groups, including religious ones (Norris and Inglehart, 2003; Putnam and Campbell, 2010; Rubin, 2012; Tepe, 2008; Turam, 2007).

In the case of Islam, a legacy of nineteenth-century essentialist conceptions of Islam that ignores its internal diversity across regions and populations and that perceives it as anti-modern has led to many scholars to argue that Islam is antithetical and incompatible with democratic politics and norms (Huntington, 1991; Lewis, 1991). Conversely, other scholars have challenged the secularist notion that the strict exclusion of religion is a necessary condition of democracy, arguing that the major challenges against democracy result not from the Islamic political movements themselves but rather from the authoritarian States that repress them (see more in Gorski and Altinordu (2008, p. 70)).

In this regard, Turam (2004: p. 270) argues that in the literature on the entwined links between political Islam and the State, "Islam is interpreted as an all-encompassing 'fundamentalist' challenge to the existing secular order and juxtaposed against secular States." Further, "utilitarian secularist approaches argue that Islamic forces adapt 'strategically' to top-down secularism or become co-opted by the authoritarian State" (p. 270). All in all, Turam asserts that "the positioning of religion with regard to the State renders it incompatible with civil society and 'modern universalistic principles'" (p. 270). Although Islam's role in either propelling or undermining civil society has been largely assumed to be in conflict with the secular State (Turam, 2004), our own conviction is that religious actors should be understood as part of civil society, as a more inclusive perception of civil society would also embrace the diversity of the Islamic Movements as an integral part of the pluralistic public sphere (Eickelman, 2000).

In the literature on the development of civil societies in the Arab world there are two main approaches to understanding the importance and roles of civil society (Al-Sayyid, 1995; Ibrahim, 1995). Religious Islamic thought maintains that civil society existed in Islam well before it developed in Europe. According to this opinion, the role of Islamic civil society differed greatly from those of its Western counterparts (Moussalli, 1993). Counter to this, secular Arab opinion holds that civil society is a new development in the Arab world and should not be associated with the various civil and social structures which existed previously in Muslim societies (Bashara, 1996).

As such, Islamic thought perceives contemporary civil society organizations to be an influence of Western modernization on Arab society, which has successfully maintained its Islamic ideals. An examination of Islamic sources shows that at Islam's nascence the prophet Muhammad formed the first political community in Madina: the second holiest city in Islam, wherein Prophet Muhammad is buried, and the political and religious base of Islam in its formative period, being widely considered as the cradle of the early Muslim community (*Ummah*). However, this school of thought does not differentiate between a political community and civil society. Rather, the political community is referred to as a civil society in Islamic sources and is influenced by the Western social contract which holds that the establishment of the State is in fact the establishment of civil society. In addition, this opinion does not recognize the separation formed later between the State and the civil societies working within it (Ismail, 2003; Ibrahim, 2004). It is worth mentioning that the definition and significance of civil society, including that of the Arab secular school, is not a political community, but rather the existence and actions of social organizations which constitute a link in the chain which connects the State to the public (Abu-Zahir, 2008). Therefore, secular Arabs reject the claim that this was in fact a civil society. Ismail mentions that "the historical reality of political and social Islam did not have what we now call 'civil society'" (Ismail, 2003).

The parallel existing between religious and secular approaches in modern Arab thought have resulted in a new conceptualization of civil society. The secular approach refers to voluntary organizations, whereas the Islamic approach sees them as communitarian social organizations. The former seeks to affect the policy of the State's political system, while the latter focuses on changing the character of the community and galvanizing it. Another characteristic of these two models is that the civil arises mostly in cities, the communal in villages or rural areas. The former expresses modern relations of power and production; the latter, however, represents the traditional relations of power and production (tribe, clan, ethnicity, social, ethical structure) (Abu-Zahir (2008). We believe that this divide is overly dichotomous and does not account for the fact that the supporters of the Islamic Movement are usually of the middle-class, while their power sources are usually located in Arab cities and not in rural areas (Ibrahim, 2004).

It is important to note that when the Islamic Movements were rejected by the Arab regimes and excluded from the government they turned to social activism within the community through the foundation of charities, welfare centers, educational institutions, and cultural activities disassociated from the Arab State. These politics, which employ social and community organizations, were intended to rally the people's support and to provide assistance to the people in areas where the State was failing to do so adequately in order to strengthen the community and the political party. As such, Islamic intellectuals and theorists coined the term "Al-Muj'tama Al-A'hli" which means "the communitarian society," considered to be more authentic and Islamic, as opposed to civil society which seeks to affect State and policy, especially regarding the community (Tamimi, 2001).

With reference to the politics of difference as Islamic politics, it is important to underscore the recent trend in the Arab world of the Islamic movements to steadily transform into National-Islamic ones. The political parties that belong to the central Islamic stream are increasingly gaining recognition and implementing modern politics that are strengthened and founded on the modern nation State. Some examples include the adoption of the rhetoric and politics of the modern nation State as a replacement for the Islamic caliphate, values of democratization and democracy instead of theocracy, adherence to citizenship rather than the division between Muslims and "Dhimmis" (the non-Muslim population in Muslim state), and a struggle to establish a representative government rather than an elitist regime of clergymen. The existence of a nation State has forced these movements to actively participate in politics, integrate into processes of democratization, and abandon political violence instead adopting civil democratic tools to transform from religious-communitarian parties to modern political ones.

In the context of the State of Israel, the Islamic Movement cannot undergo these typical processes and adjustments in terms of the nation State. This is because there cannot be an "Israeli Islamic Movement": the national, or nation-State, dimension disappears from the ideological context of the conceptual development of political Islam in Israel. The Islamic Movement in Israel is neither a Palestinian national movement nor an Israeli national movement. The former is impossible because it is not part of the Palestinian National Movement or a future Palestinian State. In contrast, the secular Arab movements and parties in Israel participate in the debate on topics such as citizenship, equality, the Constitution and the identity of the State. They consider the reality of Israel as an underlying basic assumption, and this is reflected in their political and conceptual discourse (Agbaria & Mustafa, 2012). It is difficult for the Islamic Movement to relate to this reality, so it compensates for this disadvantage by engaging in the general, and more global, Islamic political discourse, which converges on Jerusalem and the Al-Aqsa Mosque.

Additionally, over the years the Islamic Movement has cultivated the concept of building an independent community, predicated on the establishment of Arab institutions and independent from State resources in all areas, including private education. Sheikh Raed Salah, head of the Islamic Movement, called this concept 'Al-Muj'tama' Al-A'sami', namely the 'self-reliant society', which is a dependent and autonomous community (Salah, 2006: 4). It should be noted that the idea has become popular among members of the Islamic Movement on the basis of the institutionalization of the Islamic Northern Faction as an external, anti-parliamentary movement which refuses to integrate into parliamentary politics. The Movement believes that building an Arab-Muslim community is the only solution for the Arab-Muslim minority in Israel. Indeed, the movement rejects all other proposed political solutions to regulate the majority–minority relationship, such as a State of all its citizens, a bi-national State, or various autonomy proposals (Agbaria & Mustafa, 2012). In this context, the words of Rabinowitz are particularly pertinent:

> The Islamic Movement...is completely alienated from the State, and will likely remain as such. It is likely that the alienation of Palestinian Israeli citizens from

State institutions, dominant market forces and accessibility to the media, will continue to strengthen their recognition in the potential of this triple power to produce evil. Such recognition may make them a group that strives to strengthen the elements of civil activity within it. If so, the organizational example of the Islamic Movement may act as inspiration for other movements, and inspire other more equal, tolerant and essential movements…The issue of education, including non-religious institutions…signaled to the public that the association was allocating its role in initiating advancements in a broad expanse of areas. This expansion of the meaning of the term "Islamic Movement," and applying it to matters unrelated to religion, has increased the political relevance of the association. (Rabinowitz, 2001: 350, 359–360)

Returning to the "self-reliant society" coined by Sheikh Raed Salah, it is based on three principles which he recognizes as already existing within Arab society: science or human capital, the land, and the economy (Ali, 2007). In particular, Salah emphasizes the "purity of the capital" which should originate from strictly Islamic sources including charities, the Waqf, and donations from organizations and Muslim individuals. This purity also demands the rejection of contributions from non-Islamic entities due to the concern that accepting foreign funding may render the Movement vulnerable and indebted to the ulterior motives of foreign entities who seek value in exchange for their money, threatening the Movement's independence. The external-parliamentary Islamic Movement moreover claims that non-Muslim donations are explicitly "impure" and seek to change the face and identity of the Muslim community (Ali, 2004). In this context, Haklai (2004a) argues that Arab organizations that accept donations from foreign, particularly Jewish, funds are designed to strengthen the civilian dimension of the struggle of Arabs in Israel and support these organizations in the framework of a democratic Jewish State. Haklai perceives the agenda of Jewish foundations to be maintaining the Jewish character of the State by improving the status and condition of Arabs on the civil level (Haklai, 2004a). Lack of independent funding for Arab organizations is considered to be a significant challenge facing Arab civil society, because dependence on foreign funds may prove to be dangerous should an economic crisis befall or a conflict arise between the agenda of the funding bodies and that of the organization (Jabareen, 2007).

The overall Arab-Islamic dimension plays an important role in the autonomous "self- reliant society" project. Sheikh Salah argues that the establishment of such a society, or community, requires that the relationship between the Arab world and Muslim nation at large be further cemented. This may indicate that the external-parliamentary Islamic Movement sees itself as part of the Muslim nation not only in symbolic-cultural terms but also in the practical sense. The connection between the establishment of an independent Muslim community in Israel and deepening the relationship with the Islamic world points to the ideological orientation of the external-parliamentary movement as one which denies the uniqueness of the condition and status of Muslims in Israel, instead perceiving their status to be an integral part of the global political Islam movements. On the other hand, the parliamentary movement believes that Muslims in Israel are in fact in a unique situation, and political Islam in Israel is a unique political context which demands special attention from the perspective of Muslims in Israel.

Palestinian civil society in Israel and education

In many western countries, the last few decades of social policy can be characterized by increasing liberalization and privatization, leading to rising involvement of the civil society organizations (Savas, 2000). The dynamics between these organizations and the State have been pivotal to many studies that suggest different typologies to analyze the intertwined relationship between both (Anheier, 2001a, 2001b; Anheier, Glasius & Kaldor 2003; Coston, 1998; Najam, 2000; Yishai, 1991, 1998; Keane, 2004). For example, according to Najam's typology (2000), this relationship can take four forms: a) Cooperation, when the State and the civil society organization agree on goals and strategies; b) Complementarity, an agreement regarding goals but not strategies; c) Co-optation, when civil society and State disagree on goals but share similar strategies; and d) Confrontation, disagreement both on goals and strategies.

In the context of Arab civil society in Israel, Doron (1996) claims that there are two separate civil societies in Israel. These societies operate in different circles and do not maintain a meaningful relationship between them. Civil society in Israel, according to this critical approach, is not uniform but is divided along nationalistic lines. Following Payes (2005), in consideration of the fact that Arab civil society was not recognized as nor included in the Jewish-Zionist project, we would like to promote the discussion of Palestinian civil society as an "ethnic civil society" that is actively, continuously, and systematically excluded by the State (Haklai, 2004b).

Without detracting from the importance of its early days (Payes, 2005), the last three decades have witnessed considerable momentum in the formation and role of Palestinian civil society organizations in promoting processes of democratization, empowerment, and community development (Jamal, 2008). Most importantly, since the 1990s, especially after the Oslo Accords, these organizations have been major players not only in struggles for civil equality, deepening political awareness, and promoting socio-economic mobility in Arab society (Jamal, 2008), but also in gearing the recent ethno-national turn in the evolution of the Palestinian political activism in Israel to end the Jewish ethnic hegemony (Haklai, 2011). This new transformation of the political discourse among Palestinians in Israel is marked by the transition from the politics of inequality and grievance to the politics of recognition and belonging. Oded Haklai characterizes this transition as ethno-national, pointing to the politicization of indigenousness of the Palestinian minority as a platform upon which demands for collective rights, including in education, are raised to concede more power-sharing, recognition, and equality. All in all, these demands seek to end the Jewish ethnic hegemony and transform Israel into a bi-national State.

Arab civil society organizations operate in every aspect of Arab society, including education, culture, health, welfare, entertainment and leisure, religion, law, and the status of women (Chorev, 2008). Specifically, data presented by The Israeli Center for Third Sector Research shows an increase in the number of non-profit organizations listed in the field of education. For example, in 2007, a majority of non-profit organizations were listed as educational (28%), followed by organizations listed as cultural (19%), and housing and development (10%) (Balbetchan, 2008). On average, one organization exists per every thousand Arab citizens, a ratio that is one-quarter of that in the Jewish sector (Gidron & Elon, 2007). As for religious organizations, Chorev (2008, p. 43) states:

> The sector of Arab NGOs includes many religious organizations. These organizations perform religious services yet they engage in welfare, development and education activities as well. Their methods and courses of action characterize civil society organizations. However, religious goals and motives have precedence in these organizations' activity and they do not necessarily adhere to the underlying idea of civic equality.... In addition, they tend not to register officially. For these reasons, religious organizations were not included in the current survey.

As for Arab education, it is often described as suffering from inequality in the allocation of State resources, lack of recognition of the cultural needs of the Palestinian minority, and marginalizing the Arab leadership's influence on education policy (see Jabareen & Agbaria, 2010). Under these conditions, it is not surprising that Dan Ben-David (2010), who examined the educational achievements of Israeli pupils in the 2009 PISA (the Program for International Student Assessment), stated: "The achievement levels of Arab Israelis were below those of Third World countries such as Jordan, Tunisia, Indonesia, Kazakhstan, Brazil and Colombia" (p. 9).

Therefore, Palestinian civil society organizations have become increasingly more significant, varied, independent, and proactive in their campaign to improve the outcomes of Arab education and to provide alternative and complementary curricula, especially in citizenship and history studies, that counter the Israeli continuous efforts to impose the Zionist narrative (see more in Agbaria, 2010). However, the nexus between literature on Arab education (Mari, 1978; Al-Haj, 1995; Abu-Asbeh, 2007; Jabareen and Agbaria, 2010) and Arab civil society in Israel (Haklai, 2011; 2004a, 2004b; Payes, 2005; Jamal, 2008) remains unexplored. Moreover, the existing scholarship on both topics generally utilizes a top-down approach, as do the majority of social sciences research on Arab society in Israel (Sa'di, 2004). Correspondingly, research frequently focuses on State policy and practice and their implications for Arab society in Israel, often perceived as a monolithic object which has restricted autonomy, political and cultural dependence, and a limited capacity to contend. Thus, Arab education and Arab civil society have been examined only on a theoretical, macro level vis-à-vis the State and its actions. Accordingly, this chapter attempts to provide micro-level insight on the activities of two civil society organizations in the field of education, focusing on their goals and strategies of educational activism vis-à-vis the State and the local Palestinian minority. In what follows, we will present both organizations and compare the two.

Part 2: Two Case Studies

Follow-up committee on Arab education

Located in Nazareth, The Follow-Up Committee on Arab Education (FUCAE) was established in 1948 as a non-profit organization. Assuming a representative role, the FUCAE operates under the auspices of the National Committee for Arab Mayors and the Supreme Follow-Up Committee for Palestinian Arabs in Israel. Formally, FUCAE is comprised of representatives from Arab local authorities in Israel, as well as school principals, educators, and public figures. Effectively, however, many potential representatives, especially those affiliated with political parties and movements, have refrained from official membership in FUCAE due to the dominance of The Democratic Front for Peace and Equality (Hadash) on the FUCAE Board of Directors and professional staff. A number of recent media reports indicate the desire of a number of political parties in the High Follow-Up Committee for Arab Citizens of Israel to establish an alternative committee to FUCAE.[1]

The primary objective of FUCAE, according to their official website, is to advance Arab education based on the belief that each and every child has the fundamental right to education and equal opportunity to realize his or her abilities and talents and fulfillment-self. The Committee identifies four main goals: (1) equal education for Arabs and Jews in all aspects of life, including the physical surroundings and infrastructures of the educational institutions, their budgets and resources, standards, and achievements; (2) amendment of the existing framework and objectives of Arab education and initiation of educational and cultural policy in order to increase the Arab public's involvement in deciding on educational and cultural policy; (3) development of Arab students' national-cultural identity; and (4) increased Arab and Israeli public awareness regarding the condition of Arab education.[2]

Eqraa

The Eqraa Association, established in 1996, is an Islamic organization that belongs to the Northern Faction of the Islamic Movement. The Northern Faction formed Eqraa in order to improve their position among Arab students in institutions for higher education throughout Israel. In its nascence, Eqraa, based in the city of Umm al-Fahm, espoused religious ideals and provided various services including financial assistance to Arab students. During these early stages, Eqraa disassociated itself from political activity in universities, focusing instead on social and religious activism (Mustafa, 2011).

Over the years, Eqraa's horizons have expanded with the addition of new departments and a widening scope of services provided to its target audience, i.e., Arab students. This expansion included supporting scientific research, providing scholarships, and founding a new institute that specialized in preparing prospective students for the psychometric examination required for admission to most universities. As part of its expansion, Eqraa began to participate in Arab students' politics, taking part in the Arab Student Council elections in Haifa and Tel Aviv Universities, achieving remarkable results. For example, at the 2007 elections held at Haifa University, Eqraa received 34% of Arab student votes, which increased to 39% in 2011. At Tel Aviv University, Eqraa received 47% of the Arab students' votes (Mustafa, 2011: 155–156).

The objectives of Eqraa, as they appear on their official website, combine both individual and collective dimensions. Individual aspects include increasing religious and national awareness as well as providing academic and professional guidance and financial support. Goals pertaining to the collective dimension include enhancing Arab education via an aggregate composed of special educational programs, advancing future Arab leadership, and promoting culture in Arab society.

Comparison between FUCAE and Eqraa

To distinguish between different types of secular and faith-based organizations in civil society, Boesenecker and Vinjamuri (2011) suggest highlighting functional and ideological differentiation. In our case, ideological differentiation refers to how the State is conceptualized and approached. Relatedly, it also signifies the ideological perspective upon which the engagement vis-à-vis the State and the local community is predicated. The second concept, functional differentiation, refers specifically to the varied strategies different organizations in civil society employ in navigating the boundary between the State and the local community. Accordingly, we present in this section a comparison between the two organizations, Eqraa and FUCAE, based on these two categories: ideological and functional differentiation.

Ideological differentiation

FUCAE aspires to change State institutions' policies and practices of resource allocation and cultural recognition vis-à-vis the Palestinian minority in Israel, seeking specifically to realize equal rights in education. Elsewhere on its website, FUCAE states that:

> Among the principal objectives FUCAE strives to achieve are realizing equality for Arab education and enhancing it on all levels, following-up the performance of the educational Arab system in terms of organizational structure, efficacy and qualification, pedagogic policy and administration, and raising the awareness of the parents and the community to the educational process as well as promoting their involvement, aiming by this to change the condition and situation of Arab education on all levels starting with changing its objectives, structure, content, curricula, and enhancing its physical and professional infrastructure, and ending with achieving substantive equality and equality of opportunities in state budget and resource allocation."[3]

In opposition to this inclination to the citizenship framework of equality and recognition politics, Eqraa seems indifferent, as it avoids even naming Israel explicitly when referring to the Palestinian minority in Israel. Instead of "Arab society in Israel," the term used by FUCAE, Eqraa opts to use the term "Palestinian Interior" (in Arabic: al-Dakhel al- Falsteni), which does not recognize the Israeli affiliation of this minority. As for Eqraa objectives, mention of equal citizenship is absent. Thus, while FUCAE emphasizes the right to equal education, particularly demanding collective rights of self-administration and cultural autonomy that would allow a more substantial participation of the Arab leadership in education policy and decision-making cycles and substantive recognition of the Palestinian narrative,

Eqraa makes no reference whatsoever to demands of citizenship, equality or recognition.

For example, Eqraa's objectives do not compare Arab and Jewish education, nor do they seek to obtain higher budgets from the State. Instead, the first objective of Eqraa is "to support education in the Palestinian territories (i.e., the Arabs in Israel [the authors]), and address education as a central value and a tool enabling strength and stability" (Eqraa Association, Yearly Report 2006–2007: 6–7). As this quote demonstrates, Eqraa aspires to advance Arab education, without endeavoring to change State policy regarding it. The focus of Eqraa is to provide financial support obtained directly from the community. For this reason, Eqraa advocates alternative educational structures, financial and educational assistance to Arab students, and the privatization of the Arab education system (Mustafa, 2011). Eqraa's second objective is to "heighten the religious and national awareness of Arab students and preserve their Islamic and Arab identities." In an annual report published by Eqraa, their activity is said to be motivated by an attempt "to strengthen ties and restore faith between the Arab intellectuals and other social classes, especially students, in an effort to consolidate their respective roles in constructing society and become leaders in its re-establishment" (Yearly Report 2009–2010: 2).

Islamic organizations are predicated on the view that Islamic communal society organizations do not constitute a link between the individual/society and the State. Rather, they are intended to fill a void created by the State's retreat in certain areas including health, education, and welfare that the State does not sufficiently provide. Regardless of whether it derives from negligence, discrimination, or neoliberal privatization, the State's retreat is tantamount to an instrument for ethnic control which exacerbates the already weak position of the Palestinian minority by reinforcing its inferior status in the hierarchy of differential citizenship in Israel and increasing its reliance on State-provided resources. Therefore, the transition into these areas is not merely a complementary social service; it is first and foremost an act of confrontation and dissension. Islamic organizations compete with the State in instances when the latter's actions are inconsistent with their ideology. Chief among these is education, a field in which Islamic communal society competes with the State in setting goals, curricula, and determining the sociological processes required for students. Thus, the establishment of private institutions in the area of education relies on this conception of Islamic organizations (Hassan, 2000).

FUCAE, however, does perceive itself to be a link between Arab society and the State with regard to education. It sees itself as a civil-lobbying body which expresses the voice of Arab education to State authorities in an attempt to advance the status and achievements of Arab education. The desire of FUCAE to cooperate with the Ministry of Education in defining their goals and expectations is one of the committee's primary objectives.

Functional differentiation

While Eqraa's main area of activity is the Arab public and its students—Muslims in particular—FUCAE focuses on the civil arena of decision- and policy-making, such as Arab educators and school principals, the Ministry of Education, the Israeli Parliamentary Education Committee, and Israeli politicians. It should be noted that this difference does not indicate that the FUCAE disparages Arab society; rather, the direct object of its activity is the Israeli establishment. Even if certain activity is carried out directly with the Arab public, the goal remains to pressure the Israeli establishment into policy change on a given issue.

For example, in 2010, FUCAE published a study report revealing that the psycho-metric examination required for entrance into most Israeli colleges and universities was culturally discriminatory and that a significant disparity exists between the test results of Arabs and Jews (Mustafa, 2011). The report was distributed to members of Parliament, the Ministry of Education, and the National Institution for Testing and Evaluation. The various actions taken, internal and external to Arab society, in response to these findings were intended to raise awareness and apply public pressure on the Establishment in order to help improve the scores of the Arabs taking the test. In contrast, when Eqraa addressed this issue it opted not to form interest groups or undertake research and publish position papers on the subject. Instead, Eqraa formed a professional organization to help prepare Arab students for the examination, which now offers services to thousands of Arab students at reduced fees.[4] In essence, as opposed to FUCAE's wish to change policy regarding admission of Arab students to Israeli colleges and redesign the test format, Eqraa trains and prepares students for the existing format of the examination in order to increase their admission rates.

As stated in the introduction, FUCAE does not operate only in the civil arena, but the national one as well. Therefore, though the Committee does aim its activity toward achieving meaningful equality in the civil arena, it also works toward the national- communal aspects of empowering Palestinian society and strengthening its inner mechanisms, albeit to a lesser extent. For instance, Project Access, funded by the American Embassy in Israel, is a FUCAE program intended to help Arab students master the English language. Another such FUCAE project is Education for Identity. Through educational materials, newsletters, and short papers the project seeks to instill a deeper sense of national identity and familiarity with the Palestinian historical narrative.

As can be expected, the different strategies adopted by each organization derive from their respective areas of activity. Eqraa neither attempts to affect governmental policy toward Arab society nor does it coordinate its efforts with State authorities. Instead, Eqraa initiates independent programs and projects in order to advance Arab education in Israel. FUCAE, on the other hand, works primarily with the Ministry of Education and other government bodies which have influence on Arab education. The foreword to Eqraa's 2010 Yearly Report includes the following statement by Association Chair Nissim Badarna:

> Eqraa is interested in improving the educational achievements of our Palestinian children, disseminating the culture, and providing quality education on an individual basis in fields for which our community has a demand. For this purpose, the Association has initiated large- scale projects, including Torches of Light, an educational guidance project, and professional courses for students which focus on developing skills amongst our children.. All these, in order to overcome racial discrimination against Arab students...

This statement indicates Eqraa's focus on initiating independent and informal education projects aimed directly at Arab students, families, and communities without intervention by schools or the Ministry of Education. This direct approach, which supersedes the Ministry of Education, exempts Eqraa from the bureaucracy and obstacles within the education system as well as from its supervision and control. More than anything, the strategy of working in direct contact with its target community expresses Eqraa's tenet of self-empowerment, whereby the barriers of discrimination against Arab education can be overcome through corporate and communal initiatives within the Arab community in order to build an intellectual elite committed to the values of Islam and personal excellence.

For this purpose, Eqraa offers a wide array of professional courses in dozens of Arab schools in order to improve the achievements of Arab students. The aforementioned Torches of Light project is comprised of a number of informal courses intended for primary schools in the Arab education system. Likewise, Eqraa supports independent community-run schools, principally private high schools. In this sense, Eqraa is supportive of the privatization of Arab education, whereas FUCAE takes a much firmer stance against it and believes privatization is the cause of corrosion within the national community and the cohesion between its various segments. As Nabbiyh Abu Salleh, former Chair of the FUCAE, eloquently notes: "Privatization is extremely dangerous for the education of our children...some organizations come together on the basis of ethnicity, religion, politics, and tribe. These destroy our attempts to maintain universal educational values."[5]

Worthy of note is the educational activity undertaken by Eqraa to improve the academic performance of Arab students through study sessions, tutoring, and preparatory courses for the psychometric examination that conveys its underlying belief in the power and validity of the neoliberal ethos. Inherent to this ethos is the risk of a decrease in the social and political role of education, particularly in primary and high schools, in the socialization process of students. As the individual achievements of each student becomes prioritized by schools, so too declines their investment in shaping a collective identity for the student body. Nonetheless, it is important to understand that the pursuit of the goals championed by neoliberal policy depletes Arab education of its social and communal capacity and engenders a depoliticization of Arab education. Moreover, it perpetuates values of aggressive individualism manifest in the process of stratification and selectivity currently on the rise in the Arab education system (Agbaria & Mahajnah, 2009). For this reason, Eqraa promotes activity directed toward character education predicated on religious conservatism.

More specifically, Eqraa focuses on education for morality (al-Akhlak) in the limited sense of the daily behavior of people and tailors this to Islamic values as they perceive them. In recent years, this type of morality preaching has taken on a prominent role in their activity. For example, in the May 2011 elections at Haifa University, Eqraa attacked activists from the secular Arab parties (Balad and Hadash) because of the latter's inappropriate behavior (organizing parties attended by both sexes, drinking alcohol, immodest dress, etc.). This is significant as it indicates that Eqraa links together politics and morals, termed "the political discourse of morals." This discourse maintains that there is a close relationship between the ability to serve the community and the morals of those who serve. According to Eqraa, whoever does not possess these certain morals "cannot in good faith serve the community." Additionally, this discourse observes the way in which this moral dimension contributes to the political recruitment of Arab students, many of whom support Eqraa specifically because of their politics of morals and not necessarily due to ideological or political affiliation (Mustafa, 2011). The power of these politics is that they possess significant symbolic and political strength, and these are perceived to be monopolized by Eqraa. On the other hand, as previously mentioned, Eqraa also operates within the discourse of achievement. Therefore, Eqraa positions a collective value against, adjacent to, and together with a distinctly individualistic one.

As an Islamic organization which perceives itself as an internal-community organization, Eqraa emphasizes the importance of funding and the sensitivities surrounding this issue, which are not pronounced in FUCAE. Eqraa emphasizes the importance of internal and external Islamic funding from the community within which it works, as opposed to foreign funding. This is not a technical issue for Eqraa, rather a fundamental one, seen as a main contributor to its legitimization in its own eyes as well as those of the community supporting it.

The Islamic community to which the Eqraa association belongs has at its forefront the issue of funding as an essential element in its political ideology. This has increased especially in the last decade as Arab civil society organizations began to develop and take on prominence. Funding is seen as a crucial aspect of the question of the legitimacy of Arab organizations to the extent that those organizations which do accept funding from foreign sources, Jewish funds in particular, are deemed by Eqraa as illegitimate. The centrality of the source of funding is also vital to the Islamic Movement's ability to recruit from within the local community. While Eqraa's high recruitment is enabled partly by the religious aspects of its recruitment policies, the secular civil society organizations, including FUCAE, have virtually no community recruitment to speak of as a result of their foreign sources of funding. Although FUCAE is meant to represent educational policy for all Arabs in Israel, and is sponsored by representative Arab institutions, it does not perceive foreign funding as being detrimental nor as creating a conflict of interest with its activity in the areas of Arab educational policy, including projects geared to education, to national identity, or that of the pedagogical council. FUCAE depends almost entirely on foreign funding and does not emphasize its importance, while the same issue is central for Eqraa.

Part 3: Discussion

Turam (2004, p. 276) asserts:

> The key to understanding the relationship between Islam and civil society is the State…. Since democracies have the potential to become sporadically uncivil and intolerant, the proliferation of civil society depends largely on State–society interaction. This applies particularly to the actual and prospective transformations of State–Islam interaction from State repression to negotiation and cooperation in secular republics.

Accordingly, we argue that Palestinian civil society as it applies to politics of identity and difference should not be approached monolithically when its engagement vis-à-vis the State is analyzed. We believe that FUCAE is a prime example of an organization motivated by State-centered politics of difference, whereas Eqraa represents more community-centered politics. As both organizations are engaged in politics of recognition or, more precisely, the politics of demanding recognition of the difference between the group demanding recognition and other groups, both vary in three key facets: (1) the arenas in which they locate their difference—the groups they wish to differ from and within; (2) the use of difference—the politics through which they wish to accentuate and/or conceal their various distinguishing boundaries within and as opposed to the groups from, or within, which they wish to distinguish themselves; and (3) the destination of difference—the underlying goal which motivates their politics to accentuate and/or conceal their differentiation.

FUCAE represents the quintessence of the politics of contention: opposing the Jewish democratic State hegemony; calling for the establishment of an encompassing, secular Palestinian Israeli identity; and demanding national recognition and differential group rights. FUCAE and other similar organizations[6] seek to achieve these goals with capacities that the hegemonic discourse allows; they seek change from within, using the tools and opportunities that democracy—e.g., protest, litigations, and lobbying—provides based on the exclusive nature of the State as a Jewish State. In other words, organizations characterized by a "within and against" approach place the State at the center of their socio-political efforts in order to raise the quality of life and obtain equal allocation of material and symbolic resources, substantial recognition in historic and social narratives, and inclusion in decision-making within Arab society.

On the other hand, Eqraa exemplifies a different type of organization. This type also uses politics of difference; yet it is characteristic of the Islamic organizations that operate primarily through a wide network of institutions in social fields (such as community development, welfare, and education) in areas and communities that are often neglected and marginalized by the State. While it is typical of the Islamic Movement to be active in realms such as kindergartens or charity- and mosque-run youth groups (Rabinowitz, 2001), Eqraa is novel in that it represents the transition of the Islamic Movement's orientation from local to national activity. Moreover, this type of organization constitutes a new breed which places Arab society, or central parts of it, at the focus of their activity. These organizations promote politics of difference which resist the hegemonic discourse of a democratic-Jewish State from without, rather than from within. Put differently, these "without and against" organizations endeavor to empower Arab society from the inside and construct an integrative Islamic-Palestinian identity that is sectarian and specifically Muslim within Palestinian society in Israel.[7] It is important to note that this type of organization often operates in complete separation, alienation if you will, from State policy and government practices toward Arab society.

Organizations of these two types indeed initiate similar activities and projects, such as conferences, seminars, round tables, educational tours, educational programming, and use of internet and media, etc. Nonetheless, their goals and strategies greatly differ from one another. Although both make use of the tools provided by contentious politics, which have become dominant in Arab politics and civil society organizations (Jamal, 2007; 2008), each one uses these tools differently. The "within and against" type is interested in ultimately redefining the content and limits of Israeli citizenship. It demands redistribution of the common good, including material and symbolic State resources using strategies of advocacy, lobbying, applied research, and media campaigns. In contrast, the second type, "without and against," seeks to reaffirm the collective identity of Arab society as Palestinian whilst underscoring the religious Islamic facets of this identity and empowering societal capacities for resistance and self-reliance by strategies such as community development, raising national and religious awareness, professional training, and providing quality education. For the purpose of this chapter the former type is referred to as Arab civil society organizations whereas the latter as Arab communitarian organizations.

FUCAE operates in two central arenas: the national arena of the Palestinians in Israel and the civil arena of the State of Israel. In the national arena, FUCAE struggles to empower Palestinian society and strengthen it from within; whereas in the civil arena it struggles against the State's policies and practices that are geared to control Arab education and remove its curricula from national content. Eqraa, too, works in the national arena, focusing especially on the Islamic community within, but not in the civil one. Instead, it operates in the global arena of the political Islam movements. Being active in separate arenas limits the organizations' cooperation and competition. Likewise, working in the shared national arena does not seem to create tension or, conversely opportunity for collaboration.

Their ability to work in the same arena, while simultaneously maintaining independent and separate activities in different spheres within it, may be explained by their divergent use of politics of difference. FUCAE acts as a representative of the Palestinian society in Israel and thus obscures the differentiating borders between the different religious and cultural factions within it. As such, FUCAE prioritizes a joint national identity of Palestinian society in Israel, utilizing this blurring of borders in order to advance its agenda in the State arena, which is indisputably its chief area of activity, to confront State policies of marginalization and discrimination.

Overlooking the sectarian identities, whether religious or local, of the Palestinians in Israel provides legitimacy to FUCAE to speak on behalf of the entire Palestinian society, leaving a wide berth for independent and sartorial activities of other organizations. Eqraa is an example of such an organization which operates primarily within Islamic communities while highlighting Islamic religious identity. In this context, Eqraa rarely operates within the State arena and does not directly confront polices of discrimination and marginalization by, for example, trying to influence legislation, government policy, or court ruling. As such, Eqraa draws clear sartorial borders within Palestinian society and concedes the arena of Israeli society and State authorities moving instead toward a global Islamic, albeit limited, one.

As opposed to this, FUCAE confronts State policies within the State arena, employing a double technique of both marking and blurring boundaries. FUCAE highlights one overreaching national identity and obfuscates sartorial and religious boundaries to demand recognition of the collective Palestinian identity as a national and indigenous minority entitled to collective rights especially in education and cultural matters. Yet, worth noting, as it strives toward two complementary yet rival goals—civil integration and national differentiation—FUCAE indeed demands civil equality for the single Arab student as an Israeli citizen and national equality for a group of Arab students as belonging to the Palestinian–Arab nationality.

However, the goals of Eqraa, in drawing clear boundaries within Palestinian society and Israeli institutions and society, are inherently different. Eqraa employs politics of difference not in order to achieve national or civil equality but rather to internally advance the capacities of Palestinian society, and its Islamic subgroup in particular, as well as to widen the sphere of influence of the Islamic Movement in general Palestinian society in Israel. For this purpose, Eqraa seeks to advance recognition of a unique Islamic identity through education which emphasizes Islamic conduct and morality as well as by strengthening ties with the global Islamic community, specifically the Turkish model for modern Islamic politics.

Although the Islamic Movement mobilizes alternative and complementary institutions for State services that compensate for neglect and discrimination, it likewise directs the activities of such institutions, Eqraa especially, toward increasing the chances for individual economic mobility by increasing access to higher education. Eqraa is a distinctly neoliberal organization whose vocabulary is firmly rooted in Islamic education (prioritizing conduct and morality according to Islam) and which champions financial, academic, and personal excellence. In other words, Eqraa expresses an ethos of aggressive individualism: the belief that empowering the individual harbors the potential to ultimately overcome both the exclusion mechanism instituted by the State and the structural barriers which prevent upward mobility toward social and financial success. In so doing, Eqraa ascribes to the Muslim Brotherhood's doctrine of progress that maintains that individual education is the first stage in the process of Islamic resurrection of Muslim society in accordance with the teachings of Islam and nation (Mitchell, 1969). Thus, Eqraa advocates a bottom-up approach to change that perceives collective prosperity of a Muslim society as a direct outcome of the successes of the individuals who belong to that society as opposed to the top-down approach often employed by FUCAE that advocates, for the most part, changing society from above through State policies.

One should bear in mind that both FUCAE and Eqraa operate in the shadow of the various policies and practices of privatization and neoliberal education policies (Dagan-Buzaglo, 2010; Agbaria and Mahajnah, 2009). Accelerated privatization, deepening the inequality between Arabs and Jews, and the deteriorating quality of Arab education have culminated in an abandonment of Arab State education by religious and private sources in Arab society (Agbaria and Mahajnah, 2009; Keidar, 2010). For example, in the search for high quality education, the Islamic Movement has founded a selective and competitive high school (Keidar, 2010). Yet, the rising number of educational initiatives of the Islamic Movement is not merely the result of privatization and the contentious politics of identity (Ali, 2004) but also a genuine Islamic expression of the role of philanthropy and civil society organization in Islam, as outlined earlier.

To conclude, we believe that the struggle between the two approaches is ultimately a struggle for political hegemony in Arab society: the struggle between the religious-communitarian approach (represented by Eqraa and the Islamic Movement) and that of the civic-State (FUCAE and Hadash). At the center of this struggle is the issue of citizenship in Israel. While the politics of FUCAE are still disputing the boundaries and content of citizenship, the politics of Eqraa forego what they believe to be an irrelevant attempt to change the game, preferring to focus on empowering Arab society independently. This struggle also shapes two conflicting approaches with regard to the improvement of Arab education in Israel: Should Palestinian civil society seek equality and recognition from the State or should it focus more on capacity building and empowering self-reliant educational institutions? As there is no simple answer to this question, it remains a valid questions that demands further scholarly attention.

Notes

1. For example, an acerbic article by Kamal Khatib, Vice-President of the Islamic Movement in Israel, speaks out against the activity of FUCAE and its attempts to present itself as a representative committee for Arab educational matters. The article was written subsequent to FUCAE's publication of the "Arab Educational Goals" (Newspaper of the Islamic Movement, Al-hak, and Alhoria Team, "the Pedagogical Council was born illegitimately and we do not recognize its roots" 19/11/2011, p. 4). This article sharpens our claim regarding the rivalry between the Islamic Movement and the FUCAE for authority in the local arena.
2. http://arab-education.org/
3. http://arab-education.org/?page_id=663
4. On the Eqraa Association website. See the psychometric exam/psychometry-http://www.eqraa.com/projects/eqraa
5. See Yuli Harumchenko on this in the Ha'Aretz Newspaper, 20/9/05.
6. Similar organizations to FUCAE include the Masuau Institute for Arab civil rights, The Adallah Legal Institute for Arab Minority Rights, the Arab Center for Alternative Planning, and others
7. It is important to note that political Islam in the Arab world offers the Islamic, political framework as one which can encompass non-Muslims not merely on the cultural level (Islam as a regional and local culture), but on a political-governmental level as well. As such, the Islamic political platform is directed at all citizens. This can be explained by the fact that political Islam constitutes a socio-cultural alternative as well as a political and governing alternative. In Israel political Islam is not a political alternative, rather primarily a cultural one (Ayubi, 1991).

References

Abu-Asbeh, K. (2007). Arab education in Israel: Dilemmas of a national minority, Jerusalem: Florscheim Institute. (in Hebrew).

Abu-Zahir, N. (2008). Civil Society between descriptive and normative: Deconstructing a conceptual muddle. Ramaalah: Muwaten the Palestinian Institute for the Study of Democracy. (in Arabic).

Agbaria, A. (2010). Civic education for the Palestinians in Israel: Dilemmas and challenges. In H. Alexander, H. Pinson, & Y. Yonah (Eds.), *Citizenship education and social conflict: New insights and lessons from Israel* (pp. 217–237). New York: Routledge.

Agbaria, A., & Mahajnah, I. (2009). Arab education between two discourses: Achievement and recognition. *Alpayim, 34*, 111–129. (in Hebrew).

Agbaria, A. K., & Mustafa, M. (2012). Two states for three peoples: The 'Palestinian Israeli' in the future vision documents of the Palestinians in Israel. *Ethnic and Racial Studies, 35*(4), 718–736.

Al-Haj, M. (1995) *Education, empowerment and control: The case of the Arabs in Israel.* Albany: State University of New York Press.

Ali, N. (2004). Political Islam in an ethnic Jewish state: Its historical evolution, contemporary challenges and future prospects. *Holy Land Studies, 3*(1), 69–92.

Ali, N. (2006). *Religious fundamentalism in ideology and practice: The Islamic movement in Israel in a comparative perspective.* Ph.D. Thesis. Haifa: Department of Sociology, Haifa University. [In Hebrew].

Ali, N. (2007). The Islamic movement's perception of the 'Independent Community.' In A. Reches (Ed.), *The Arab minority in Israel at the elections for the 17th Israeli parliament* (pp. 100–110). Tel Aviv: Tel Aviv University. (in Hebrew).

Al-Sayyid, M. K. (1995). The concept of civil society and the Arab world. In R. Brynen, B. Korany, & P. Noble (Eds.), *Political liberalization and democratization in the Arab World: Theoretical perspectives* (pp. 48–131). Boulder, CO: Lynne Rienner.

Anheier, H., Glasius, M., & Kaldor, M. (Eds.). (2003). *Global civil society.* Oxford: Oxford University Press.

Anheier, H. K. (2001a). Dimensions of the third sector: Comparative perspectives on structure and change. *Journal of Youth Studies, 4*(2), 1–23.

Anheier, H. K. (2001b). Foundations in Europe: A comparative perspective. *Civil Society Working Papers* 18. London: London School of Economics.

Ayubi, N. (1991). *Political Islam: Religion and politics in the Arab World.* London: Routledge.

Balbetchan, E. (2008). Trends in the registration of new third sector organizations in 2007. *Aloan, 30*, 3. (in Hebrew).

Bashara, A. (1996). Critique of civil society. Ramallah: Muwaten Palestinian Institute for the Study of Democracy. (in Arabic).

Ben-David, D. (2010). *State of the nation report 2009: Society, economy and policy.* Jerusalem: Taub Center. Retrieved on 24 April 2013 from http://taubcenter.org.il/tauborgilwp/wp-content/uploads/PR_E2010_State_of_Nation_Report.pdf. (Hebrew).

Boesenecker, A. P., & Vinjamuri, L. (2011). Lost in translation? Civil society, faith-based organizations and the negotiation of international norms. *International Journal of Transitional Justice, 5*(3), 345–365.

Casanova, J. (2001). Civil society and religion: Retrospective reflections on Catholicism and prospective reflections on Islam. *Social Research, 68*(4)1041–1080.

Chorev, E. N. (2008). Arab NGOs civic and social change in Israel: Mapping the field. Jerusalem: The Van Leer Jerusalem Institute.

Clarke, G. (2006). Faith matters: Faith-based organisations, civil society and international development. *Journal of International Development, 18*(6), 835–848.

Coston, M. J. (1998). A model and typology of government-NGO relationships. *Nonprofit and Voluntary Sector Quarterly, 27*(3), 358–382.

Dagan-Buzaglo, N. (2010). *Privatization in the Israeli School System: Selected Issues.* Tel-Aviv: Adva Center.

Doron, G. (1996). Two civil societies and one state: Jews and Arabs in the State of Israel. In A. R. Norton (Ed.), *Civil society in the Middle East.* The Netherlands: Koninklijke Brill NV, Leiden.

Eickelman, D. F. (2000). Islam and the languages of modernity. *Daedalus, 129*(1), 119–135.

Eqraa Association. (2010). Yearly report. Nazereth: Eqraa.

Emerson, M. O., & Hartman, D. (2006). The rise of religious fundamentalism. *Annual Review of Sociology*, 127–144.

Friedland, R. (2001). Religious nationalism and the problem of collective representation. *Annual Review of Sociology, 27*: 125–52.

Fukuyama, F. (1995). *Trust: The social virtues and the creation of prosperity*. New York: Free Press.

Gidron, B., & Elon, Y. (2007). *Israeli third sector Database 2007: Patterns and developments*. Be'er Sheva: Israeli Center for Third Sector Research.

Gorski, P. S., & Altinordu, A. (2008). After secularization? *Annual Review of Sociology, 34*, 55–85.

Grzymala-Busse, A. (2012). Why comparative politics should take religion (more) seriously. *Annual Review of Political Science, 15*, 421–442.

Habermas, J. (2006). Religion in the public sphere. *European Journal of Philosophy 14*(1) 1–25.

Habermas, J., & Mendieta, E. (2002). *Religion and rationality: Essays on reason, God, and modernity*. Cambridge, MA: MIT Press.

Haklai, O. (2004a). Helping the enemy? Why transnational Jewish philanthropic foundations donate to Palestinian NGOs in Israel. *Nation and Nationalism, 14*(3), 581–599.

Haklai, O. (2004b). Palestinian NGOs in Israel: A campaign for civic equality or 'ethnic civil society'? *Israel Studies, 9*(3), 157–168.

Haklai, O. (2011). *Palestinian ethnonationalism in Israel*. Philadelphia: University of Pennsylvania Press.

Hassan, A. (2000). Political Islam and civil society. Cairo: Al-Dar Al-Thakafie Lnasher. (in Arabic).

Huntington, S. P. (1991). *The third wave: Democratization in the late twentieth century*. Norman: University of Oklahoma Press.

Ibrahim, S. E. (1995). Civil society and prospects for democratization in the Arab world. In A. R. Norton (Ed.), *Civil society in the Middle East* (pp. 27–54). Leiden: E. J. Brill.

Ibrahim, S. E. (2004). *Egypt, Islam and democracy*. Cairo: The American University in Cairo Press.

Ismail, S. A. (2003). *A critical comparison between civil and communitarian society from an Islamic perspective: From theory to practice*. Damascus, Dar Al-Fakar. [In Arabic].

Jabareen, Y. T. (2007). NGOs as political alternative: Critical perspectives. In E. Reches (Ed.), *The Arab minority in Israel and elections for the 17ᵗʰ parliament* (pp. 93–99). Tel Aviv: Tel Aviv University and Conrad Edenower.

Jabareen, Y., & Agbaria, A. (2010). *Education on hold: Israeli government and civil society initiatives to improve Arab education in Israel*. Haifa: The Arab Minority Rights Clinic, Faculty of Law, University of Haifa & Dirasat, Arab Center for Law and Policy.

Jamal, A. (2007). Strategies of minority struggle for equality in ethnic states: Arab politics in Israel. *Citizenship Studies, 11*(3), 263–382.

Jamal, A. (2008). The counter hegemonic role of civil society: Palestinian Arab NGOs in Israel. *Citizenship Studies, 12*(3), 283–306.

Kaplan, S. (2005). Religious nationalism: A textbook case from Turkey. *Comparative Studies of South Asia, African and the Middle East, 25*(3): 665–676.

Keane, J. (2004) *Civil society: Old images, new visions.* London: Polity Press and Blackwell Publishers Ltd.

Kedar, M. (2010). Twentieth century privatization trends in Arab education. In O. Ichilov (Ed.), *Twentieth century privatization trends in Arab education.* Tel-Aviv: Ramot. pp. 209–236. [In Hebrew]

Kumar, D. (1993). Civil society: An inquiry into the usefulness of an historical term. *British Journal of Sociology, 44*(3), 375–395.

Lewis, B. (1991). The political language of Islam. Chicago, IL: University of Chicago Press.

Mari, S. (1978). *Arab education in Israel.* Syracuse, NY: Syracuse University Press.

Markman, N., & Yona, Y. (2009). Nationalism, multiculturalism and core curriculum in Israel: Between inclusion and exclusion. *Alpayim, 34*: 65–81. [In Hebrew].

Mitchell, P. R. (1969). *The society of the Muslim Brothers.* London: Oxford University Press.

Moussalli, A. (1993). Modern Islamic fundamentalist discourse on civil society, pluralism and democracy. In A. R. Norton (Ed.), *Civil society in the Middle East* (pp. 79–119). Leiden: E. J. Brill.

Mustafa, M. (2011). *Arab student movements in Israeli universities.* Umm al-Fahm: The Center for Contemporary Research.

Najam, A. (2000). The four-c's of third sector—Government relations cooperation, confrontation, complementarity, and co-optation. *Nonprofit Management & Leadership, 10*(4), 375–396.

Norris, P., & Inglehart, R. (2011). *Sacred and secular: Religion and politics worldwide.* Cambridge, UK: Cambridge University Press.

Payes, S. (2005). *Palestinian NGOs in Israel: The politics of civil society.* Library of Middle East Studies. Tauris Academic Studies London. New York.

Philpott, D. (2009). Has the study of global politics found religion? *Annual Review of Political Science, 12*(1), 183–202.

Putnam, R. D., & Campbell, D. E. (2012). *American grace: How religion divides and unites us.* New York: Simon and Schuster.

Rabinowitz, D. (2001). De Tocqueville in Umm al-Fahm. In A. O. Adi, & Y. Peled (Eds.), *From mobilized society to civil society.* Israel: Hakibbutz Hameukhad and VanLeer Jerusalem Foundation. [In Hebrew].

Rubin, A. 2012. Toward conceptual integration of religious actors in democracy and civil society: Turkey and Israel compared. In B. Turam (Ed.), *Secular state and religious society: Two forces in play in Turkey* (pp. 167–193). New York: Palgrave Macmillan.

Sa'di, H. A. (2004). Trends in Israeli social science research on the national identity of the Palestinian citizens of Israel. *Asian Journal of Social Science 32*(1), 140–160.

Salah, R. (2006, March 31). Towards an independent community. *The Sueth Al-Hakual-hurria Newspaper*, p. 4. (in Arabic).

Savas, E. S. (2000). *Privatization and public private partnership*. New York: Chatham House.

Sherkat, D. E., & Ellison, C. G. (1999). Recent developments and current controversies in the sociology of religion. *Annual Review of Sociology*, 363–394.

Stake, R. E. (2000). Case studies. In N. K. Denzin, & Y. S. Lincoln (Eds.), *Handbook of qualitative research* (pp. 435–454). Thousand Oaks, CA: Sage.

Stark, R., & Bainbridge, W. S. (1985). *The future of religion: Secularization, revival, and cult formation*. Berkeley, CA: University of California Press.

Stark, R., & Bainbridge, W. S. (1987). *A theory of religion*. New York: Peter Lang.

Tamimi, A. (2001). Rachid Ghannouchi: A democrat within Islamism. Oxford: Oxford University Press.

Taylor, C. 1994. The politics of recognition. In Amy Gutmann (Ed.), *Multiculturalism and the politics of recognition*. Princeton, NJ: Princeton University Press, pp. 25–73

Tepe, S. (2008). *Beyond sacred and secular: politics of religion in Israel and Turkey*. Stanford, CA: Stanford University Press.

Turam, B. (2004). The politics of engagement between Islam and the secular state: Ambivalences of 'civil society.' *The British Journal of Sociology, 55*(2), 259–281.

Turam, B. (2007). *Between Islam and the state: the politics of engagement*. Stanford, CA: Stanford University Press.

Wald, K. D., Silverman, A. L., & Fridy, K. S. (2005). Making sense of religion in political life. Annu. *Rev. Polit. Sci., 8*, 121–143.

Yin, R. K. (2003). *Case study research: Design and methods (3rd ed.)*. Thousand Oaks, CA: Sage.

Yishai, Y. (1991). *Land of paradoxes: Interest politics in Israel*. Albany: State University of New York Press.

Yishai, Y. (1998). Civil society in transition: Interest politics in Israel. *Annals American Academy of Political and Social Science, 555*(1), 147–162.

Yonah, Y., & Shenhav, Y. (2000). The multicultural situation. *Theory and Criticism*, 17, 163–188. [In Hebrew].

9. Post-Secular Ethnography: Religious Experience and Political Individualism among Neo-Hasidic Religious Zionists in Israel and the West Bank

Nehemia Stern

Introduction: The Prayer of the Scream

Rabbi Menachem Froman, the Chief Rabbi of the West Bank settlement of Tekoa, sat in the front of his small prefabricated synagogue. It was a wintery Sunday night in 2012, and a sizable crowd had gathered for a weekly lesson in Jewish mysticism. The rabbi with his large white knitted *kippa* was wearing slippers and white socks and had one swollen leg propped up and resting on a plastic chair. His once full long white beard was now short and scraggly, his white side locks that once flowed down his shoulders had largely disappeared. He was pale and gaunt, his body wracked with the stomach cancer that would later take his life.[1] Despite his terminal illness, he still had the ability to enthrall crowds with his short, pithy, and mysterious interpretations of the *Zohar*, a classic text of Jewish mysticism.

On this particular evening the Rabbi was commenting on the different kinds of prayer experiences that were common within Israeli religious Zionist educational institutions. Surrounded by two of his sons at his side, and musical accompaniment behind him, he leaned into the black microphone.

> "There are three methods of prayer," he said "the prayer of a *Gushnik*, the prayer of a *Mercaznik*, and the prayer of the 'scream.'" [*Tefillah shel Tze'aka*]

The terms '*Gushnik*' and '*Mercaznik*' refer to two different religious Zionist educational/rabbinic seminaries. By "*Gushnik*" Rabbi Froman was referring to students who attend the seminary in the Gush Etzion Bloc of West Bank settlements called *Har Etzion*. "Mercaznik" refers to students who attend the seminary in Jerusalem known as *Mercaz Harav*. The "scream" refers to individuals who are drawn to Neo-Hassidic modes of religious Zionist thought and practice. The Rabbi was using institutionalized modes of prayer and textual study to offer a description of different kinds of religious and social experiences.[2]

In societies where textual study is a central focus of everyday life, textual practices bear with them strong social, moral, and political implications (Seeman, 2010). People engage with texts in ways that move beyond efforts to "comprehend" the straightforward meaning of their words (Bielo, 2009: 73). The place one studies and the methods one uses to study are central components in shaping social, political, and religious experiences.

Through the prism of institutions of textual study, Rabbi Froman attempted to place religious Zionism in Israel into three separate religious, social, and political categories. The first two categories are classical theological modes of how Zionist thought has been assimilated into Israeli religious communities. The *Gushnik* is generally stereotyped within religious Zionist communities as a student who is pragmatic and rational and whose Zionism follows this pattern. For the *Mercaznik*, on the other hand, loyalty to the State of Israel and its institutions is deeply rooted in mystical and messianic principles. The last category—of the 'scream'—references a distinct Neo-Hasidic religious and political subjectivity. Neo-Hasidism in its religious Zionist context is relatively new, and emerged out of a certain disillusionment with classical religious Zionist thought and practice. The reference to the "scream" stresses the different—and sometimes contradictory—ways in which a person may experience both individual divinity as well as state loyalty. Here a theological stress is placed on an individual relationship with God, one that mirrors a political outlook that highlights individualism against State collective nationalism.

This chapter concerns the "scream." It will ethnographically explore the wider social, political, and religious context of post secularism within Neo-Hasidic religious Zionism in Israel and the occupied West Bank. Through descriptions of neo-Hasidic educational and settlement practices it will show how a classical theological and political emphasis on collective nationalism has shifted to a more individualist focus. This shift towards an individual and nuanced form of religious experience and practice can be used to sharpen scholarly understanding of how religious and social experiences interact with one another in a post-secular age. As Fischer, Hotam and Wexler argued, "[I]ndividualism...may serve as the new religion, enabling the production of the necessary collective forces and meanings, by replacing the tribal totem with the ideal of the individual..." (2012: 264).

In a post secular society religious individualism has replaced the Durkheimian model of symbolic collective effervescence.

This kind of post-secular individualism is unpredictable and allies itself with political forces in ways that can be surprising and counterintuitive. Habermas has classified "post-secular" societies as ones where "religion maintains a public influence and relevance, while the secularistic certainty that religion will disappear worldwide in the course of modernization is losing ground" (2008: 21). Some—including Habermas himself (2008: 18)—locate the mass of this public influence within a politically reactionary, and religiously zealous social context. Indeed, most studies of Neo-Hasidism in Israel have focused on right-wing political practices and on the violent behaviors that inhabit those practices. Steinhardt (2010: 28), Weiss (2010), and Feige (2009) link this new spiritual ethos to right-wing political extremism that finds expression in acts of violence against West Bank Palestinians. This study hopes to add ethnographic context to studies of religious activity within a post-secular context by showing how the Neo Hasidic attributes of individualism and personal spiritualty can be found throughout the Israeli political spectrum. An ethnography of post-secular religion can add depth to our understandings of how individualist expressions of religious experience exist amidst a complex and fertile field of various kinds of political subjectivities.

Israeli Religious Zionism and the History of the Settlement Movement

Contemporary religious Zionism in Israel is primarily organized around the theological concepts of Rabbi Abraham Isaac HaCohen Kook (1865–1935) and his son Rabbi Tzvi Yehuda Kook (1891–1982) (Ravitzky, 1996). These rabbinic thinkers posited a mystical interpretation of Jewish nationalism that stressed theological, collective, and political statism. For these thinkers, their disciples, and the political movement that they inspired, Jewish settlement in the Land of Israel served as a stepping stone to a messianic age that promised to redeem the Jewish People and the world at large (Mirsky, 2014). For Rabbi Kook, secular socialism played an (albeit unwittingly) central role in the redemptive process. In his Kabbalistic-theological view, ritual transgression takes on redemptive significance. For Kook, as redemption draws near, human nature becomes audacious and angry. There is discord and sin. The meek, the moderate, and the pious become intimidated by this phenomenon. This contrary energy, however, has the capacity to animate not just the nation of Israel, but humanity as well. Eventually the energy that causes transgression invigorates the righteous and produces a truly sacred phenomenon

(Ravitzky, 1996: 102). This is only one formulation of Rabbi Kook's theological and kabalistic thinking. But it highlights his distinctly dialectical approach. Redemption is a process that leaves room not just for secular transgressors but for the inevitable "bumps in the road" towards a straightforward redemptive process.

Rabbi Kook's theological outlook took on practical implications after Israel's victory in the 1967 Arab-Israeli War. The capture of Biblical territories in the West Bank, the Golan Heights, and East Jerusalem lent credence to the religious Zionist eschatological belief in a progressive and messianic redemption.

As the war concluded, Israelis—both secular and religious—began to re discover areas of the Holy Land that were cut off to them for close to two decades. Moreover, after 19 years of Jordanian control Jerusalem was reunited, and for the first time in 2,000 years, under Jewish auspices. The famous radio communication of General Mota Gur, "*har habayit b'yadeinu*" (the Temple Mount is in our hands), sent excited messianic shockwaves throughout world Jewry, the Israeli public, and within religious Zionism in particular.

Settlement activity within the newly captured areas really only began however, after Israel's near loss in the 1973 Arab-Israeli War. The surprise of the war, coupled with the heavy casualty rate, introduced a sense of malaise into Israeli life (Leibman, 1993). *Gush Emunim* (the Bloc of the Faithful), a religious Zionist non-governmental body, offered one response to this existential sense of loss. For their members, the settlement project in the newly captured areas of Judea, Samaria, and Gaza offered a means through which the People of Israel could return to their ancestral lands and revitalize their religious and ideological principles. As Gush Emunim's first position platform stated,

> Our aim is to bring about a large movement of reawakening among the Jewish
> people for the fulfillment of the Zionist vision in its full scope.... The sources of
> the vision are the Jewish tradition and its roots, and its ultimate objective is the
> full redemption of the Jewish people and the entire world. (Sprinzak, 1991: 114)

Gush Emunim's push to restore an ideological vision for the State of Israel produced hundreds of settlements in the lands captured during the 1967 war. Early on however, the settlement project confronted many political pressures that challenged its existing theological and social structures. These include: the 1982 withdrawal from the Sinai Peninsula in return for a peace treaty with Egypt, the 1993 Oslo Peace Accords, and most recently the 2005 disengagement from the Gaza Strip.

For many religious Zionists in Israel and the West Bank the disengagement from the Gaza Strip was a distinct breaking point with the classical mode of progressive and collective religious nationalism. The political and social outcome of the disengagement reinforced a kind of religious uncertainty within religious Zionist communities (Newman, 2005; Inbari, 2007, 2008; Tabory & Sasson, 2007; Waxman, 2008). The youth were particularly affected by this event, having been told by rabbinic figures that the disengagement was a religious and political impossibility (Cherlow, 2008, 2010).

This kind of religious disenchantment coincides with a distrust of rabbinic and political authority. Many religious Zionists pointed to the seeming fecklessness of the established settler political leadership (many of whom were involved with Gush Emunim in the 1980s). The established leadership was ultimately unable to stop the evacuations. A bitter feeling was left in the hearts of some religious Zionists. As one woman who worked in the Gush Katif Museum in Jerusalem told me in 2010,

> We felt like, not that we lost the struggle, but that we didn't properly fight. Look at how the Ultra-Orthodox react to moves against them. Hundreds of thousands come out in protest, they burn down garbage cans and riot in the middle of streets. We never did anything close to that.

The movement towards a more individualist and distinctly Neo-Hasidic understanding of Judaism and Jewishness follows in the path of these political and theological challenges. Religious Zionism has formed a new manner of experiencing religion, spirituality, and political authority. Steinhardt (2010) characterized this Neo-Hasidic spiritual experience among religious Zionists in Israel as a "combination of environmental consciousness, 'back-to-the-land' ethos, attraction to non-Western 'alternative' spiritualties, and traditional or premodern lifestyles" (2010: 23–4). From a theological perspective these individuals focus on specific Hasidic schools of thought (mainly Breslov and Lubavitch) that highlight individual affective experiences.

Socially, Neo-Hasidic religious Zionists can generally be spotted wearing distinctive fashions. Males wear a style of large knitted skull caps (*kippit*) that fit over the majority of the head almost like a bowl. They also tend to grow out their side locks (in Hebrew *Peyot*), some wearing them very long down the sides of their shoulders. Women tend to wear multi layered skirts, and married women tend to cover their hair using layers of colored fabric that produces something that one informant described as a tall turban.

Beyond ideology, political angst, and social dress codes rests another element that impacts the everyday lives of religious Zionists and their communities in Israel and the West Bank. Education and educational choices serve as the social background to the post secular individualist shift occurring within religious Zionism in Israel and the West Bank. As Rappaport, Garb, and Penso write, "Religious educational frameworks act simultaneously as educational institutions and as religious socializing agencies" (1995: 48). Formal and informal educational (*chinuch* in Hebrew) paradigms are an essential element to religious Zionist socialization. As Sprinzak notes, "The long process of socialization often starts at home, and continues through kindergarten, religious primary school, high school yeshiva, Yeshivat Hesder, or advanced yeshiva." (1991: 108).

Religious Zionists in Israel and the West Bank understand themselves and relate to each other through the prism of educational and service options. Religious and political shifts, both within the movement and Israeli society more broadly, happen against this educational background. Yeshivas, youth groups, and rabbinic figures become the ethnographic locus for religious and political change. In this way education serves as the background to post secular shifts within religious Zionist thought and practice.

The Theological Vectors of Neoliberalism

In the eyes of many young religious Zionists the classical messianic and collectivist model of redemption has been unable to confront political challenge and change. Rabbi Kook's progressive process towards a universal redemption, for example, is one that is saturated with certainty. The return of the Jews to their homeland *must* usher in a redemptive era. The power of secularism within Jewish nationalism will *certainly* add a spiritual force that mystically strengthens the nation. Society marches indelibly through theological and social stages to finally emerge redeemed. Yet as Rabbi Yoel bin-Nin, a one-time leader within the Settler Movement, said in a yeshiva class I attended in 2004, "what at one point seemed so certain and obvious actually turns out to be very complicated and problematic."

This disenchantment with classical religious Zionist theologies mirrors a larger disenchantment that is occurring within Israeli society as a whole. The early Zionists who arrived in Palestine were deeply rooted in socialist values (Cohen, 1992). Social justice and equality, workers' rights (sometimes international workers' rights) and communalism were common ideals that later became an important part of the State of Israel's social and legal framework.[3] Israel has a centralized healthcare system, a centralized Rabbinate, a social security system that is famed and feared for its *bureaucracy*, and extremely powerful workers unions in almost every sector of the economy.[4] In the 1980s, however, Israel introduced certain neo-liberal reforms into its economy in the wake of a severe economic recession.

Indeed beginning in the 1970's, Israel's communal values began to lose sway in the hearts and minds of the populace. One small example of this shift can be seen by the fate of Israel's famed kibbutz movement (Simons and Ingram, 2003). Nearly all kibbutzim have now privatized their industries. Where once all kibbutz members received the same wage regardless of employment position, most now receive differential wages dependent on position. The all-important communal dining halls have also privatized on most kibbutzim. They have either closed entirely, or members are forced pay for the food they eat. The idea of communal values, sacrificing for the good of the collective, simply is not as compelling a call as it once was (Weiss, 2011: 38).

Israeli social and economic shifts are paralleled by theological shifts within religious Zionism. The redemptive vision—otherwise known as Mamlachtiyut—for these religious Zionists was predicated upon progressive political, social, and theological unity. As Rabbi Kook wrote in the Lights of Holiness,

> The affirmation of the unity of God aspires to reveal the unity in the world, in man, among nations, and in the entire content of existence, without any dichotomy between action and theory, between reason and imagination.... In the content of man's life this is the entire basis of holiness. (Bokser, 1978: 225)

The Jewish State is viewed as a sacred entity because a Jewish national existence is one stage towards this ultimate unity. This redemptive vision—otherwise known as *mamlachtiyut* (statism or Israeli Republicanism)—was predicated upon progressive political, social, and theological unity.[5] As Moshe Koppel argues, "Mamlakhtiut—and its economic twin, socialism—both involve centralizing in the hands of the state powers and resources that would otherwise be left to the free market or to voluntary associations" (2008: 124). The disenchantment with classical religious Zionist theologies implies then a deep distrust of centralization, communalism, and messianic progressive redemption.

Gershom Scholem argued that early Hassidic theology worked to 'neutralize' the messianic impulses within Lurianic Kabbalah. For Scholem the Sabbatianism of the 17th century turned the mystic desire to unite the different aspects of divinity from a general theological principle into a real-world political effort. The early Hasidic focus on "cleaving to god" or *dvekut* turned this political push into a personal religious experience. In this way early Hasidism worked to neutralize the political (or real-world) messianic impulse among adherents. It transformed that impulse towards collective national redemption into one that focused on a personal relationship with divinity. "It [Early Hasidism] did not deny the original doctrine of redemption by the raising of the sparks, but it removed from it the acute Messianic tension" (Scholem, 1995: 195).

The national religious community is shifting its focus from collectivism towards more individualistic modes of experience. This is true in the domain of politics and the economy but particularly so in the realm of religious experience. In the process, ideas like messianism and collective redemption are being neutralized in favor of a more individualized spirituality. I term these shifts from theological and political collectivism towards individualism the "theological vectors of neo-liberalism."

For anthropologists, the settler emphasis on collectivism stands in contrast to the current Israeli neo-liberal ethos. Settlers must then somehow deal with this cognitive dissonance (Feige, 2009; Weiss, 2011; Dalsheim, 2011). By analyzing shifts in religious experience, a somewhat different story emerges. In a post-secular age, settlement activity is increasingly becoming a part of (and not a contrast to) the neoliberal shift within Israel. This is particularly so in the outlying areas of the West Bank and within satellite communities of much larger settlements. For those who live in such communities, such endeavors are not "messianic" in the classical religious Zionist sense of the term. Their neighborhoods and communities are not meant to progressively unify the nation to reach a transcendental redemption.

While the importance of the Messiah, and the Messianic age is not "negated" in this post-secular individualist subjectivity, these religious Zionists are doing something very different from messianic eschatology. For them Neo-Hasidism is a practice that frees them from government control. In so doing, it neutralizes the progressively messianic forces inherent within classical religious Zionism.

This neutralization of the political messianic impulse within contemporary Israeli religious Zionism in favor of an individualist Neo-Hasidic subjectivity can be seen merging with different vectors of the Israeli political spectrum. In the ethnography that follows I will offer three examples of how the theological vectors of neoliberalism impact a diverse array of individuals and communities. I saw the more violent face of post-secular neoliberalism on a visit to Homesh one Sabbath with individuals identified with the "Hilltop Youth." These are youngsters who rebel against the growing bourgeois nature of religious Zionism.[6] In contrast, in Beit Rimon, a premilitary rabbinic seminary situated in the Galilee, I experienced a kind of post-secular neoliberalism that was more concerned with individual piety than it was with specific political subjectivities. Finally I will return to the case of Rabbi Froman (from the introduction) to briefly describe a kind of neoliberal religious experience that attempts to move beyond stark political boundaries.

Example A: Violence among the Hilltop Youth in Homesh

Homesh was one of four settlements in the northern West Bank that were removed as part of Israel's disengagement plan in 2005. Homesh, the closest community to larger Jewish settlement blocs, has been a focus for activists who call for a return to these evacuated communities. There are both formal (legally sanctioned by the IDF) gatherings at Homesh during holidays and smaller illegal gatherings that are usually organized on the Sabbath.

A rabbinic seminary called "Yeshivat Homesh"—which has a permanent presence in the nearby settlement of Shavei Shomron—illegally sent its students a couple of times a week to study among the ruins of the destroyed settlement. In addition they used to spend the Sabbath there about once every other week. Jewish civilians are only allowed inside Homesh and its surrounding areas with special military permission. The army sometimes puts a checkpoint on the main road to deter Jewish entrance into the area. Those students who do visit Homesh are in violation of the law.

Yeshivat Homesh in the settlement of Shavei Shomron is a rather ramshackle structure. It was really only several caravans placed together, to make a large building. There were about three rooms with beds in them, a kitchen, a small dining hall, a study hall (Beit Midrash), and a shower/bathroom. The building was far from clean, there were some large holes in the walls, and the bathroom did not have proper locks on it.

The study hall featured a large Hasidic section, which included texts from various Hasidic traditions. That Shabbat there were 13 people going up to Homesh. These included myself, 4 young ultra-orthodox men, a newly married couple, a former student who was a soldier on leave that brought an M-16 short rifle and one magazine with him, and five other yeshiva students. Most of the Homesh students wore large knitted *kippot* and they all had longer curled side locks.

These students were all from religious Zionist families. They attended a yeshiva (Yeshivat Homesh) that extolled the virtues of the Land of Israel. Yet they had a complex relationship with the army. For them the I.D.F. was not a sacred institution. Rather, it was an institution that forbade them from visiting "their" settlement. Over the Sabbath I sat with some of these students and rarely heard anything positive said about the I.D.F. During one of our conversations I expressed how important the military is for most religious Zionists; How many people feel that it does not matter where one serves; the essence (Ha'Ikar) is that one serve the State.[7]

Uri, a student with long blonde side locks down to his chest, turned to me and asked argumentatively, "*Ha'Ikar*, the essence?" For him that phrase echoed Breslov Hasidic concepts of faith in God. Breslov Hasidism is extremely popular among religious Zionists. For them "the essence" is an individual experience of God.[8] Uri went on, "I think there are other things which are essential, maybe even more essential." The unifying, sacred nature of the Israeli army that is so common in Rabbi Kook circles was distinctly absent among this group.

Homesh is located on top of a mountain, and the only permanent structure that survived the 2005 evacuation is the large water tower at the summit. When we arrived at Homesh we unloaded the jeep and brought all the stuff down a drainage ditch into a clearing that was relatively concealed from the road. As the I.D.F sometimes patrolled the area on Friday afternoons the group along with the gear had to remain hidden within the ditch until right before the onset of the Sabbath. I was told by one of the yeshiva students that if we hear a military Jeep we were to quickly run and hide.

While we were waiting to set up the gear, we heard a vehicle drive up the hill. All our heads perked up. Would we have to run and hide? Would we get arrested? We knew it was not our Jeep however, and by the sound of the motor it was not a military jeep either. The only possibility that remained was that it was a vehicle of Palestinians.

The leader of the group, David, who before this was sitting down relaxing, said "we have to get them out of here!" He looked around and found a long iron pipe. Picking it up, he started sprinting up the drainage ditch towards the main road. Everyone else started picking up large stones, and began running after David.

I heard David scream, "Give me your identity card! Give me your identity card.[9] Get out of here!" One of the Palestinians screamed back in Arabic, and then I heard the vehicle turn and with a loud screech, speed down the mountain. I was in the back, and I did not see the incident, I just heard what was happening. I learned later that David had broken one of the vehicle's windows with the iron pipe. These were people who seconds earlier were learning Talmud or building a box in which to place a Torah scroll. After the incident they all went back to what they were doing as if little had happened.

Violence is a difficult thing to describe and anthropologists have produced few actual descriptions of violence. Violence "escapes easy definition" and is also a formative aspect of the human condition, both for the informant as well as the ethnographer (Nordstrom & Robben, 1996: 6). It is difficult to see people take up a pipe and bricks and charge towards a car. I was told there were three men in the vehicle. But what if it contained children? I was told by the group that families sometimes go up to Homesh for picnics. Amidst all the running and shouting, it did not seem like anyone was very discerning as to who was in the car.

This violence that I had witnessed, however, was not tinged with messianism. David's call to us "we have to get them out of here" was not truly messianic. National and transcendental redemption had no place on that hill. Indeed the national and "sacred" army was just as much an adversary as were the Palestinians. Homesh was simply David's mountain and he was going to defend it with an iron pipe and bricks.

We prayed that night in the makeshift hut that also served as the dining hall, a shady spot for a nap in the middle of the day. One student, Dvir, with a soft gentle voice and a quick smile went off into the surrounding trees and prayed alone, without a minyan. Every once in a while we would hear him scream. He was crying out to his God, on his mountain. The phenomenon of young men choosing to pray by themselves and not with a *minyan* was not new to me. I often encountered religious Zionist men, influenced by Hasidut, who preferred the individual experience of prayer, over that of the collective. The religious collective is less important than the individual relationship with his (or her) creator.

As I walked back down the drainage ditch after the confrontation, my pulse racing, Gershom Scholem's words echoed within my heart. "When the Baal Shem Tov and his pupils made it [*dvekut*] the very center of Hasidic life, the emphasis shifted from Luria's stress on the Messianic action of man...toward a strictly personal relation of man to God" (1995: 186). These Neo-Hasidic youth on Homesh had neutralized the messianism of their religious Zionist forbearers. The political push towards harmony and unity that led to the occupation and settlement of the West Bank was not present. In its place I found a strictly personal drive to cleave to our mountain. Through that *dvekut* (devout attachment), they were also attempting to cleave, in a very personal sense, to God.

Example B: Personal Experience beyond Politics in Beit Rimon

This kind of individualism that is steeped in both Hasidism and contemporary politics is not exclusive to the West Bank, nor is it only expressed through violence. In many ways it is also implicated within the *sturm und drang* of young adulthood. An acquaintance, Amichai, was a religious teacher in a pre-military seminary (*mechina*) called *Carmei Chayil* (Vineyards of Valor). *Carmei Chayil* is located in a privatized religious Zionist kibbutz in Israel's north called Beit Rimon. Amichai had studied in the *mechina* as a young man ten years earlier, and returned to teach there.

In mid-2013 I decided to visit Amichai and the *mechina* for a Sabbath. Traveling up to the community I was expecting to find classical yeshiva students. This included young adults who were *kippot* and maybe even have the long Hasidic side locks. What I found was something very different and surprising. When we entered onto the grounds of the yeshiva I noticed that many students lacked the classical garments that mark religious observance within the national Religious community.

I met Amichai in the study hall of the *mechina*. With his long sidelocks, bushy beard, and wide friendly smile, Amichai ignored my tentative outstretched hand and gave me a large bear hug. "Shalom! How are you? Thank you for coming!" he exclaimed. After organizing a few things around campus Amichai took me into his car for the short ride up to his house for lunch.

"I don't know if you noticed what's here, but maybe I should explain" Amichai said as he started the engine. "The students in Beit Rimon, some are religious, some aren't. Like...they all come from religious homes, but somehow they fell away.

Laughing a little, I said "Yeah I think I noticed, a lot aren't wearing kippot." "We don't push them here. We don't allow public violations of the Sabbath, but we don't force what they do privately. It doesn't come from a position of pluralism mind you. We just let them come to religion in their own way." Amichai's students have "fallen away" or grown disenchanted with the religiosity of their families as well as with the modes of classical religious Zionist thought and practice. What is important for Amichai (and presumably his students) are their very personal and individual religious desires.

As we entered into his house I immediately took a look at his bookshelf.[10] It included a wide variety of religious thinkers. I noticed several texts by Rabbi Joseph Soloveitchik, a rabbinic philosopher who is very popular among American religious Zionists. Rabbi Soloveitchik's views on Zionism were pragmatic and skeptical of the messianic and statist claims made by Rabbi Kook and his students.

"Amichai I'm sort of surprised. Rabbi Soloveitchik? That's interesting," I chided a little.

"Surprised huh? What's so surprising?" Amichai said smiling back and taking the ethnographic bait.

"I don't know, it's just not something one normally sees in Israeli households, certainly not with a bookmark in one of them!"

"Yeah I guess it is kind of unique. I try to read a lot of things. I didn't grow up with Rabbi Soloveitchik, but he sort of echoes my Zionism."

"His Zionism is sort of more critical," I added. "The State is only sacred so long as it advances Jewish interests."

of "Exactly, it expresses a lot of what I've been thinking and feeling. I'd like to read more of what Rabbi Soloveitchik has to offer."

Sitting down to lunch in Amichai's house and listening to him talk about Rabbi Soloveitchik (with some of, Rabbi Ginzburg's texts in the background and a portrait of Rabbi Kook staring down at us) it became clear how eclectic religious individualism could be. Theological and even political opposites could coexist under the same roof. That kind of coexistence only echoed the myriad ways in which individuals could mix and mingle religious experience, political expression, and personal beliefs in surprising and paradoxical ways. This individualism which emerges alongside political critique and personal religious quest was expressed very poignantly in the Friday night prayer service and in the ritual meal that followed.

Most yeshivot and mechinot incorporate some kind of singing and even dancing into their Friday night prayers. The singing is not coordinated like a choir, but everyone knows the tunes and follows them. The dancing is also usually done in concentric circles around the center of the synagogue. The prayers in Carmei Chayil were very different. Individual students—in the middle of a tune—would invent their own variation. The dancing was completely free. Students would swing their arms, jump around, and yell out in their own individual and unique ways. No one seemed to be afraid to do something different, and unique, no matter how off beat it might appear. The *mechina* was encouraging individual self-expression as a means toward divnity. Amichai was insistent that I take part in the effort, so I stood up and tried my best.

During the meal Amichai gave a homily based on the weekly Torah reading alongside a Hasidic text. This particular discourse was interactive. All 20 students or so had to go around the table and offer two pieces of information. We had to say something which makes us feel truly happy and fulfilled, and then something which makes us feel terrible, something which holds us back from fulfilling our individual potential. Students shared around the dinner table some very personal information. One student revealed how masturbation made him feel terrible. Amichai's wife and children were present at the table, yet this personal revelation was accepted calmly and with understanding.

Amichai walked me back to my room that night, and I had a chance to talk to him about the issue of individual and (sometimes very) personal expressions in the mechina and their relationship to Hasidism. Hasidic theology (especially the Lubavitch variant) stresses self-negation and the nullification of ego as disciplinary tools for the preservation of the soul's connection with a divine source. I asked Amichai how he can reconcile this idea with the mechina's strong emphasis on self-expression. "Before you negate yourself," I was told, "you have to accept that you have a self. People tend to jump to the last step, and they never really get to know themselves."

That Sabbath in Beit Rimon offered a good illustration of several factors influencing the Neo-Hasidic shift within religious Zionism as it relates to the nature of individualism within post-secular subjectivities. Firstly, it showed how religious Zionist youth who turn towards Hasidism are responding to political, social, as well as personal rifts. Secondly, an interest in politics or the use of violence is only one aspect of Neo-Hasidic religious Zionism. These students in Israel's north were far more interested in self-development than any political or even messianic message. Thirdly, as Fischer, Hotam and Wexler argue, postsecularism denotes a breakdown in the traditional ideological and religious divisions within society (2012: 263). It allows a space for individuals to be very creative in the ways they meld different theologies and ideological persuasions into their everyday lives. Individuals on the ground rarely follow the scripts laid out for them by ideological dogma.

Example C: Freedom and Neo-Hasidism Beyond State Boundaries

Rabbi Menachem Froman passed away from stomach cancer in March of 2013. One of the founders of the Israeli Settlement Movement, Froman grew out of the Kookian tradition of ultimate progressive unity and collective redemption. At the same time, he was also very different from many of his rabbinic colleagues. Moving away from the collectivism of his peers, Rabbi Froman turned to a kind of Neo-Hasidism that focused on an individual faith in God that went beyond the political and social boundaries of state nationalism. This theological view led Rabbi Froman to (according to his critics, naively) conduct private talks with Palestinian militants including Yassir Arafat (the former head of the PLO) and Sheikh Ahmed Yassin (the former spiritual leader of Hamas). It also led him to come out very strongly against any State evacuation of settlements and removal of Jews from their homes (Dalsheim, 2011).

The rabbi's funeral took place in the settlement of Tekoa on a Tuesday afternoon in March. It was a cool day, one where the heat of the midday sun seems to be tempered by a steady, strong, and chilling breeze. The funeral procession began with several speeches by friends and family inside the community's main Ashkenazi synagogue. There was standing room only; women were standing on one side of the room and men on the other. Individuals were pressed tightly together, everyone trying to get a few inches closer to the center of the room. As his students carried their rabbi's body into the synagogue wrapped in a *tallit* (Jewish Prayer Shawl), the crowd began to intone slow and melodic Hasidic *nigunim* (wordless tunes). Bodies swayed back and forth and wails could be heard as the immediate family entered the room.

His eldest son Yossi stood behind the synagogue's lectern surrounded by fellow mourners. Through his grief he tried to express what he felt to be the core of his father's thought:

> The freer a man is, the closer he is to God. A man and woman meet in freedom. Religion and heresy meet in freedom. My father tried to connect us and our neighbors the Arabs, not around borders, boundaries, and political arguments, but in freedom!

Freedom for Rabbi Froman was indicative of an individual connection to God. This individual bond is just as much a political perspective as it is a religious experience. The freedom that follows a uniquely post-secular individualism allowed Rabbi Froman to look beyond historical and theological boundaries. Throughout Israel more and more religious Zionists are searching for their own personal connection to *their* God as well as to *their* land. These people tend to question (though most do not completely disregard) the collective, statist, and messianic vision of religious Zionism that was extremely popular in the previous generation.

Conclusion: Post-Secular Ethnography

Charles Taylor characterizes the notion of secularism within the nation state as one of transcendence. The nation state transcends divisions based on race, class, and religion in favor of a unifying (and in so doing, secularizing) principle of citizenship (Asad, 2003: 5; Taylor, 1998). Peter Berger understood secularization as the slow process through which religion becomes transformed from an overarching framework of experience into just one of many societal institutions that influence socio-political practice (Bracke, 2008; Berger, 1969). The post secularist paradigm disturbs these frameworks by rethinking the ways in which new kinds of secular and religious attachments may be imagined and structured within the public sphere.

Current events in the Middle East have shown quite clearly how religion and religious practices can act as a strong force for modern political action. What deserves more attention, however, are the multifaceted ways in which religion experience itself is oftentimes affected by and responsive to socio-political changes and upheavals. In this chapter for example, socio-political crisis and upheaval paved the way for a Neo-Hasidic shift in religious Zionist thought and practice. This Neo-Hasidic shift makes possible a wide range of social and political positions within an area that is besieged by ethnic and religious conflict.

Relatedly, Lieven Boeve has noted the impacts post secular shifts have had on Christianity and Christian theology in contemporary Europe. As he argues, "recontextualizing theology in a post secular context…offers opportunities to profile Christian faith anew both for contemporary believers as well as the public forum (2008: 296). I would argue that ethnographic ac counts of religious experiences, practices, and ideologies can uncover the particular quotidian details of how theology is actually lived in post secular contexts. An ethnographic approach to the study of post-secularism can signal far more than just a "contested claim about the resurgence of religion" (Gorski et al., 2012: 1). It can trace how the specific ways in which that resurgence influences and relates to the experiences and political loyalties of religious practitioners themselves. In this unique position ethnography can explore and add depth to the kinds of personal dilemmas and moral ambiguities that have been so greatly influential in the lives of political pietists in the contemporary Middle East.

This chapter has explored the ways in which a distinct kind of post-secular religious experience becomes implicated in a variety of social and political subjectivities. Hotam and Wexler have argued that "a post secular emergent society is about the return of religion" (2014: 1). Ethnographic analysis has the capacity to uncover the true complexities of this paradigm. Ethnography moves to empirically document and represent the circuitous and culturally specific ways in which religious experience "returns" to society. Such an analysis allows for unique social and political formations to coalesce.

Notes

1. His passing will be discussed in the concluding remarks.
2. Marcel Mauss noted the centrality of prayer in religious life "Of all religious phenomena there are few which, even when considered from the outside, give such an immediate impression of life, richness, and complexity as does the phenomenon of prayer … It has filled the most varied roles: here it is a brusque demand, there an order, elsewhere a contract, and act of faith …" (2008: 21).
3. This was true for both the secular as well as for religious Zionists. In the first decades of the State (and well into the 1990s) religious Zionist political parties regularly joined coalitions with secular socialists. These alliances were not merely based on a pragmatic confluence of interests. Religious Zionism had deep roots within the Kibbutz movement (Katz, 1995).

4. For an informed analysis of Israel's nationalized healthcare system and its neoliberal reform, see Dani Filc's, "Circles of Exclusion: The Politics of Health Care in Israel" (2009).
5. The concept of Mamlachtiyut enjoys a broad history within Israeli political thought. For an excellent overview of the history and philosophical content of Mamlachtiyut, see Nir Kedar's (2002) *Ben-Gurion's Mamlakhtiyut: Etymological and Theoretical Roots.*
6. Scholars often relate the Hilltop Youth to Second or Third generation Israeli settlers (Susskind et al., 2005; Feige, 2009; Weiss, 2010). While second and third generation settlers are represented within the hilltop youth, I found the primary contention to be the bourgeois atmosphere of contemporary religious Zionism. Most of the youth I met were from Israel's middle to upper class economic and geographical center.
7. For the importance of the military within religious Zionism, and the conflicts that inspires see Stuart Cohen's (2007) "Tensions between Military Service and Jewish Orthodoxy in Israel: Implications Imagined and Real."
8. The phrase '*Ha'Ikar*' may have echoed for Uri the popular Breslov song about faith in God "The entire world is a very narrow bridge. And the essence [*Ha'Ikar*] is not to be afraid."
9. Jibil Awiye in Arabic. This is the first thing soldiers at checkpoints ask of Palestinians. This is a phrase most Jews living in the West Bank are familiar with.
10. This was a common practice for me. I would often look to see what Jewish political pietists were *reading*. I felt it gave me some insight into how they viewed their world.

Bibliography

Asad, Talal. 2003. *Formations of the Secular: Christianity, Islam, Modernity.* Stanford, CA: Stanford University Press.

Berger, Peter. 1969. *The Sacred Canopy: Elements of a Sociological Theory of Religion.* New York: Anchor Books.

Bielo, James. 2009. *Words Upon the Word: An Ethnography of Evangelical Group Bible Study.* New York: New York University Press.

Boeve, Lieven. 2008. *Religion after Detraditionalization: Christian Faith in a Postsecular World.* In *The New Visibility of Religion: Studies in Religion and Cultural Hermeneutics.* Edited by Michael Hoezl and Graham Ward. Manchester, UK: Continuum Resources in Religion and Political Culture.

Bokser, Ben-Zion. 1978. *Abraham Isaac Kook: The Lights of Penitence, The Moral Principles, Lights of Holiness, Essays, Letters, and Poems.* Mahwah, NJ: Paulist Press.

Bracke, Sarah. 2008. Conjugating the Modern/ Religious, Conceptualizing Female Religious Agency Contours of a 'Post-secular' Conjuncture. *Theory, Culture & Society.* 25: 6. pp. 51–67.

Cherlow, Yuval. 2008. The Disengagement Plan as Reflected in Virtual FAQ in *Religious Zionism Post Disengagement: Future Directions.* Edited by Chaim Waxman. New York: Yeshiva University Press.

Cherlow, Yuval. 2010. Shut Hahitnatkut. (Hebrew).

Cohen, Mitchell. 1992. *Zion and State: Nation, Class, and the Shaping of Modern Israel.* New York: Cambridge University Press.

Cohen, Stuart. 1993. The Hesder Yeshivot in Israel: A Church-State Military Arrangement. *Journal of Church and State. 35:* 1. pp. 113–130.

Cohen, Stuart. 2007. Tensions between Military Service and Jewish Orthodoxy in Israel: Implications Imagined and Real. *Israel Studies. 12:* 1. pp. 103–126.

Dalsheim, Joyce. 2011. *Unsettling Gaza: Secular Liberalism, Radical Religion, and the Israeli Settlement Project.* New York: Oxford University Press.

Feige, Michael. 2009. *Settling the Hearts: Jewish Fundamentalism in the Occupied Territories.* Detroit: Wayne State University Press.

File, Dani. 2009. *Circles of Exclusion: The Politics of Health Care in Israel.* ILR Press.

Fisher, Shlomo; Hotam, Yotam; and Wexler, Phillip. 2012. Democracy and Education in Postsecular Society. *Review of Research in Education. 36.* pp. 261–281.

Gorski, Philip S.; Kim, David Kyuman; Torpey, John; and VanAntwerpen, Jonathan. (Eds.) (2012). *The Post Secular in Question: Religion in Contemporary Society.* New York: New York University Press.

Habermas, Jurgen. 2008. Notes on Post-Secular Society. *New Perspectives Quarterly. 25:*4. pp. 17–29.

Hotam, Yotam, and Wexler, Philip. 2014. Introduction: Education in Post-Secular Society. *Critical Studies in Education. 55:* 1. pp. 1–7.

Inbari, Motti. 2007. Religious Zionism and the Temple Mount Dilemma—Key Trends. *Israel Studies. 12:* 2. pp. 29–47.

Inbari, Motti. 2008. *Messianic Religious Zionism Confronts Israeli Territorial Compromises.* New York: Cambridge University Press.

Jackson, Michael. 1998. *Minima Ethnographica: Intersubjectivity and the Anthropological Project.* Chicago, IL: University of Chicago Press.

Katz, Yossi. 1995. The Religious Kibbutz Movement and Its Credo, 1934–1948, *Middle Eastern Studies 31:* 2, pp. 253–280.

Kedar, Nir. 2002. Ben-Gurion's Mamlakhtiyut: Etymological and Theoretical Roots. *Israel Studies. 7:* 3. pp. 117–133.

Koppel, Moshe. 2008. The Demise of Self Negating Religious Zionism. In *Religious Zionism Post Disengagement: Future Directions.* Edited by Chaim Waxman. New York: Yeshiva University Press.

Leibman, Charles S. 1993. The Myth of Defeat: The Memory of the Yom Kippur War in Israeli Society. *Middle Eastern Studies. 29:* 3. pp. 399–418.

Lichtenstein, Aharon. 1981. *The Ideology of Hesder: The View from Yeshivat Har Etzion. Tradition. 19:* 3. pp. 199–217.

Mauss, Marcel. 2008. *On Prayer.* New York: Berghahn Books.

Mirsky, Yehuda. 2014. *Rav Kook: Mystic in a Time of Revolution.* New Haven, CT: Yale University Press.

Myers, Jody. 2003. *Seeking Zion: Modernity and Messianic Activity in the Writings of Tsevi Hirsch Kalischer*. Oxford: Littman Library of Jewish Civilization.

Newman, David. 2005. From Hitnachalut to Hitnatkut: The Impact of Gush Emunim and the Settlement Movement on Israeli Politics and Society. *Israel Studies*. 10: 3. pp. 192–224.

Nordstrom, Carolyn, and Robben, Antonius C. G. M. 1996. *Fieldwork Under Fire: Contemporary Studies of Violence and Culture*. Berkeley, CA: University of California Press.

Rappaport, Tamar; Garb, Yoni; and Penso, Anat. 1995. Religious Socialization and Female Subjectivity: Religious-Zionist Adolescent Girls in Israel. *Sociology of Education*. 68: 1. pp. 48–61.

Ravitzky, Aviezer. 1996. *Messianism, Zionism, and Jewish Religious Radicalism*. Chicago, IL: University of Chicago Press.

Scholem, Gershom. 1995. *The Neutralization of the Messianic Element in Early Hassidism*. In *The Messianic Idea in Judaism: And Other Essays on Jewish Spirituality*. New York: Schocken Books.

Seeman, Don. 2010. Does Anthropology Need to 'Get Religion'? Critical Notes on an Unrequited Love. *Practical Matters 3*. pp. 10–14.

Simons, Tal, and Ingram, Paul. 2003. Enemies of the State: The Interdependence of Institutional Forms and the Ecology of the Kibbutz, 1910–1997. *Administrative Science Quarterly*. 48: 4. pp. 592–621.

Sprinzak, Ehud. 1991. *The Ascendance of Israel's Radical Right*. New York: Oxford University Press.

Steinhardt, Joanna. 2010. American Neo-Hasid's in the Land of Israel. *Nova Religio: The Journal of Alternative and Emergent Religions 13*: 4. pp. 22–42.

Susskind, Laurence; Levine, Hillel; Aran, Gidon; Kaniel, Shlomo; Sheleg, Yair; Halbertal, Moshe. 2005. Religious and Ideological Dimensions of the Israeli Settlements Issue: Reframing the Narrative? *Negotiation Journal*. 21: 2. pp. 177–191.

Tabory, Ephraim, and Sasson Theodore. 2007. A House Divided: Grassroots National Religious Perspectives on the Gaza Disengagement and Future of the West Bank. *Journal of Church and State*. pp. 423–443.

Taylor, Charles. 1998. Modes of Secularism. In Rajeev Bhargava (ed) *Secularism and Its Critics*. New York: Oxford University Press

Waxman, Chaim. 2008. *Religious Zionism Post Disengagement: Future Directions*. New York: Yeshiva University Press.

Weiss, Erica. 2014. *Conscientious Objectors in Israel Citizenship, Sacrifice, Trials of Fealty*. Philadelphia: University of Pennsylvania Press.

Weiss, Hadas. 2010. Volatile Investments and Unruly Youth in a West Bank Settlement. *Journal of Youth Studies 13*(1). pp. 17–33

Weiss, Hadas. 2011. On Value and Values in a West Bank Settlement. *American Ethnologist 38*(1). pp. 34–45.

Contributor Biographies

Philip Wexler is Professor of Sociology of Education (emeritus) at the Hebrew University of Jerusalem and Unterberg Chair of Jewish Social and Educational History. Currently, he is Visiting Professor of Social Pedagogy and Social Politics at the Bergische University, Wuppertal, Germany. He works on questions of education and religion and society, and has recently published *Mystical Sociology* (Peter Lang, 2013). He is writing at the intersection of critical theory and Jewish mysticism and working (together with Heinz Sünker) on a forthcoming book on critical theory and education.

Yotam Hotam is a Lecturer at the University of Haifa and the head of the MA program for the Study of Alternatives in Education. His current area of research covers different themes and aspects which relate to the relations between the 'secular' and the 'religious' in modern society, culture, politics and education. He is the author of *Modern Gnosis and Zionism: The Crisis of Culture, Life Philosophy and Jewish National Thought* (Routledge, 2013), and *Space Theodyssey: Science Fiction, Education and Religiosity in a Post Secular Age* (Resling, 2011).

Ayman Agbaria is a Lecturer in the Department of Leadership and Policy in Education at the University of Haifa. He specializes in education amongst ethnic and religious minorities and researches policy and pedagogy for civics education, Islamic education and teacher training. He is the editor of two books: *Teacher Education in the Palestinian Society in Israel—Institutional Practices and Educational Policy* (Resling) and *Commitment, Character, and Citizenship: Religious Schooling in Liberal Democracy* (with Hanan A. Alexander, Routledge, 2012).

Hanan A. Alexander is Professor of Philosophy of Education at the University of Haifa, where he serves as Dean of Students and heads the International School and the Center for Jewish Education. He is also a Senior Research Fellow at the Van Leer Jerusalem Institute and has served as a Lecturer in Education at UCLA, Visiting Professor at the University of California Berkeley, and a Visiting Fellow at the University of Cambridge. His new book *Reimagining Liberal Education: Affiliation and Inquiry in Democratic Schooling* appeared from Bloomsbury Press in 2015.

Robert A. Davis is Professor of Religious and Cultural Education and Head of the School of Education at the University of Glasgow. His current work is in the areas of the effectiveness of religious education, the cultural history of early childhood and Scottish children's literature.

Oren Ergas lectures at the Hebrew University's school of education and at a number of teacher colleges in Israel. His research focuses on curricular and pedagogical aspects of contemplative education from sociological and philosophical perspectives. His work has been published in peer-reviewed journals and books, including *Critical Studies in Education, Paideusis, The Journal of Transformative Education* and *The Routledge International Handbook for Education, Religion and Values* (2013). His co-edited book (with Sharon Todd), *Philosophy East/West: Exploring Intersections between Educational and Contemplative Practices,* is forthcoming from Wiley-Blackwell.

Jürgen Habermas is a German sociologist and philosopher in the tradition of critical theory and is widely recognized as one of the world's leading intellectuals. His extensive written work addresses topics stretching from social-political theory to aesthetics, epistemology and language to philosophy of religion, and his ideas have significantly influenced not only philosophy but also political-legal thought, sociology, communication studies, argumentation theory and rhetoric, developmental psychology and theology.

Muhanad Mustafa is a Lecturer in the Department of Society, Culture and Education at the Center for Academic Studies-Or Yehuda. His research fields are political Islam, democratization and politics in the Arab world, Palestinian politics and the Arab minority in Israel.

William F. Pinar teaches curriculum theory at the University of British Columbia, where he holds a Canada Research Chair. The author, most recently, of *Experience as Lived* (Routledge, 2015), Pinar has also served as the

St. Bernard Parish Alumni Endowed Professor at Louisiana State University, the Frank Talbott Professor at the University of Virginia, and the A. Lindsay O'Connor Professor of American Institutions at Colgate University.

Suzanne Schneider received her PhD from the Department of Middle East, South Asian and African Studies at Columbia University. As a scholar affiliated with both the Center of Religion and Media at New York University and the Brooklyn Institute for Social Research, her research concerns the development of religious modernism in Islamic and Jewish contexts, the "reform" projects forwarded by these movements, and their relationship to the material and epistemic dimensions of European colonialism. In addition to numerous scholarly articles, she is the author of *The Politics of Denial: Religious Education and Colonial Rule in Palestine* (forthcoming).

Nehemia Stern is an anthropologist and a religious studies scholar. His research focuses on the relationship between religious experience, affect and political practice among Jewish religious Zionists in Israel. He has published articles on both the practice of hitchhiking in the West Bank, as well as the nature of sanctity among contemporary religious Zionists in Israel. He received his PhD from the Graduate Division of Religion (Jewish Religious Cultures Track) from Emory University in 2014. He is currently a Postdoctoral Fellow in the Department of Sociology and Anthropology at Bar Ilan University.